Microsoft Access 2003 Database by Examples

By

Sheila Ababio

authorHOUSE™

1663 LIBERTY DRIVE, SUITE 200
BLOOMINGTON, INDIANA 47403
(800) 839-8640
WWW.AUTHORHOUSE.COM

First published by AuthorHouse 06/30/05

ISBN: 1-4208-2735-9 (sc)

Printed in the United States of America
Bloomington, Indiana

This book is printed on acid-free paper.

TABLE OF CONTENTS

INTRODUCTION xiii
   What is a Database? xiii
   Examples of Database Systems xiii
   What is Access 2003? xiv
   An Access Database File xv
   The different objects in a Database File xv

PLANNING YOUR DATABASE APPLICATION 1
   The different approaches to designing and building a database 1
   The Systems Development Lifecycle 1
   A Simple approach to designing a database 5
   A sample database application 5
   Things to avoid in designing your tables 10

STARTING AND QUITTING ACCESS 13
   Quitting Microsoft Access 14

GETTING HELP 15
   Type a question for help box 15
   Microsoft Access Help Menu 16
   The Office Assistant 18
   Getting help from other sources 20

CREATING AN ACCESS DATABASE 21
   Create A Blank Database Without A Wizard 21
   Creating A Database Using A Wizard 23

TABLES 29
   Create A Table With A Table Wizard 30
   Create A Table In Design View (Without A Table Wizard) 33
   Setting Up A Primary Key 36
   Create A Table By Entering Data 37

CUSTOMISING A TABLE IN DESIGN VIEW 42
   Adding Fields To A Table 42
   Deleting A Field From A Table 43
   Renaming A Field In Design View 44
   Rearranging A Field In Design View 44
   Copy A Field 45
   Changing The Data Type For A Field 45
   Changing Or Setting Fields Properties 46

Default Value Property 55

RELATIONSHIPS IN ACCESS DATABASE **63**

Setting up a relationship 64
Types of Relationships 64
Creating A Relationship 67
Referential Integrity 70
Viewing Existing Relationship 72
Editing an existing relationship 72
Deleting a relationship 73

ADDING AND EDITING DATA **74**

Adding Records..74
Editing a field 76
Saving Data 76
Selecting a field 77
Selecting Record 77
Deleting a Record 78
Copy records in a datasheet 79
Move records in a datasheet..79
Navigating Between Fields 80
Navigating between records 80

CUSTOMIZING A TABLE IN DATASHEET VIEW **82**

Changing the Column Width 82
Changing row height 82
Formatting a datasheet 83
Changing the font of a datasheet...84
Formatting a datasheet with gridlines 84
Adding Special Design Effects 85
Rearranging columns 86
Hide a column...87
Unhide Columns 87
Freeze a column 88

FORMS **89**

Creating a form...89
Creating a form using the AutoForm 89
Creating a form with the form Wizard 90
Creating a form in the Design View..92
Adding a new Record to a form 93
Navigating through records 94
To move to specific record 95
Editing records in a form 95

Deleting records in a form 95

ADDING CONTROLS TO A FORM **98**

Adding a bound Text Box Control to your form 99

Creating Unbound or Calculated Controls 100

To create an unbound control 101

To create a calculated text box 101

Creating a label...102

Setting Control Properties 102

Changing the Properties of a control...103

Validating or restricting data entry in a form...104

Validation Rule and Validation Text Properties 105

Changing the Tab Order 107

Forms Sections..108

Resizing a form 108

Setting Section Properties 109

Setting Form properties 110

Setting the Default View for a form 110

IMPROVING THE APPEARANCE AND LAYOUT OF YOUR FORM **114**

Moving Controls...114

Resizing a Control 115

Changing the fonts and font size...116

Aligning text within a control 116

Adding Rectangles 118

Drawing a line...118

Creating a three dimensional effect 119

Adding Background Color to your form...119

Changing the color of the text 119

CUSTOMISING YOUR FORM WITH CONTROLS AND COMMAND BUTTON **121**

Creating a List Box or a Combo Box 121

Creating a List Box or Combo Box with a Wizard...................................122

Creating a List Box or Combo Box without a Wizard..............................123

Examples of Data Properties..124

Setting the properties for a List Box or Combo Box...............................124

Restricting users to values on the list 126

Creating Check boxes, Option Buttons and toggle Buttons 127

Creating a Check Box 127

Creating an Option Group..127

Change a control from one type to another..130

Creating Command Buttons..131

To create a command button with a Wizard 131

Creating a Command Button Without a Wizard 133
Creating a form with multiple pages 136
To add a page break to a form 136
To add a Tab Control to a form 136

ADDING GRAPHICS TO FORMS 138
Add a bound object frame 138
To create an embedded object in a bound object frame 139
To embed or link an existing object in an unbound object frame 140
Resizing an object 141
To make the object fit its frame 141

TO FIND SPECIFIC VALUES IN A FIELD 143
Using the Replace Feature 145
Filtering Records 147
Filter by selection 148
Filtering by forms 149
Saving Your Filtered Data as a Query 151
Filtering with Expression 151
Advanced Filter 152

QUERIES 154
Creating a Query 155
Creating a Select Query with a wizard 155
Creating a Select Query without a wizard 157
Adding Fields to a Query 158
Saving a Query 159
Exploring the different views in a Query window 160
The Design View 160
The Datasheet view 160
The SQL view 161
Switching between view 161
Opening a query 161
Opening a query in Design view from the Database window 162

CUSTOMISING A QUERY 163
Adding a column to a query 163
Inserting a field 163
Deleting a field 163
Rearranging or moving a column 164
Add a table to a query 165
Removing a table from a query 165
Viewing and setting properties for queries 166
To view and set the properties of a field or query 166

Showing unique values in a query.. 167
Adding Criteria to Your Query 168
Specifying the criteria 168
Viewing your Query Results from Design View 168
To specify criteria for a field using the Expression Builder 169
Comparison Operators 169
Specifying more than one criteria 170
Using Or 171
Using And 172
Using the Date, Year and DatePart function...................................... 172

PERFORMING CALCULATIONS IN A QUERY 175
Using predefined functions to calculate total 175
Calculate Total on all records in a table.. 175
Calculating on a group of records... 176
Create a calculated field in a query 177
Using the & Operator to join text and fields...................................... 178
Group Query.. 178
Sorting your records 179

OTHER TYPES OF QUERIES 183
Parameter Query 183
Creating a parameter query 183
Specifying the data type for a query parameter 184
Crosstab Query.. 186
Creating a Crosstab Query with a Wizard.. 187
Creating a crosstab query without a Wizard 189
Modifying your column Headings... 192
To Modify the Column Headings 193
Action Query 193
Make-Table 193
Creating a Make-Table 194
Delete Query 195
Creating a Delete Query... 195
Append Query.. 196
Creating an append query 197
Appending Records with Autonumber fields...................................... 198
Update Query 198
Creating an Update Query 198

REPORTS 200
Creating a Report.. 200
Creating a Report Using AutoReport 200

Creating a Report With the Report Wizard 201

Create a report without a wizard 205

CUSTOMISING A REPORT **208**

Adding Controls to your report 208

Adding bound Controls to a report 208

Adding bound control using the toolbar 209

Adding an unbound control 209

Calculated control 210

To change an expression in a text box 214

Creating a label 215

Change the Text in a label 215

Deleting Controls 215

Resizing controls 217

Formatting a control 217

Properties 218

To change the field that a text box or control is bound to 218

The different sections of a report 219

Adding Sections to a report 219

To show or Hide a section 220

Add Page Breaks 221

Adding Page Numbers to your report 222

To Add Page Numbers using the Expression Builder 222

To add page numbers to a report using the Insert Menu 223

Adding a date to your report 223

Enter a date using the expression builder 224

Changing the size of a section 225

To set the property of a section 226

Setting Report Properties 226

To set property for a Report 227

SORTING AND GROUPING DATA **228**

Sorting 228

Setting a sort order 228

To change sorting and grouping order 229

Deleting a sorting or grouping field or expression 230

Inserting a sort or grouping field or expression 230

Grouping Data 231

To add a group header or footer 231

To remove a group 234

Calculating Totals for a group of records 234

To calculate a group total 235

Calculating Totals on Several Groups 235

Printing One Group of Record Per Page 236

SUBFORMS AND SUBREPORTS 237
Subform 237
Creating a form/subform 238
Subreport 248
Adding a sub-report to a report 248
Printing your report 252
To set the error checking feature 252

USING CHARTS TO ANALYZE YOUR DATA 254
Creating a chart in a form 254
Create a chart report 256
Create a new chart report 256
Previewing a chart 258
Saving a chart 258
Printing a chart 258
Customize a chart 259
Change the type of chart 259
To Format the look of a chart 260
To Format the Chart Title 260
Objects 262
Open a database Object 263
To copy a database object 264
Renaming a database object 265
To delete a database object 266
To Preview Data in a report 266
To Preview Data in the Design view 267
Magnifying the view of the report. 267
Previewing a report from the database window 268
Printing a database object 268

USING MICROSOFT ACCESS AND THE INTERNET 270
Creating a hyperlink 271
Adding a hyperlink to a form or report. 272
Publishing your data on the web 274
Using Static pages to publish your data 274
Using Dynamic pages to publish your data 275
Creating a Data Access Page 275
Modifying a Data Access Page 281
Viewing or modifying records 283
Customize a Group 286
Customizing a section 287

Customize a page... 288

ANALYSING YOUR DATA ON THE WEB....................................... 290

TURNING YOUR DATABASE INTO AN APPLICATION........................ 297

SHARING DATA AND SECURING YOUR DATABASE........................ 316
Sharing Data in a network environment 316
Ways of sharing data.. 316
Setting up options to open a database in shared or exclusive mode 317
Editing Data in a multi-user environment 317
Securing your database.. 319
Protecting your database with a Password 320
User-Level Security 321
Creating an MDE file 340
Encrypting your database 343

MAINTAINING AND IMPROVING THE PERFORMANCE OF YOUR DATABASE 345
Maintaining your database Backing up your data...................... 345
Restoring your Backup copy.. 349
Compacting and repairing your database................................ 354
Improving the performance of your database 355
Documentation.. 356

IMPORTING AND EXPORTING DATA 359
Importing Data.. 359
Importing Information from Excel 360
Importing from a Delimited or Fixed-width Text File.................. 363
Importing Data from another Database file into Access Database 365
Importing a Data Access Page from a Microsoft Access file into Microsoft Access... 366
Importing data from an HTML FILE 368
Importing data from an XML file 369
Exporting Data 370
Linking a Database 372

INDEX 380

INTRODUCTION

Welcome to Microsoft Access 2003. Microsoft Access 2003 is a Relational Database Management System for Microsoft Windows particularly for Windows XP. Microsoft Access 2003 is user friendly and easy to use. Its new features like autocorrect, error checking in forms and reports, Windows XP themes and a new improved help facility makes it easier to use.

This book, **Microsoft Access 2003 database by examples** is a step-by-step approach to designing and building a database. It will give you an understanding of databases and teach you how to design and build professional and easy to use databases. With screen-by-screen illustration you can learn fast. It is full of practical examples, which you can use to build your database.

Whether you are a beginner or an expert user, this book is for you, because it explains and illustrates all the procedures in simple language without any jargons. The visual images makes learning easy and fun.

What is a Database?

A **Database** is an organized collection of related information about a particular subject or purpose.

Databases are used in schools, supermarkets, stock market, retail shops, libraries, local council or anywhere where people need to organize and retrieve information.

You can use a database to manage contact information, employees' information, inventory, schedule flights and reservations.

A Database is designed to meet the information needs of an organization. For example the order database system is designed to track orders, keep information about customers and to monitor sales. A retailer may need to keep information about its customers, the orders they have placed, who took the orders and other information relevant to the order to track orders, monitor sales and meet other information needs. Information is collected about the customers, order details, employees and any other information relating to the order. This information can be organized into one single file known as a **Database file.**

A Database can also help retrieve and analyze information quickly and easily. For example using queries and reports you can retrieve and analyze data easily with a database.

Examples of Database Systems

A good example of a database system is an order-tracking database system. The order tracking database system is an organized collection of information relating to orders. Information about different aspects of the order are collected and organized into separate tables and stored in a database file. For example information about customers are organized into a customer table, information about orders are organized into orders tables, information about all the products that the retailer sells are organized into products tables.

Another example of a database system is a telephone directory system. Addresses and telephone numbers are kept in a database. Individuals wishing to know the telephone number or address of a company may call directory enquiry and give the operator the name of the company they wish to find the address or telephone number of, this information is used to search the database and retrieve the information they are looking for.

How can we store and organize data to meet our information needs?

A software program is needed to store, retrieve and organize the data. There are many software programs that can help you organize and store your data. For example there are software programs like Oracle, Ingress and Microsoft Access. Microsoft Access is by far the most poplar software program. It is part of the Microsoft Office suite and can run on any Personal Computer or network computer.

What is Access 2003?

Microsoft Access 2003 is a relational Database Management System. There are different versions of Microsoft Access, but the current version of Microsoft Access as at the time of writing this book is Microsoft Access 2003. Microsoft Access 2003 includes the following new features.

Error checking in forms and reports: In Microsoft Access 2003, when the **Error checking** feature is enabled, common errors are highlighted in forms and reports.

Viewing information on Object Dependencies: With the Object Dependency feature, you can view information on dependencies between different objects in a database. For example, the Daily Sales query is used to create the Monthly Sales Report, Annual Sales Report and the Employees Crosstab Query, if you decide to delete the Daily Sales query, you can use the **object dependency** feature to view all objects that depend on this query. You can then decide to change the record source of the dependent objects before deleting the Daily Orders Query. This will minimize errors and save time.

Smart tags: you can add smart tags to fields in your tables, forms, reports or data access pages to track dates, names and addresses.

Autocorrect Options: use the Autocorrect feature to correct common errors. You can also control how the autocorrect works. For example if Microsoft Access automatically uses the autocorrect feature to correct something you don't like, you can easily undo it.

Immediate fields properties Update: In Microsoft Access 2003, if you change the property of some inherited field property like the Format property in a table, Microsoft Access gives you the opportunity to update the property of all or some of the controls that use that field in their forms or reports. You don't have to manually modify all the objects that use this field, as was the case in previous versions of Microsoft Access.

Backup with this new feature you can easily backup your files using the File Menu in Microsoft Access 2003.

Improved Sort Feature

You can now use the improved sort feature to sort up to about four fields in ascending or descending order in the List box and Combo Box Wizard in forms and reports and the Lookup Wizard in an Access Database.

Context base Help: You can press F1 to get help relating to the current selected text.

Enhanced capability for importing and exporting data: Microsoft Access 2003 supports XML (Extensible Markup Language). With this feature you can specify a transform file when you import or export data to XML.

Pivot Table and charts you can create pivot table and charts to summarize and analyze data.

Supports windows XP Theme: Microsoft Access supports windows XP themes and gives you the flexibility to change inherited themes from the operating systems in your database. Microsoft Access 2003 offers many different themes, which you can apply to your views, dialog boxes and controls.

An Access Database File

A database file is a container that holds all the objects in a database. With Microsoft Access you can collect, organize and manage information about your database into one single file. You can use the different objects in a database to store, collect and manipulate data in your database. For example you can collect and store data in a table.

The different objects in a Database File

The different objects in a database file are Tables, Queries, Forms, Reports, Data Access Pages, Macros and Modules.

Tables: Tables are the fundamental structure in a database. You can use tables to collect and store data. Data is organized into fields (columns) and records (rows) in a table.

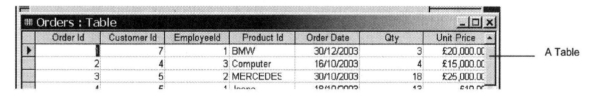

	Order Id	Customer Id	EmployeeId	Product Id	Order Date	Qty	Unit Price
▶	1	7	1	BMW	30/12/2003	3	£20,000.00
	2	4	3	Computer	16/10/2003	4	£15,000.00
	3	5	2	MERCEDES	30/10/2003	18	£25,000.00
	4	5	1	Icono	18/10/2003	12	£10.00

A Table

Queries: you can use queries to retrieve information from tables. This query retrieves information from the employees and orders tables.

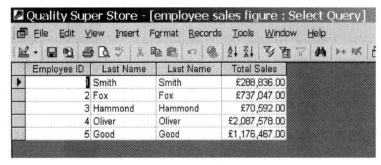

A Query

Forms: you can use forms to view information and enter data into a table.

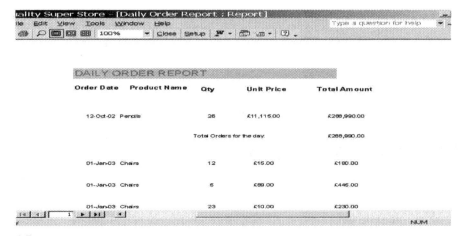

A Forms

Reports: you can use a report to analyze and print information in your database.

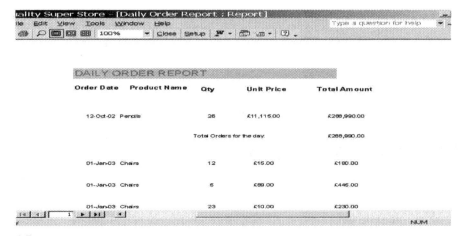

A Report

Data Access Page: you can use a Data Access page to view and analyze data on the web.

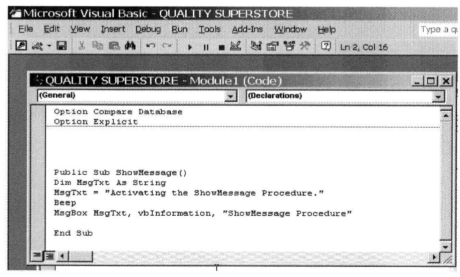

A Data Access Page

Macros: you can use macros to automate common tasks like opening or closing a form.

A Macro

Modules: you can use modules to write windows programs i.e. use Access Visual Basic for Applications to develop Database programs.

```
Option Compare Database
Option Explicit



Public Sub ShowMessage()
Dim MsgTxt As String
MsgTxt = "Activating the ShowMessage Procedure."
Beep
MsgBox MsgTxt, vbInformation, "ShowMessage Procedure"

End Sub
```

A Module

1

Chapter

PLANNING YOUR DATABASE APPLICATION

If you want to build a good database that is easy to maintain and retrieve the kind of information you want, you must spend time planning the database before you build it. You need to plan and design the database carefully or else you will run into difficulties later on. A developer or a database designer will spend considerable time planning and designing the database before using a software program like Microsoft Access to implement the design.

A well design database makes your database easy to maintain. Microsoft Access stores data in tables. A well design database stores information about each subject separately. In Microsoft Access data about each subject is stored in one table and each table contains data about a particular subject. Because each table contains information about a particular subject, updating information is easy because all updates takes place at only one place.

A well design database provides accurate and efficient information. To provide efficient and accurate information, you need data from different sources. Microsoft Access is capable of combining data from different tables to provide accurate and efficient information.

A well-designed database provides easy and quick access to information. With a well design database, less time is spent building the database and access to information is quick and accurate.

The different approaches to designing and building a database

There are many approaches to building a database application, for example, the Rapid Application Development approach and the System Development Life Cycle approach. The System Development approach is a top-down systematic approach to designing a database. Some Designers do not follow any approach they just create the database file, create tables and create the other objects in the table. In an ideal world, a systematic approach is needed to develop a database application suitable for the needs of an Organization.

The Systems Development Lifecycle

The System Development Lifecycle consists of the following steps.

o   NEEDS ASSESSMENT/REQUIREMENTS GATHERING

o   DESIGNING THE APPLICATION

o   BUILDING THE APPLICATION

o   DOCUMENTING THE APPLICATION

o   TESTING THE APPLICATION

o   IMPLEMENTING THE APPLICATION

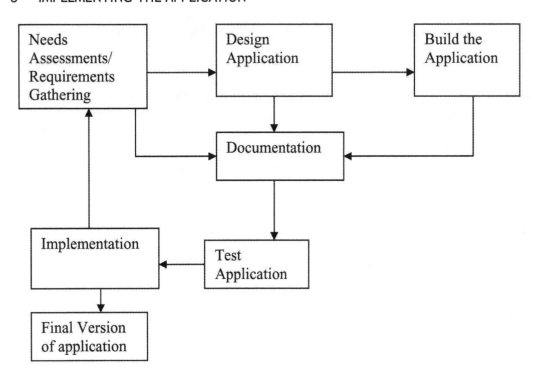

1.   **NEEDS ASSESSMENT /REQUIREMENTS GATHERING**

The first stage of the systems development cycle is to assess the needs of the organization and to gather requirements. By the end of this stage, the designer should be clear about the purpose of the database, who will be using the application and what information will be stored in the database.

- **Determining the purpose of the database.**

In determining the purpose of the application, you need to ask yourself "what do you want to achieve in building the database". For example a retailer may want to create a database to keep track of customers order and to monitor sales. You can also talk to the people who will use the database to determine the purpose of the database and how they want to use it.

- **Find out what information you need to store in order to achieve your purpose.** For example to keep track of customers order you may need to store and retrieve information about customers, orders, employees and products.

Using a brainstorming session, determine the information you would like the database to store and the kind of reports you would like it to produce.

- **Find out who will use the database**

Is the database application going to be used by the sales staff only, or by other departments also?

- **Identify the forms and reports that the current system uses to record data.** The current system may be using a receipt book or a spreadsheet to record sales transactions.

- **Determine the forms and report you will need to build the new system.** For example you will need forms for taking orders, entering customer details and employees details. You will need reports like daily order report, sales analysis report and product list.

2. **DESIGN THE APPLICATION**

Based on the information that you want to store and retrieve and the output you want from the database, you can identify the subjects you need to represent in your database.

- Identify the subjects that you need to store information about. For example, you want the database to be able to store and retrieve information about your customers, employees, orders and products and provide you with a list of customers and the orders they have placed you would therefore like to represent the Customers, Employees, Products and Orders as subjects in your database.

- Identify the tables you need. Each subject you identify will become a table. Information about each subject will be stored in a separate table in the database.

- Identify what information you need to keep in each table. For example in the Customer Table you will need to keep information about the customer i.e. customer name, address, telephone number and postcode. This becomes the fields in the tables. Each field in a table contains individual attributes or characteristics about the subject of the table.

- Determine the field type for each field in the tables. For example the field type for the customer name will be text.

- Determine the primary keys for the tables. The primary key is a unique column, or set of columns, which identifies each row in a table. Microsoft Access uses the primary key to relate information stored in separate tables. Each table in your database must have a primary key which uniquely identifies each individual record in the table.

- Determine the relationships between the tables. Microsoft Access uses the relationship between the tables to find related information.

- Refine your design. Normalize your tables. You can also use Microsoft Table Analyzer to analyze the design of your tables. It will give you feedback and suggestions about the design of your table.

3. **BUILD THE APPLICATION**

- Create the Database.

- Create the tables.

- Create the relationship between the tables.

- Create other database objects i.e. create the queries, forms, reports, data access pages, macros and modules.

- Create roles and privileges for users to limit access to database to only authorize users.

- Analyze your design for errors. You can use the Table Analyzer in Microsoft Access to analyze your table.

4. **DOCUMENTATION**

It is good practice to document every stage of the development process. Documentation creates continuity, accuracy and consistency. If you don't document your system more time will be spent dealing with problems. Also it will be difficult to rebuild the database if something goes wrong. Document the requirements, the design, the relationships diagrams, tables, other objects, codes etc. You can use the Documenter in Microsoft Access to document your database. This Microsoft Access tool produces detailed report of your database.

5. **TEST THE APPLICATION**

At this stage the application undergoes user acceptance and testing. Obtain users approval for the general user interface, menus and forms and reports.

Use sample data to test the application to see whether it can give you the expected results. Test the forms and report.

Test if the application will accept valid inputs and reject invalid inputs.

6. **IMPLEMENT THE APPLICATION**

Install the application by creating directory on users machine and copying all the necessary files into one directory. If the application is going to be used in a network environment install the application on a file server, which is accessible by all users.

Train Users for users to make effective use of the system, users need to know how to use the application properly.

7. **MAINTAINING THE APPLICATION**

Poor maintenance of application results in poor performance. Once the system becomes functional you must expect feedback from users. You can use the feedback to enhance and refine the system. You must also monitor the database performance so that you can make improvement. Nothing is so irritating as a slow application. You can improve the performance of an application by using performance tools provided by Microsoft Access (i.e. Performance Analyzer). Periodically you can also use the Compact and Repair tool to repair corrupt files, forms, reports and modules. Compacting and repairing your database can improve the database performance.

A Simple approach to designing a database

If you find the system development cycle difficult to follow, you can use the following steps to build a database.

- Create a new database file.

- Add tables to the database.

- Define the relationship between the tables.

- Create other database objects.

A sample database application

The sample database used throughout this book is a database about a fictitious retailer known as Quality Superstore. Quality Superstore is a retailer who aims to provide its customers with quality products at competitive prices. Before the database was setup, the retailer recorded all transactions on paper and receipt books. The retailer wants you to design a database to help keep track of its customers order and to monitor sales. Follow the steps below to design the database.

1.   Determine the **purpose** for building the database.

     The purpose of the database will be to keep track of customers order and to monitor sales.

2.   Find out **what information you need to store** in order to achieve your purpose.

     Store, maintain and retrieve information about customers.

     Store, maintain and retrieve information about orders.

     Store, maintain and retrieve information about order details

     Store, maintain and retrieve information about employees.

     Store, maintain and retrieve information about products.

     Store, maintain and retrieve information about suppliers.

     Store, maintain and retrieve information about contacts with customers.

3.   Identify the **tables** to store this information.

In Microsoft Access information about each subject is stored in a table, therefore translate the subjects that you have identified in step 2 into tables.   For example in step 2 you identified the need to store information about customers, translate this requirements into a table and it becomes customers table. Information about all customers will be stored in the customers' table.   Information about orders will be stored in the orders table etc.   Each table should contain information about one subject.

Tables identified: Customers, Suppliers, Orders, OrderDetails, Contact, Employee and Products.

The Customers table will contain information about all the customers.

The Suppliers table will contain information about all the suppliers.

The Orders table will contain information about all the orders.

The OrderDetails table will contain details about an order.

The Employees table will contain information about all the employees.

The Products table will contain information about all the products.

The Contacts table will contain information about contacts with customers.

4.   Decide **what information you need to keep in each table.** For example in the customers table you may want to store details such as the customers first name, last name, phone number and address.   These are attributes, which describes customers.   These attributes become the fields in a table.   Examples of tables used in the Quality database with their attributes.   This is not an exhaustive list; you may have to add more fields to the table.

Customers Table	Suppliers Table	Products Table
Customer Id	SupplierId	Product Id
FirstName	SupplierName	ProductName
LastName	ContactName	ProductPicture
Address	Address	Product UnitPrice
City	City	
PostalCode	PostalCode	
PhoneNumber	PhoneNumber	

OrderDetailTable	Order Table	Contact Table	Employees Table
OrderDetailId	Order Id	Contact Id	EmployeeId
Order Id	Order Date	Date	DeptId
Product Id	EmployeeId	Time	FirstName

Quantity	Comments	LastName
Unit Price	Title	

5. Determine the **data type** for each field in the tables.

   The data type you choose depends on the kind of information you want to store in the field. For example you can use text fields to store text or a combination of text and numeric numbers. You can use number to store fields that requires numbers and calculation. The following is an example of the Products table and its data types with examples of data it can contain.

Products Table	Field Type	Example of Data
Product Id	Text	C1003
Product Name	Text	Barbie Doll
Unit Price	Decimal	50.99
Qty	Number	15

6. Determine the **primary key** for each table.

   The primary key is a field or set of fields in the table, which uniquely identify an individual record. Think about a field that will uniquely identify each record or row. This is often a unique number like an employee number or social security no. The name of a person is not a good choice because you can have two or more people with the same name. Using a unique number is the best way of identifying an employee in the employee table. Each employee in the **employees** table is given a unique identification number, which is stored in the **Employee Id** column. This field is known as a primary key and it uniquely identifies each employee, so that in situations where two or more employees have the same name, you are able to distinguish between them.

Primary Key

Employee ID	DeptId	First Name	Last Name	Title	Extension	Work Phone
1	2	James	Smith	Doc	333	0207-3456
2	5	Susan	Fox	Ms	4445	0207-563-123
3	3	Emmanuel	Hammond	Doc	21455	0201-566-7845
4	6	Kemp	Oliver	Mr	2233333	0207-556-5244
5	2	Kenneth	Good	Doc	2564	0214-562-9882
6	2	Sarah	Babbie	Mrs	2888	0215-623-5894
7	1	Abraham	Smith	Mr	2569	0215-653-5982
8	3	Abraham	Smith	Mr	3568	0214893-53267
(AutoNumber)	0					

EMPLOYEES : Table

Different Employee Id   Same name but different Employee Id

The employee Id will distinguish between the two Abraham Smiths' in the Employees table.

   In some situations one field is not enough to uniquely identify a row, you may have to choose two fields as the primary key.

7. Determine the **relationships** between the tables.

Not all the tables in a database relate to each other. You need to look at the tables and determine whether a relationship exist between the two tables. You determine whether or not a relationship exist by considering what will be stored in the table, actions that will take place with the tables and who is going to take the action. Consider the examples below.

Table	Action	Who/What
Orders	Order will be placed	By Customer.
Orders	Orders will be taken	Employee
Suppliers	Suppliers will supply Products	Suppliers
Order	may consist of different items	Order details
Contact	will be made	By Customers/Employees

Looking at the above activities you can say for example that there exist a relationship between the Customers Table and the Orders Tables, because a customer places an order, there is also a relationship between the **employees** table and the order table because an employee takes an order. However, there are no relationships between the employee table and the suppliers; no relationships between the employees table and the products table. There are also no relationship between the **customers** table and the employees, no relationship between the customers table and the suppliers; no relationship between the customers table and the products table.

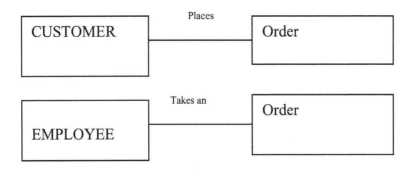

The type of relationship

After determining whether or not a relationship exist between the tables, you will need to find out what type of relationship exist between the tables which are related.

There are three types of relationships between tables. They are

One-to-many: each record in a table (A) can have many records in a relating table (B), a record in a relating table (B) can only have one record in table (A).

Many-to-many: each record in a table (A) can have many records in a relating table (B) and a record in the relating table (B) can also have many records in that table (A).

One-to-one a record in a table (A) can only have one record in a relating table (B) and a record in the relating table (B) can also have only one record in that table.

Example of a one-to-many relationship

The relationship type between the Employees and Orders table is one to many. A record in the **employees** table can have many matching records in the Orders table, and a record in the Orders table can only have one matching record in the employees table.

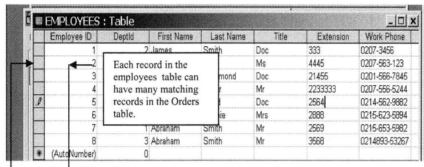

And each record in the Orders table can have only one matching record in the employees table.

You can apply the same principle to determine the relationships between the other tables in the database. The one side of the relationship, is represented by the number **1** and the many side of the relationship is represented by the infinity symbol Refer to chapter 6 for full discussions on how to create a relationship.

An example of a Relationship Diagram in Microsoft Access

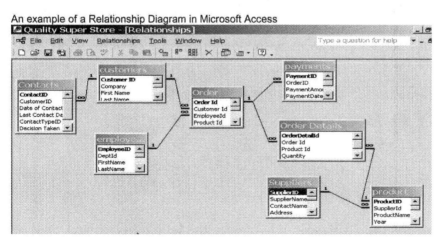

8. Determine the **forms** you will need to perform all the actions to keep track of your orders. For example you may need the Order Entry Form to enter information

about orders.   You may also need the following forms Employee Form, Products Form, Contacts Forms, Suppliers Form and Order Details Form.

9.   Determine what **reports** you will need.

- Sales Analysis Report

- Product List

- Daily Order Report

- Monthly/Annual Sales Report

- Sales Summary Report

- Products Analysis Report

- Employees Sales Analysis Report

- Order Analysis Report

10.   Create the **Database** i.e. Quality Superstore.

Create the tables i.e. Customers, Order, Order Details and Products.

Create the queries i.e. Daily Sales query etc..

Create the forms i.e. Order Entry form and Products Forms etc.

Create the reports i.e. Sales Analysis Report, Order Analysis Report etc.

Add sample data to your database, use the forms, queries and report to see if your can get the results you want. If not refine you design.

Things to avoid in designing your tables

- **AVOID REPEATING INFORMATION.**

If for example in designing your tables, you decided to keep information about suppliers and the products they supply all in one table.   You will have to repeat the supplier's details each time you enter a new transaction. This leads to more errors and repetition and waste of memory space.

Supplier Name	Address	Tel No	Product	Qty/Box	Unit Price
ATC	28 Avenue	333 1336	Staples	10	£15
XBERRY	13 Row	445 1421	Pencils	15	£20
ATC	28 Avenue	333 1336	Ribbons	12	£10
ATC	28 Avenue	333 1336	Paper	5	£12

Repeated information

Avoid this   Table 1

To avoid this problem you will have to normalize the table. **Normalization** is the process of breaking down the table so that it contains information about only one subject. In the above example you will have to break the table into two separate tables one table to contain information about the supplier and the other table to contain the product information.   Remember always to keep each subject in a separate table.

Supplier Table

SupplierId	Supplier Name	Address	Telephone No
1	ATC	28 Avenue	333 1336
2	XBERRY	13 Row	445 1421

Product

P01	Product Name	Qty/Box	Unit Price
P02	Staples	10	£15
P03	Pencils	15	£20
P04	Ribbons	12	£10
P05	Paper	5	£12

Table 2

By breaking the table into two separate tables you can enter the supplier's information once, and if the supplier address changes you can update it once in the supplier's table.

- **AVOID REDUNDANT DATA**

Avoid having fields that are left blank because they are not applicable to all the records. For example you designed a table to hold information about employees and their dependants. Not all employees have dependants; therefore fields for employee without dependants will always be left blank. This will waste storage space.

Name	Address	Dependants	No of Dependants
John Smith	12 Hale St.	Yes	2
Rose Fall	69 Needle St.	No	0
Samuel Flee	111 Goods St.	No	0
Mary Kettle	200 Light House	No	0

Table 3

A better approach will be to create a separate employee table and a separate Dependants table.   The employee table will only contain information about employees, and the dependant's table will only contain information about employees with dependants.

- **AVOID DELETING VALUABLE INFORMATION.**

Each table should contain information about one subject. When you store information about each subject in a separate table, you can maintain information about each subject independently and avoid deleting valuable information.

Suppose you have a table, which stores both the employee and the department information all in one table. If an employee leaves the company, you may decide to delete that employee's details from the table. By deleting the employee's details you end up deleting the department the employee works in from the table. The Department information is very important information and you don't want to delete this information. Even though you may want to delete the employee details you don't want to delete details about that employees department.

Employee ID	Name	Address	Department Id	Department
0001	John Smith	12 Hale St.	01	Accounts
0002	Rose Fall	69 Needle St.	02	Finance
0003	Samuel Flee	111 Goods St.	03	Sales
0004	Mary Kettle	200 Light House	04	Catering

Table 4

To avoid deleting valuable information you will have to separate the table into two separate tables. Each table will contain data on just one subject. One table will contain the employee information and another table will contain information about the department. Keeping the information in two separate tables will prevent you from deleting important information that you need. For example when an employee leaves your company you can delete the employee information from the employee table without deleting the employee's department.

STARTING AND QUITTING ACCESS

STARTING ACCESS

1. Click on the **Start** button.

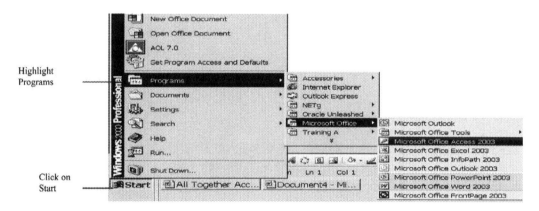

Highlight Programs

Click on Start

2. Highlight **Programs**, click on **Microsoft Office** and then click on **Microsoft Access 2003** from the list of Programs.

The Microsoft Access main screen is displayed with **Menu bars**, **Tool bar** and a **Task pane** to help you in building your database.

THE MICROSOFT ACCESS MAIN SCREEN

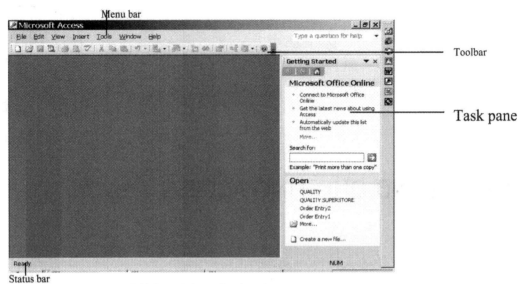

The Initial Microsoft Access Database Screen

Quitting Microsoft Access

When you finish using Microsoft Access, you should exit from the program. Exiting from Microsoft Access would return you to windows where you can click on **Start** and **Shutdown** to turn off your computer. Follow the instructions below to exit from Microsoft Access.

1.   Click on the **File Menu**.

2.   Click on **Exit**.

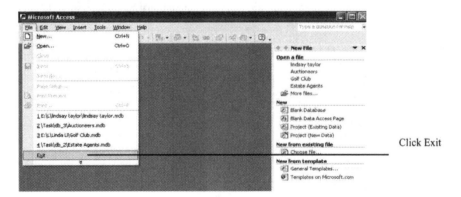

Many of the options on the menu may not be available instantly, you may have to highlight the Extended Menu symbol to display all the items on the menu. For example you may have to highlight the Extended Menu to display the Exit command.

Chapter

3

GETTING HELP

You can get help as you work with Microsoft Access 2003. There are about three ways to get help in Microsoft Access 2003. They are

• Type a question for help box

• Microsoft Access Help Menu

• Office assistant

Type a question for help box

To get help quickly, you can use the **Type a question for help box** located at the right end of the menu bar. Follow the steps below to get help with the **Type a question for help box.**

1. Click inside the box labelled **Type a question for help box.**

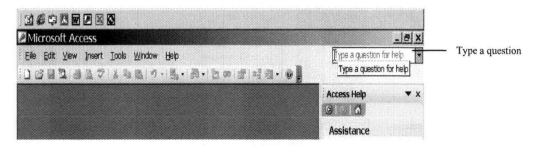

2. Type a question. For example type **"How do I get help"**.

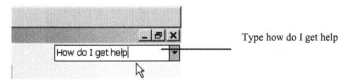

3. Press **Enter**.

   Microsoft Access returns the results of your search in the **Search Results Task Pane.**

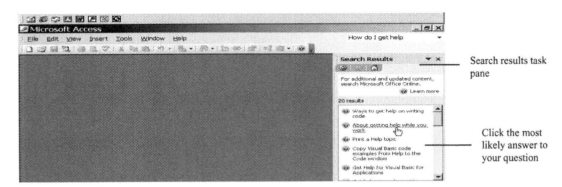

Search results task pane

Click the most likely answer to your question

4. Click the answer from the **Search Results Task Pane** that most likely answers the question you typed in the **Type a question for help box**. The content is displayed on your screen.

Microsoft Access Help Menu

You can use Microsoft Access Help Menu to search for help. This method gives you a variety of options to choose from. For example you can choose help by clicking on the **Table of Content**, or type specific phrase or word in the **Search** box to return a list of possible answers, relevant to the topic. To get help from Microsoft Help Menu follow the steps below.

1. Click on the **Help Menu** and select **Microsoft Access Help F1**.

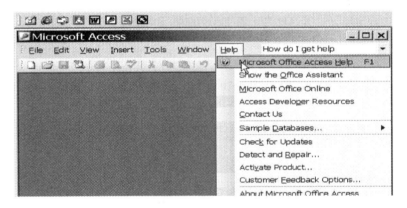

The help window is displayed, you can type the word you want to search help on in the **search for box** or click the **Table of content**.

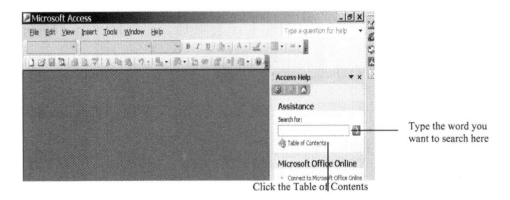

Type the word you want to search here

Click the Table of Contents

To Use the search for box to find help

2. To use the **search for** box to find help, type a specific words or phrase in the box labeled **Search for** and click on the green arrow

    (the **Search button**) next to the **Search for** box.

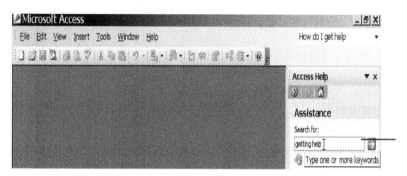

    Click on the search button or press **Enter**. The results of your search are displayed in the search results window.

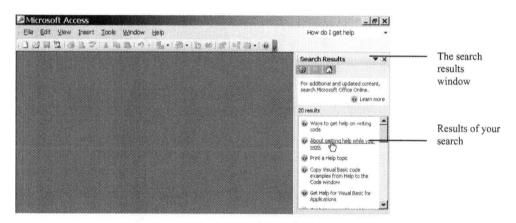

The search results window

Results of your search

    Click the most likely answer to your questions. The help window opens to display information about the topic you selected. Click the **back** arrow on the **Search Results** window to return to the **Access Help** screen. The **Back** and Forward buttons allow you to review topics. The Back button displays the help topic viewed before the current topic. The forward button displays the help topic viewed after the current topic.

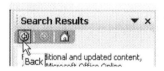

To use the Table of Content method to search for help

3. To use the **Table of content** to search for help, click on **Table of Contents**.

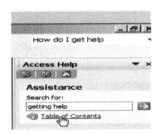

A list of help topic organized into different categories is displayed in the **Search Results** window.

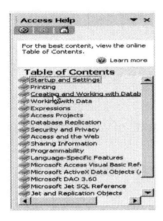

4.   Click on the category relating to the topic you want help on. A list of topics is displayed underneath the category.

5.   Choose a topic that relates to the help topic you want

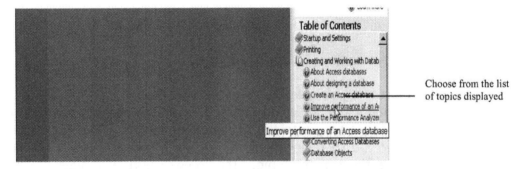

Choose from the list of topics displayed

The result of your search is displayed in the Microsoft Access window.

The Office Assistant

You can also ask for help from the office assistant. For example you can ask for help on **"how do I create a pivot table"**. The office assistant needs to be displayed before you can ask help from it.

To ask help from the office assistant follow the instructions below.

1.   If the **Office Assistant** isn't visible, click on the **Help Menu** and select **Show The Office Assistant**. The **Office Assistant** appears.

The Office Assistant

2. Click on the **Office Assistant**. The Office Balloon appears.

3. Type a question into the Office Balloon and press **Enter** or click **Search**.

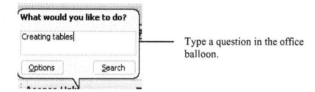

Type a question in the office balloon.

4. The results of your search are displayed in the **Search Results** window.

5. Click the answer that most likely answers your question. When you finish click the **close** icon **X** button to close the help window.

Not everyone wants to work with the office assistant appearing now and then on his or her documents. Follow the steps below to hide or turn off the office assistant.

To hide office assistant

To hide the office assistant, click on the **Help Menu**, and select **Hide the Office Assistant**.

Turning off the office assistant

1. Click on the **Options** button on the Assistant balloon. The Office Assistant dialog box appears.

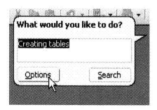

2. Click the **Options tab** and clear the check box next to **Use the Office Assistant**.

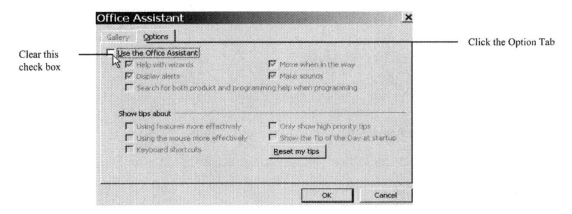

Clear this check box

Click the Option Tab

3.   Click **Ok**. The office assistance disappears.

Getting help from other sources

If you are connected to the Internet you can get more help from Microsoft Online.   The Microsoft Online help includes up-to-date help topics, links to templates, training and Downloads.

You can also search for help by scrolling down the results of your search.   Under **Other places to look**, there are a number of options you can click to extend your search.

Chapter

CREATING AN ACCESS DATABASE

The first step in creating a database is to create the database file. In practical terms, when you create a database you create the structure or file that holds the different objects in the database. This file will hold all the tables, queries, forms, reports, pages, macros and modules for your database.

You can create a blank database without a wizard or use the database wizard to create a database.

Microsoft Access provides wizards, which makes the task of creating a database easier. If any of the sample databases meets your needs then it is much quicker to use the wizard to create a database and customise it to meet your needs. However, if none of the sample databases meet your needs, then it is better to create a blank database.

Example

Suppose we want to create a database for Quality Superstore, we will first have to create the database file, the structure which will hold all the different database objects like the table, forms, query, reports etc. We can create a blank database file with or without the wizard.

Create A Blank Database Without A Wizard

When you create a database without a wizard, you will have to create the tables, forms and the other objects yourself. Follow the steps below to create a blank Database without a wizard.

1.   Clickon **New** ⬜ on the toolbar or choose **New** from the **File Menu**.

2.   In the Task pane under **New File**, Click on **Blank Database**.

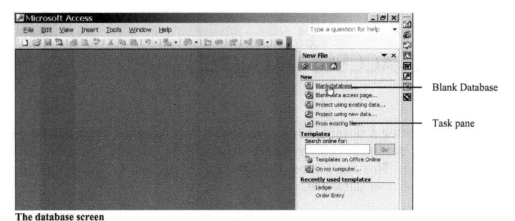

The database screen

The **File New dialog** box appears.

File New Database dialog box

3.   In the **File New Database** dialog box, select a folder in the **Save In** box and enter a name in the **File Name** box.

4.   Click on **Create**.

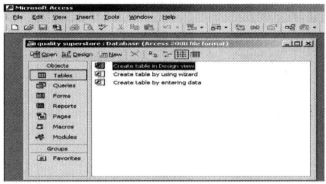

The Database window

The database window appears on the screen. You can create your own tables, queries, forms and report to populate the database.

Creating A Database Using A Wizard

If you can find a sample database that matches the database you want to create, then it is much quicker and easier to use the wizard to create a database. Suppose for example that Quality Superstores needs a database to manage its accounts and finances, it can choose the Ledger database in the sample database to create a similar database to manage its accounts. Using the Database Wizard, Quality Superstores can create a Ledger database to manage its accounts in less time. When you create a database with a wizard it comes pre-loaded with tables and the other objects in the database. Follow the steps below to create a database with the Wizard.

1.   Click on **New** on the toolbar.

2.   Under Templates in the task pane, click on **My Computer** ...

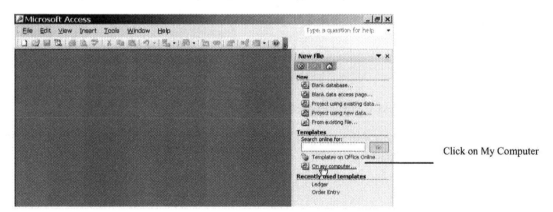

Click on My Computer

3.   Click on the **Databases** tab to display a number of sample databases.

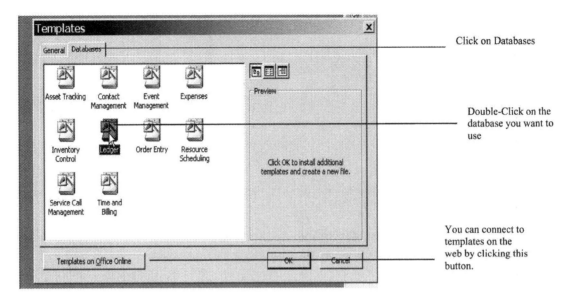

4.   Double-click the **Ledger Database** from the Sample databases displayed.

5.   The **File New Dialog box** appears.

6.   Select a folder and enter a name for the database. You can accept the default name Ledger or type in a new name in the **File name** box.

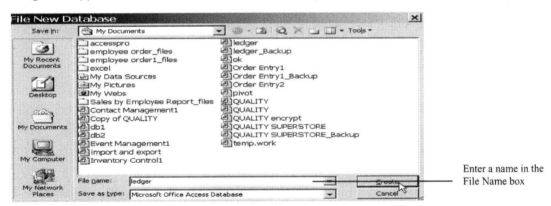

7.   Click on **Create** to create the Ledger database.

The Database wizard appears on the screen describing the information that would be stored on your database.

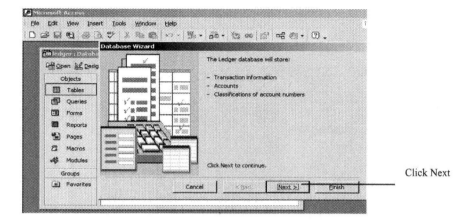

Click Next

8. Click **Next** to continue.

The database Wizard appears again with a list of the tables that will be used in creating the Ledger database. On the left side of the dialog box are the tables and on the right side are the fields of the highlighted table.

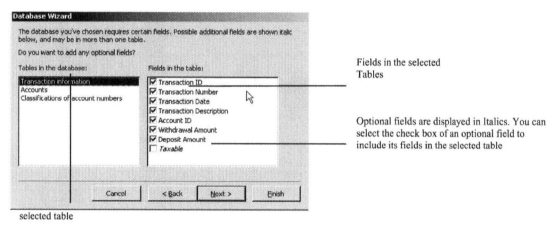

Fields in the selected Tables

Optional fields are displayed in Italics. You can select the check box of an optional field to include its fields in the selected table

selected table

9. Click **Next** to continue.

The **Style page** is displayed with a list of styles. There is a preview window on the left side of the list of styles. Select from the list of styles displayed and you will notice a preview of the selected style displayed in the preview window.

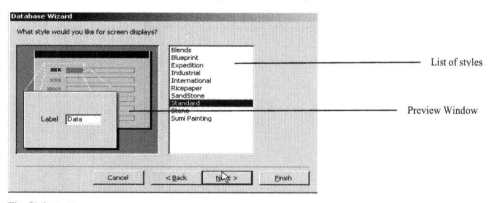

List of styles

Preview Window

The Style page

10. Click **Next** to continue.

The report style page appears. Chose a report style.

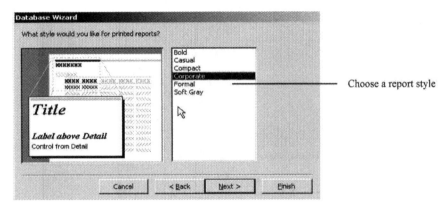

Choose a report style

The Report Style Page

11. Click **Next**. On the next page the wizard requests for a name for your database.

Accept the default name Ledger. Click the box next to **Yes, I'd like to include a picture**, if you want to include pictures in your database. For this sample database leave this box clear, as we do not want to include pictures in our database.

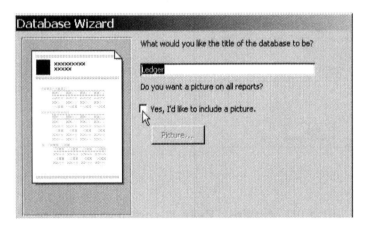

12. Click **Next**.

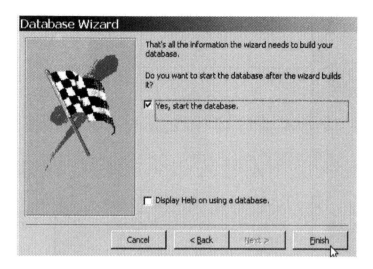

13. Click **Finish**.

The wizard starts creating the database. This may take a few seconds. Microsoft Access creates the objects including the tables, queries, forms and reports. When the wizard finishes creating the database, it displays the Main Switchboard with a Menu. A dialog box may appear requesting you to enter your company information before using the database. Click **Ok** to enter your company's information. After you have entered your company information etc. the main switchboard for the Ledger database appears.

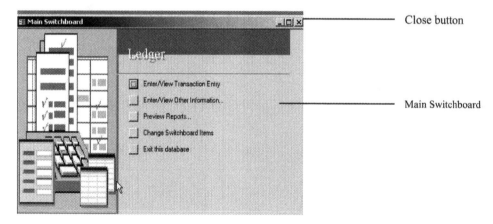

You can use this sample database to enter your accounts information, your cash withdrawal and deposits or any other transactions you may want to record in your ledger. You can also print and preview your reports. You may have to modify the ledger database to suit your needs. For example you may want to include and delete certain fields in the tables and customize the forms and reports to meet your needs.

You can also start entering data into your database straight away by choosing **Enter/View Transaction Entry** from the menu or close the database. Following the remaining steps to close the database.

14. When the database opened the Database window was minimized. You can maximize the database window by clicking on the maximize button.

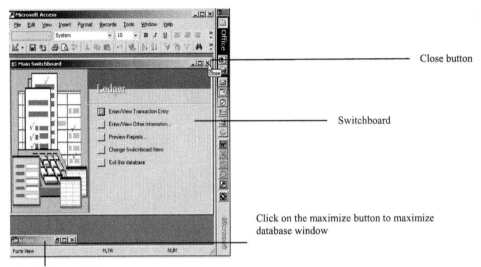

Close button

Switchboard

Click on the maximize button to maximize database window

The database window

15. You can close the database by clicking on the close (x) button in the Database window below.

Note: When you use the wizard to create a database, the database is created with tables and other objects in the database.

Chapter

TABLES

A **Table** is the basic storage unit of a Relational Database Management System and it consists of columns and rows.

A Relational Database Management System like Microsoft Access stores data about particular subjects in tables. Each table contains information about a specific topic or subject and each table has attributes, which describes the table. For example the Customer table has attributes like Customer ID, Customer Name, Customer Address, which describe the Customer table. Microsoft Access stores this attributes in **columns** called **fields**. The **fields** in a table make up a **record**, which describes an individual item. For example John Smith's record contains information about his address, city, postcode and company's details. This record contains information about John Smith only and no other person.

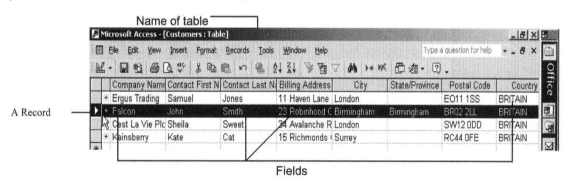

Examples of tables you can create for your database

- Suppliers table to store data about all your suppliers.

- Customers table to store data about all your customers.

- Orders table to store data about all your orders.

Data Integrity

According to Relational Database theory, every subject has a set of attributes, which uniquely identifies each row in that subject. Relational Database theory also states that no duplicate rows can exist in a table. This means that every row in a table must be unique. To ensure each row's uniqueness, a column or sets of columns are identified and assign a unique number(s), which identifies each row, and make it unique. This column or set of column, which uniquely identifies each row, is known as a **primary key**.

Primary Key

A primary key is a field or set of fields in the table, which uniquely identify an individual record or row.

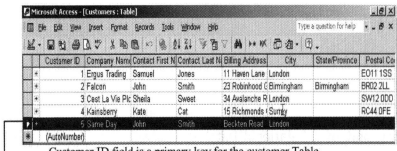
Customer ID field is a primary key for the customer Table

Quite often an ID number is chosen to represent a **primary key**. For example you can choose the Social Security Number as a primary key for the employee table or the vehicle registration number as the primary key for the vehicle table. When you enter data into a table with a primary key, Microsoft Access stops you from entering records with the same primary key value. So for the employee table, you cannot enter an employee with the same Social Security Number. This will ensure accuracy of data and prevent duplication. A primary key is unique and should not be empty. You can enter numbers or a combination of numbers and letter in your primary key field. You can also ask the computer to generate consecutive numbers for your table. The consecutive numbers generated by the computer is known as autonumber.

Foreign Key

A foreign key is a column in table whose value must exist as primary keys in another table. Primary and foreign keys work together to enforce referential integrity.

CREATING A TABLE

There are about three ways of creating a table. They are as follows:

- Create a table with the table wizard

- Create a table in Design view.

- Create a table by entering data in a data sheet.

Example

Suppose we want to create a table to hold information about all our customers, we can create a table with or without a wizard. If we can find a table with similar structure and fields like the customer table we want to create in the sample tables, then we can use a wizard to create the table, if not we may have to create the table from scratch.

Create A Table With A Table Wizard

The quickest and easiest way to create a table is to use a Wizard. Access comes with sample business and personal tables from which you can choose the one that best meets your needs. Follow the steps below to create a table with a wizard.

1. In the Database window click **Tables** under **Objects**.

2. Choose the **New** button.

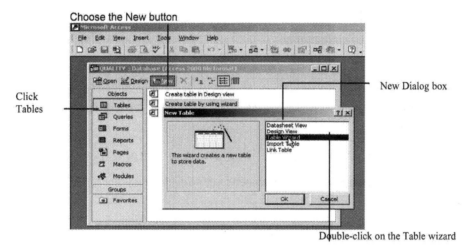

3. Double Click the **Table Wizard** in the New Table dialog box.

   The Table Wizard appears on the screen, click on either **Business** or **Personal** to display a list of either business or personal tables.

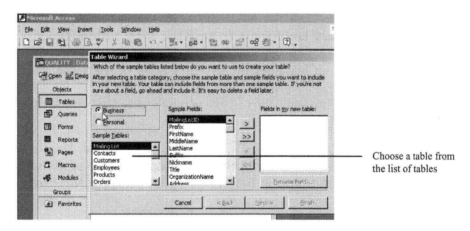

4. Choose a table from the list of tables and select the fields you want to add to your table from the **Sample fields**. Click the > button to move a field to the **Fields in my new table**, Click < to move a field back to the Sample fields. Click >> to move all the fields to **Fields in my new table** and click << to move all the fields back to Sample fields. You can rename the fields by click on **Rename field.**

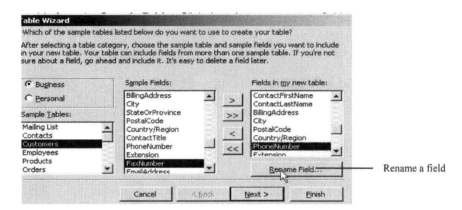

Rename a field

5. Repeat step 4 until you have selected all the fields for your table. Click on **Next** to continue.

6. Microsoft Access prompts you for a table name. Enter a name for your table.

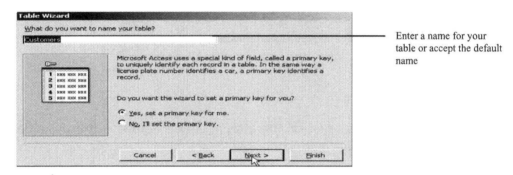

Enter a name for your table or accept the default name

7. Click **Yes, set a primary key for me** to have the wizard choose your primary key field, or **No, I'll set the primary key** to set the primary key yourself. If you click on **Yes**, skip to step 9. If you click on **No**, Click **Next** to continue.

    Hint If you are not sure about how to set primary keys click Yes to let Access set the primary key for you.

8. The Wizard next asks for a field you will like to be the primary key for your table. It also presents you with different options to choose the data type for the primary key field from. Choose from the following options and click **Next** to continue.

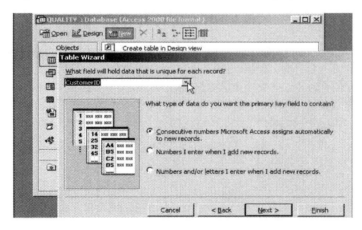

Options to choose the Data type for the primary key from

Consecutive numbers Microsoft Access assigns automatically to new records:
Choose this option if you want Access to automatically generate consecutive
numbers for your primary key.

Numbers I enter when I add new records: Choose this option if you want to
enter your own numbers for the primary key column.

Numbers and/letters I enter when I add new records: Choose this option if you
want to enter both numbers and letters in the primary key field.

9. The next page is the Wizards last screen. It presents you with the option to
Modify the table design or **Enter data directly into the table, Enter data into
the table using a form the wizard creates for me.** Accept the default option if
you want to enter data directly into the table. If you want to modify the table
choose **Modify the table design.** For this example choose **Enter data directly
into the table.**

10. Click on **Finish.**

If you accepted the default option, which is **Enter data directly into the table,**
your screen will look similar to the screen below.

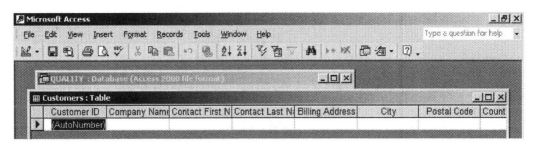

Create A Table In Design View (Without A Table Wizard)

Microsoft Access Wizards can be convenient and the quickest way to create tables,
however, sometimes you may find that the sample tables do not meet your needs, in a
situation like this you may have to create the table from scratch. Follow the steps below
to create a table in Design view.

1. In the Database window click **Tables** under **Objects.**

2. Choose the **New** button.

Microsoft Access displays the New Table Dialog.

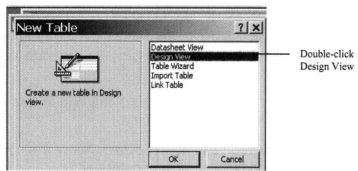

The New Table Dialog box

3. Double-click **Design View.**

    Microsoft Access opens a blank Table window in Design view.

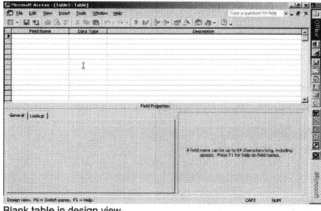

Blank table in design view

4. Type a field name in the **Field Name** column. Press Tab to move to the **Data Type** column.

5. In the **Data Type** Column you can accept the default data type or select a data type from the drop down list. See **Understanding Access Data Types and other field properties** later on in the chapter for a list of data types and how to use them.

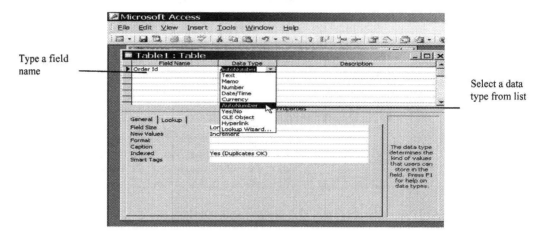

6. In the lower bottom of the dialog box are the field properties. Use this section to format the fields. You can format the **field size**, **input mask** and other properties in the lower bottom of the dialog box. For example you can format the UnitPrice field by selecting the Unit Price in the Upper section and clicking the **General Tab** in the lower bottom and then selecting the **Format** property.   You can then select the format you want from the drop-down list as indicated below.

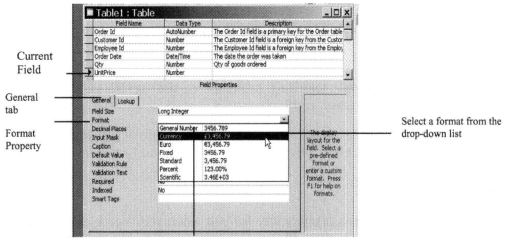

Click the format property box and select currency from the list.

7. Press tab to move to the **description column**. This is an optional field; you can describe the fields in your table in this column. For example you could describe the Order Id field in this column. Type, **The Order Id field is a primary key field for this table** in the description field.

    Press the **Tab** key to move to the **Field Name column**.

8. Repeat step 4-7 until you finish creating the fields in your table.

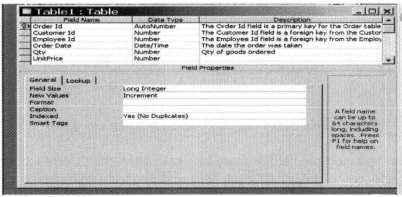

A table in design View

9. When you finish creating all the fields for your table Click on the save button to save your table. Enter a name for your table in the **Save As** dialog box and click **ok** to save your table.

    A dialog box appears advising you about the need to have a primary key for your table.

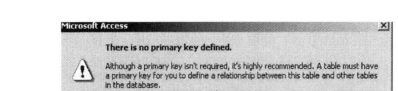

10. Click on **Yes** to allow Access to create a primary key for you.

    Note that you can create your own primary key

    If you want to create your own primary key, click on **No.** Creating a primary key will be discussed later in the chapter.

11. Click on the close icon on the upper right hand side of the design window to close the table in the design view and return to the Database window.

Setting Up A Primary Key

Microsoft Access can set the primary key for you when you create a table or you set the primary key field yourself. Follow the steps below to set a primary key yourself.

1.   Open the table in **Design View.**

2.   Select the **field(s)** you want to use as the primary key.

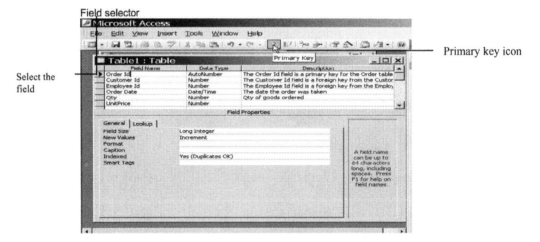

    Tip: To create a multiple field primary key, hold down the **Ctrl key** and then click the **field selector** to the left of each field that you want to include.

3.   Click the **primary key icon** on the toolbar or choose **Set Primary key** from the **Edit Menu.**

The primary key icon appears next to the designated primary key field.

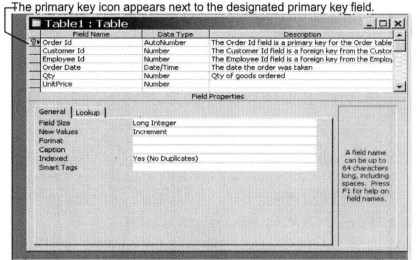

The Order table with the Order Id field set as the primary key

To remove the primary key

To remove the primary key, select the field or fields designated as primary keys and then click the **Primary key icon** on the toolbar or choose **Primary key** from the **Edit Menu.**

Create A Table By Entering Data

1. Press **F11** to switch to the **Database Window.**

2. In the Database Window, click on **Tables** under **Objects** and click on **New.**

3. Double-click on **Datasheet View.**

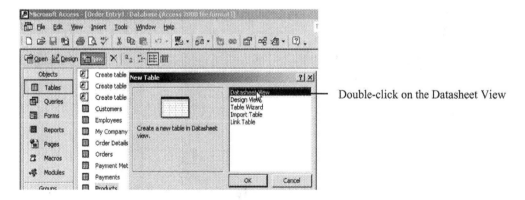

Double-click on the Datasheet View

A blank table appears with the default fields field1, field2, field3 and so on.

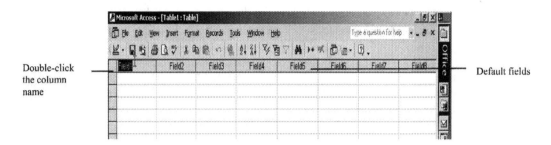

Double-click the column name

Default fields

4. Double-click the **column name**. You will observe the fieldname highlighted. Rename the column by typing a new name for the column on the highlighted text and then press the **Enter** key.

5. Repeat step 4 until you finish renaming all the fields.

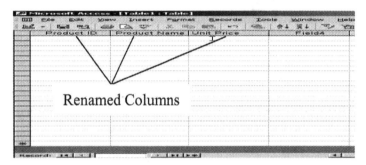

Renamed Columns

6. Enter data in the datasheet. Type the data that correspond to each field for example enter **Product Id** in the **ProductId** field. Press the **Enter Key** and enter **Products name** in the **product name** column. Press Enter to move to the next column and enter the **Unit price** in the **Unit price** column.

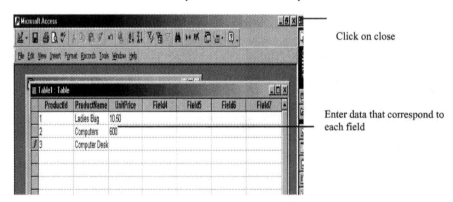

Click on close

Enter data that correspond to each field

When you finish entering all the data, click on the close button or the save icon ![save icon] to save your table.

The **Save As dialog** box appears.

7. Enter a name for your table and click **Ok** to save your table.

A dialog box appears advising you on whether to let Microsoft Access create a primary key for you or not.

8. Click **Yes** to have Microsoft Access create a primary key for your table or **No** to create the primary key later.

Taking a Break

You may want to take a break and return to your work later on. Follow the steps below to close the database.

1. Form the File **Menu**, click on **Close**.

For confidential reasons, you may want to turn off your computer. If you want to turn off your computer, you will have to exit from Microsoft Access.

2. Click on **File** and then click on **Exit** to quit Microsoft Access.

Returning from Break

1. Start Microsoft Access as discussed in the section on **Starting Microsoft Access**.

2. Click on **File** and select the database file you want to open from the list of recently opened files displayed at the bottom of the file menu.

You can also click on the **File Menu** and select **Open** and then click on the folder that contains the file you want to open, select the file from the list of files displayed in that folder and then click on **Open** to open the file.

UNDERSTANDING ACCESS DATA TYPES AND OTHER FIELD PROPERTIES

Microsoft Access stores information in different formats. The data type determines the type of information that can be stored in the field.

ACCESS DATA TYPES

The following are a list of some of the data types in access and the type of data they can store.

Data Type	Type of Data Access Stores	Size
Text	Stores text or a combination of text and numbers.	Up to 255 characters
Memo	Use for lengthy text. Stores text or combination of numbers and text	Up to 65,536 characters
Number	Numeric values	1,2,4 or 8 bytes
Date/time	Dates and times	8 bytes

Currency	Currency values or any monetary values.	8 bytes
Auto Number	A numeric value that Microsoft Access automatically assigns to each record. It can be increase sequentially by 1.	4 bytes
Yes/No	Use for Yes/No, True or False, On or off.	1 bit
OLE Object	Use for graphic, pictures, sound, Word document, Excel sheet or other binary data.	1 gigabyte
Hyperlink	Use for hyperlinks i.e. the location of another database object or a page on the web.	64,000 characters
Lookup Wizard	Use for creating a field whose values come from another table or a list of values using a combo box.	4 bytes

Working with tables in different views

When you work with tables you can view your table in Design view and Datasheet view.

The **Design view**: you can create a new table in design view or you can make changes to the design of an existing table. In the Design view of a table, you can specify the structure of the table and modify the field properties. The design view gives you more flexibility over the table's design than the Table wizard. You may want to use the Design view to create tables that are not available in the sample tables or to customize existing table

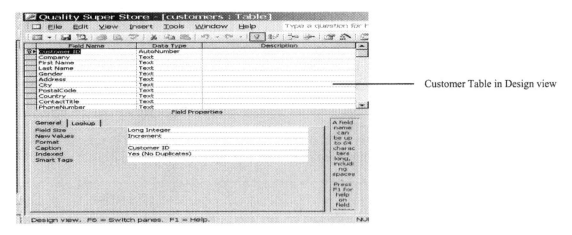

Customer Table in Design view

Datasheet view

The **datasheet view** is where you view the data in your table. The datasheet view displays the data in your table in rows and columns.

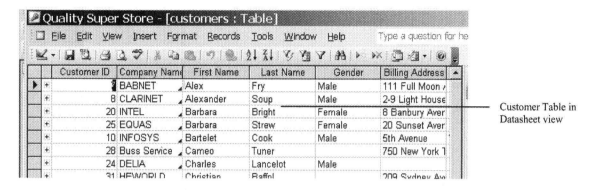

Customer Table in
Datasheet view

Switching between different views

You can switch between the different views in a table by using the view ![icon] tool button on the toolbar. Follow the steps below to switch between the different views in a table.

1. Click on the **View** ![icon] tool button on the toolbar.

2. Select from the drop-down list the view you want. For example to switch to Design view, click on **Design View**

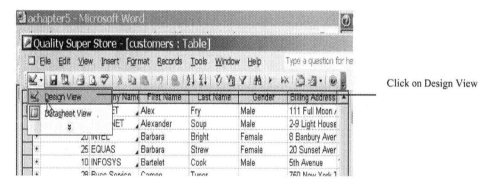

Click on Design View

Chapter

CUSTOMISING A TABLE IN DESIGN VIEW

You can customise a table in Design view by adding, removing and re-arranging fields. You can also set and change the data type and other properties of a field to ensure accurate and valid data are stored in your tables.

The Design view is used to customise the design of a table.

Adding, Deleting And Rearranging Fields In A Table

Access is quite flexible; you can add fields, delete and rearrange fields in your table.

Example

Suppose after creating the customer table, you decide that you may need an additional field to store information about customer's e-mail address, you can add an additional field to the table in design view.

Adding Fields To A Table

You can add additional fields to the end of the list in your table or add a field between two fields.

To add a field to the end of a list

1. Open the table in **Design View**.

2. Click in the **first blank row**.

Click in field Name   Click Data Type Click in the Description

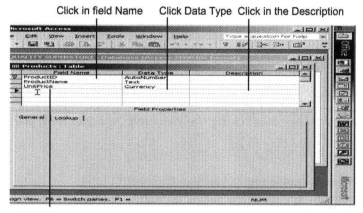

Click inside the first blank row

3.   Click in the **Field Name** column and enter a name for the field.

4.   Click in the **Data Type** column and select a data type for the field.

5.   Click in the **Description** field and type a description for the field, the description field is an optional you can leave it blank.

Add a field between two existing fields

1.   Open the table in the **design view**.

2.   Click in the row below where you want to insert the field and then click the insert row button on the toolbar. Microsoft Access inserts a blank row between the fields.

Click the row below where you want to insert the field

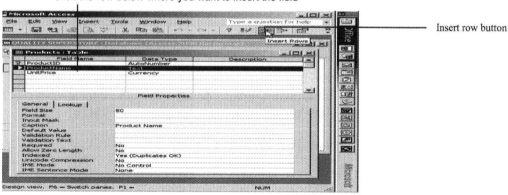

Insert row button

3.   Click in the **Field Name** column and type a name for the field.

4.   Click in the **Data Type** column and select a data type for the field.

5.   Click in **the Description field** and type a description for the field, this field is optional you can leave it blank.

Deleting A Field From A Table

Sometimes after creating a field, you may find that you don't need that field again. Redundant fields can waste space and slow down performance. You can improve the performance of a table by removing any field(s) that you no longer need. Unwanted fields can be deleted to improve performance. Follow the steps below to delete a field.

1.   Open the Table in **Design View**.

2.   Select the Field(s) you want to delete by clicking the field selector and then press the

Delete Key or click the Delete Row button ⬛ on the toolbar.

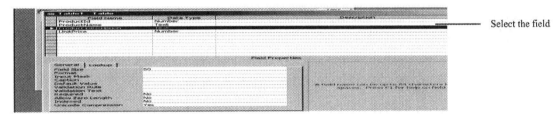

Select the field

Renaming A Field In Design View

You may decide to rename a field after using the wizard to create a table. Follow the steps below to rename a field.

1.   Open the Table in **Design View**.

2.   Double-click the field name you want to rename.

3.   Type the new name and save ⬛ the changes you have made by clicking on the save button on the toolbar.

Rearranging A Field In Design View

Microsoft Access uses the same order in which the fields are arranged in the Design View to display data in the Datasheet View or in forms or report. It is therefore necessary to arrange the fields in the order you want them to appear in the forms or datasheet view. If you are not happy with the order of the fields in design view you can always rearrange them. Follow the instructions below to rearrange the fields in your table.

Follow the steps below to re-arrange the fields in a table.

1.   Open the table in **Design View**.

2.   Select the field by clicking the field selector on the left of the field name.

3.   Click the Field Selector again holding down the mouse and drag it to the desired position.

Select the field

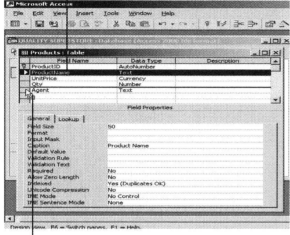

Drag field selector to the desired position

If you change your mind about an insertion or deletion, you can undo the changes by clicking on the Undo button. You can also choose Edit ➤ Undo.

Copy A Field

The quickest way to create a field with similar field properties is to copy the field and give it another name. Follow the steps below to copy a field.

1. Select the field(s) you want to copy.

2. Click on the copy button 🗐 on the toolbar and click in a blank row.

3. Click the paste button 🗐 on the toolbar. Another field with the same name as the field you have copied replaces the blank row.

4. Type a new name for the new field you have just copied.

    Note: The original field property will be copied into this new field, but not the data contained in the original field

Changing The Data Type For A Field

The data type controls the type of data that is entered into a field. The different type of data you can enter in a field ranges from text, numbers, date, memo etc. For example if the data type is set to number, you cannot enter text into that field. Microsoft will refuse the entry and display and warning.

Example

The data type for the supplierId field was initially created as number data type. You may decide to change the SupplierId field from number to text so that you can store both numbers and text in that field. Follow the steps below to change the data type.

1. Open the table in **Design View**.

2.   Click the **Data Type** column of the field whose data type you want to change.

3.   Click the drop-down list and select the data type from the list displayed.

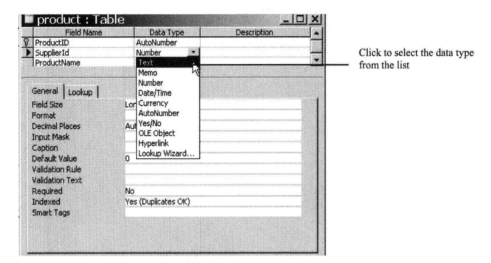

Click to select the data type from the list

Caution: if your table contains data, the data in your table will be converted to the new data type that you have selected. In some instances you may lose data. Microsoft Access will inform you about any errors that occur in the conversion.

4.   Click **Ok** to save the changes.

Changing Or Setting Fields Properties

The field property determines what data can be entered in a field and how the data will be displayed. When you create a table, Microsoft Access sets the default field properties for the field. Sometimes, you may find that the default values do not meet your needs. You can customise the field properties to meet your needs.

You can also set a fields property to ensure that valid data is stored in your table. For example you can ensure that the value in a field is always entered by setting the **required property** to **Yes**. You can also control the display of data and specify default values with the field's properties. It is good practice to set fields property in the Table Design View so they can be automatically applied to a query, form or report.

With Access 2003 when you change certain inherited property, you will be presented with the option to update all controls in forms and reports that depend on the field whose property you have changed. For example when you change the **Input Field Property** in a table, Microsoft Access presents you with the option to update all controls that use this field.

Properties can be set or change in the **Design View** using the **General** and the **Lookup** Tab. The **General Tab** allows you to set properties. The **Look up tab** allows you to set up values for a lookup list. Follow the steps below to set the properties for the field.

In the Database window, click on the table you want to customise.

1. Switch to **Design View**. In the upper section of the window, click the field whose property you want to set.

2. Click the **General** tab in the lower section to set the general properties or click the **look up** tab to set properties relating to look up fields.

3. Click inside the property box that you want to set and enter the new value or select the values from a drop down list.

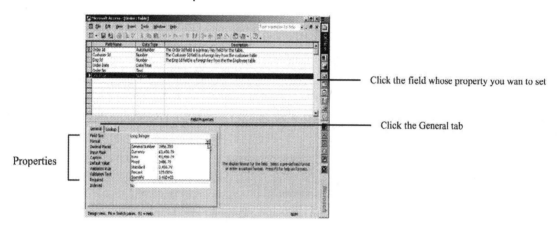

The properties available for a field depend on the field data type.

The following describes some of the field properties available in Microsoft Access.

Field Size Property

The Field Size property is used to set the maximum size for data stored in a field with a data type set to Text, Number or AutoNumber. If the field data type is set to Text you can enter a value between 0 and 255.   If the field data type is set to AutoNumber you can set the field size property to Long Integer or Replication Id. If the field data type is set to Number you can select Decimal or any value from the drop down list as indicated below.

Text fields

For fields with text data type you can specify the maximum number of characters you can enter in that field. For example you can set the Product Name field to 20 characters. This means that the Product Name field can only store a maximum of 20 characters. If you try to enter more than 20 characters in that field, a message is displayed warning you.

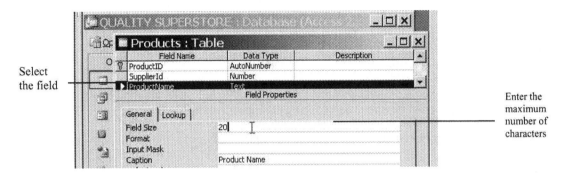

Select the field

Enter the maximum number of characters

Number Fields

The field size property for a number field determines the values that can be stored in the field. A number field can be set to Byte, Integer, Long Inter, Single, double, Replication ID and Decimal. For a field that stores large numbers an **Integer** or **Long Integer** will be a suitable field size property. You can also set a field that stores numbers with decimals to Double or Single.

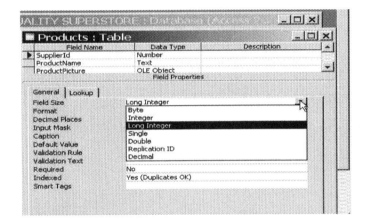

Format Property

The **format property** determines how a value is displayed on the screen or printed. You can use the format property to customise the way text, memo, numbers and dates are displayed and printed.

Text and Memo

You can use the following characters to create custom text and memo fields.

Character	Description
>	Displays text in uppercase.
<	Displays text in lower case
@	Displays a character or a space
&	Displays a character if a character exists, if not it doesn't display anything.

Example

For example to display the department name in capital, you select the DeptName field and put the > sign in the **format** property in design view, this will cause all Departments to be displayed in capitals.

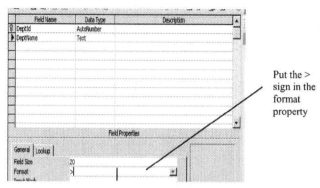

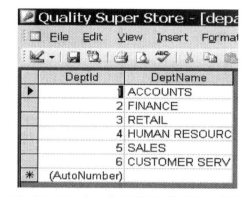

Put the > sign in the format property

The Greater than character will display all departments in capitals

Results of applying the > format to the DeptName field

Number and currency fields

Character	Description
General Number	Displays the number you entered in the field.
Currency	Displays a number according to the windows regional settings. For example Access will display amount with a comma separator, currency symbol and decimals. $1,562.23
Euro	Displays amount in Euro. The position of the Euro sign and decimal is according to the windows regional setting. €1,562.00
Fixed	Displays a specific number of decimal places for the number. For example displays a number with two decimal places. If you want to change the number of decimal places, use the Decimal Places settings below to set the number of decimal places you want. 53.20
Standard	Displays a number according to the regional setting for numbers. Uses the thousand separators and a comma to format your number. 6,236.45
Percent	Multiplies the value by 100 and displays the value with a percent sign (%). For example .856 will displayed as 85.60%
Scientific	Applies scientific notation to the number. 1.23E+5

Date/Time fields

The following format is available for date and time data type

Format	Descriptions
General	Displays a number as a date. If the number has a fraction, the fractional part is displayed as time. 09/02/78 00:19
Long Date	Displays the date in full according to the windows regional setting. Monday, February 28,2004.
Medium Date	Displays the date in abbreviation, using hyphens to separate month, day and year. Feb-28-2004.
Short Date	Displays the date according to the regional setting for short dates. 2/28/2004.
Long Time	Displays the time in full according to the windows regional setting for long time. 1:23:15 am
Medium Time	Displays a time in 12 hours format, with the AM or PM and the seconds omitted. 1:23 AM.
Short Time	Displays a time in 24 hours format omitting the seconds. 1:30 PM will be displayed as 13:30.

Example of a date format

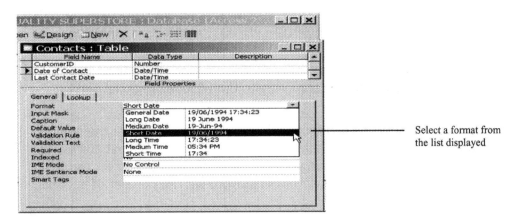

Select a format from the list displayed

When you change a format field, Microsoft Access presents you with the option to update all fields that depend on the field whose format you have changed.

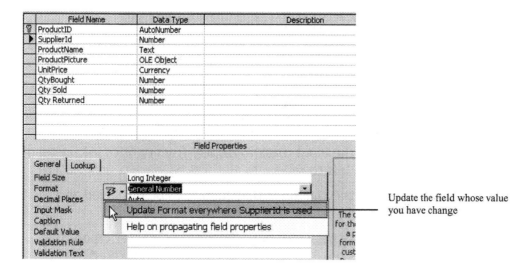

Field Name	Data Type	Description
ProductID	AutoNumber	
SupplierId	Number	
ProductName	Text	
ProductPicture	OLE Object	
UnitPrice	Currency	
QtyBought	Number	
Qty Sold	Number	
Qty Returned	Number	

Field Properties

General | Lookup |

Field Size   Long Integer
Format   General Number
Decimal Places   Auto
Input Mask   Update Format everywhere SupplierId is used
Caption   Help on propagating field properties
Default Value
Validation Rule
Validation Text

Update the field whose value you have change

Decimal Places Property

You can use the decimal places property to display the number of decimal places after the decimal point. Microsoft Access uses the decimal places property to display the number of decimal places for a field with a **Number** or **Currency** data type.

Input Mask Property

If the data you enter in a field always follows the same pattern, you can create a field template, which Microsoft Access can use to display, and control how data is entered into a field. Input Mask Property are generally used in Text, Date/Time and the settings include literal characters such as spaces, dots, dashes and parentheses. An input mask will automatically show literal characters in a field. It will also prevent you from entering inappropriate character in a field. For example if you always enter the first three characters of a telephone number in parenthesis followed by a dash, you can create an input mask that will display the parentheses and a dash in your data entry form, this will simplify data entry and ensure accuracy in your data. With input mask, you can ensure that the data you enter fits into the input mask and match the data type you have specified.

Examples of common input mask

Characters	Description
0	Digit required, (0-9)
9	Digit or Space (Entry not required) (Optional).
#	Digit, +, - sign or space. (Optional). Blank positions are converted to spaces.
L	Letter (A-Z entry required)
?	Letter (A-Z entry not required).
A	Letter or digit (entry required)
&	Any character or space (entry required)

C	Any character or space (entry not required)
.,:;-/	Decimal placeholders, thousands, date and time separators. The character used depends on the regional windows settings.
<	All characters that follows are converted to lower case.
>	All characters that follows are converted to upper case.
!	Causes the input mask to display from right to left instead of from left to right.
\	Causes the character that follows to be displayed as a literal character.
Password	Creates a password entry box. Any character typed into this box is displayed as asterisk * and stored as the character.

You can enter the input mask directly into the input mask property box, or use the wizard to apply any of standard formats supplied by Microsoft Access.

Example

You want to create an input format that will accept the telephone numbers of your clients in the following input format i.e. (_ _ _)-_ _ _-_ _ _ Follow the steps below to create an input mask.

Creating an input format by hand

1. Open the table in **Design View**

2. Select the field you want to create an input format for in the upper section of the dialog box.

3. Click inside the **Input Mask** property box (in the lower section of the dialog box), and enter the input mask you want to apply.

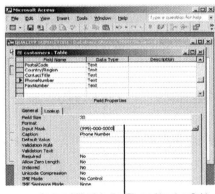

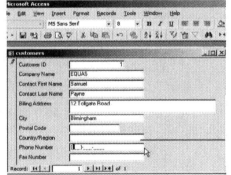

An Input Mask in the Phone Number field   Results of applying the input mask

A parenthesis and a hyphen is displayed in the Phone Number field during Data Entry

Create an input mask with the wizard

1. Open the table in **Design View**.

2. Select the field whose input format you want to set or change.

3. Click the Build button ... next to the **Input Mask** property box. The Input Mask Wizard appears.

Select
the

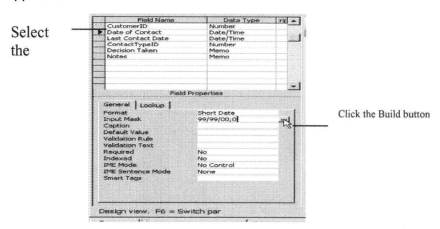

Click the Build button

4. Select an input mask from a list of input mask and click **Next** to continue.

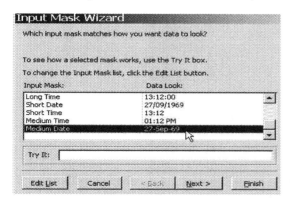

5. On this page, you can change the input mask and placeholder for the date or accept the default format displayed.   Click the box labeled **Try It** to preview the changes. Click **Next.**

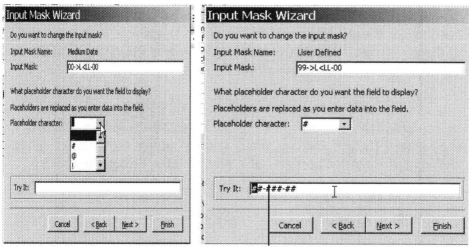

A preview of the changes you have made

6. Click **Finish**. The new input mask is displayed in the Input Mask box.

7. Press Enter. The Property Update box appears next to the Input Mask.

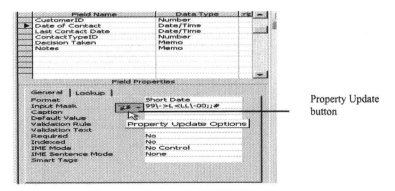

8. Click the **Property Update** button to display a list of options.

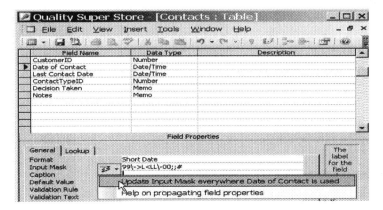

9. Click on **Update Input Mask everywhere Date of Contact is used**. This will apply the new changes anywhere Date of Contact is used.

10. Save your changes.

Caption Property

The **Caption property** is used to specify a label for a control in a form or report or is used as a column heading for the field in a table or query in Datasheet view. If the **Caption** Property is left blank, Microsoft Access uses the field name as the default value. You can change the caption property to meet your need.

Example

For example you created the customers table using the table wizard, you want to change label or column heading for the PhoneNumber field to Telephone Number. Follow the steps below to change the caption property of a field in Table Design View.

1. Open the table in **Design View**.

2. Select the field whose Caption you want to change.

3. Select the Caption label you want to change.

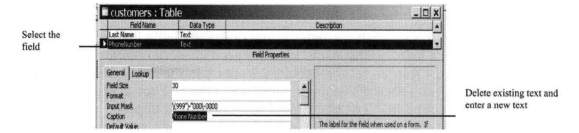

Select the field

Delete existing text and enter a new text

4. Delete the existing text and enter a new text in the Caption field.

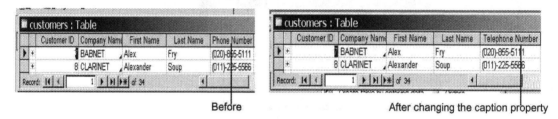

Before

After changing the caption property

Default Value Property

If from experience you know that certain fields always contain the same value, you can set a default value, which will always be displayed whenever you create a new record.

Example

For example in the Order form the order date will always be the same as the system date. You can set the default value property to the system date. For example you can enter = **Date() or =Now()** in the **Default field** property to insert the system date or time into the Order Date field. Each time you add a new record to the Order table, the system date is displayed in the Order Date field.

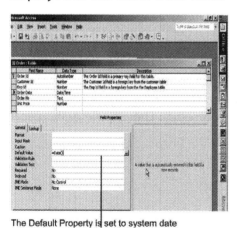

The Default Property is set to system date

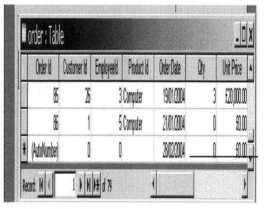

A default date is displayed in the Order Table

Default date displayed in a new record

Required Property

The Required Property is used to ensure that a field contains a value for every record you enter. If you set the Required Property to **Yes**, Microsoft access will ensure that that field is not left blank.

Example

For example, even though each customer in the Customer Table has an Id, you may still want the Customer's first and last name to be entered in every record you create before you save the record. You can set the Required Property in the First Name and Last Name to **Yes**. When you set a record's Required Property to Yes and you try to save the record with any of the required field left blank, Microsoft Access will display a message and will not save the record until you enter data in the First Name and Last Name field.

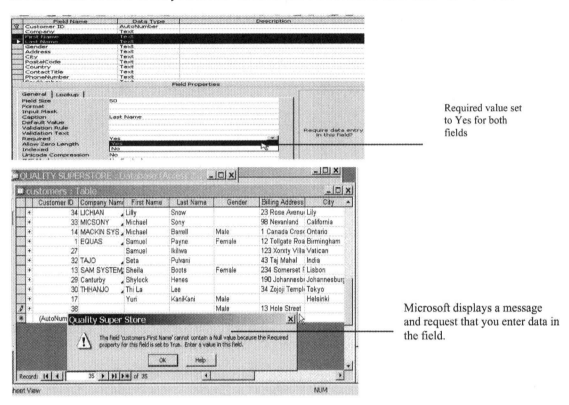

Required value set to Yes for both fields

Microsoft displays a message and request that you enter data in the field.

Validation Rule Property

A field's Validation Rule Property is used to check the value entered in a field. For example in the Products Table you can set the validation rule property for the Qty field to accept only values less than 80. If a value greater than 80 is entered in the Qty field Microsoft Access displays a message.

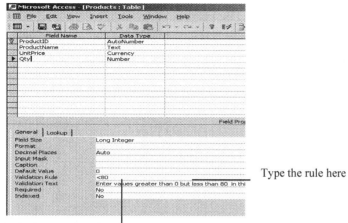

Type the rule here

Enter the text you want to display in the Validation Text field

Validation Text Property

The Validation Text Property is used to enter a message that will be displayed when the validation rule is broken.

Example

For example in the previous example when a number greater than 80 is entered in the Qty field the message "Enter values greater than 0 but less than 80 in this field" is displayed. This text you want to display is entered in the Validation Text Property field.

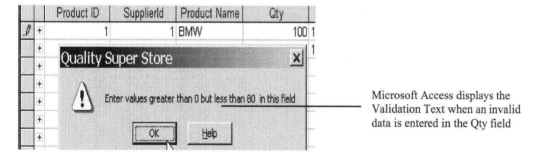

Microsoft Access displays the Validation Text when an invalid data is entered in the Qty field

Indexed Property

An Indexed field is a field Microsoft Access uses to search a table or sort records with. Indexes speeds up searches, however sorting and running of queries on an index field, require more space and can slow down data entry. For example when you add data to a table with an index, Microsoft will have to update the index each time a record is added to the table this can slow down data entry. You can create an Index on a single field or on multiple fields. Multiple-field Index is used to distinguish between records in which the first field may have the same values. For example in the customer table you can have many people with the same last name. In order to distinguish between two records with the same names you could create a multiple-field index which will include both the first and last name field, this way records with the same last name can be distinguish by the second field (first name).

> Note: The primary key of a table is automatically indexed, and you can't index a field whose data type is memo or OLE object.

Example

In the Order Entry database you may find from experience that it is easier and quicker to search for a customer using the customer's postcode but as the table gets bigger searching for a customer takes longer. You can speed up your search by creating an index on the Post Code field.

Creating a single-field Index

1.   Open the Table in the **Design View**.

2.   Click the field you want to use as your index field in the upper section of the window.

3.   In the lower section of the window, click on the **Index** property box and select from the drop-down list. Microsoft Access gives you the following options.

   •   **Yes (Duplicates Ok)** this option allows you to enter the same value in more than one record.

   •   **Yes (No Duplicates)** this creates a unique index and does not allow the same value in other records.

   •   **No** choose this option if you don't want to create an index on this field. You can enter the same value for more than one record.

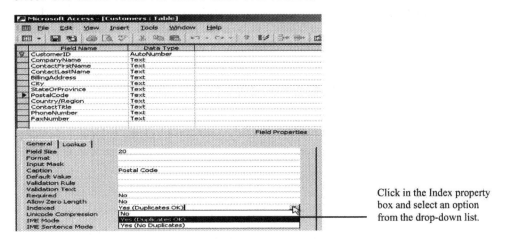

Click in the Index property box and select an option from the drop-down list.

4.   When you finish, click on the close (x) button and when asked whether or not to Save the table, click **Yes**.

Creating Multiple-field Indexes

In the Order Entry database you may realize that when you do the search for a customer by the Postcode, you may end up with customers with the same postcodes and same last names. You can improve your search by creating a multi-field index based on more than one field. For example you can search first on the postcode and narrow your search using the last and first names.

When you create a multiple-field index, Microsoft Access sorts first by the first field listed in the Indexes windows. If there are records with the same values in the field, Microsoft Access sorts next by the second fields listed, followed by the 3rd and 4th etc. until it finishes sorting the table. You can include up to 10 fields in a multiple-field index. Follow the steps below to create a multiple-field index.

1. In Table **Design View,** click on the Index button 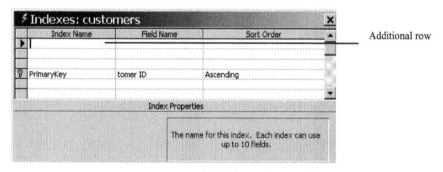 on the toolbar. The Indexes window is displayed.

Additional row

Use the Insert key or insert row button on the tool to add additional rows if you need to.

2. Type a name for the index in first blank row in the **Index Name** column.

3. Press tab to move to the next column, which is the **Field Name** column. In the **Field Name** column, click the down arrow to select the first field for your index.

4. Press tab to move to the next column. Select the sort order for this field. You can select Ascending or Descending.

5. Press tab to move to the next row. Leave the **Index Name** blank and click the **Field Name** column, select the second field for the index. Select the sort order. Repeat this step until you have included all the fields you want to index.

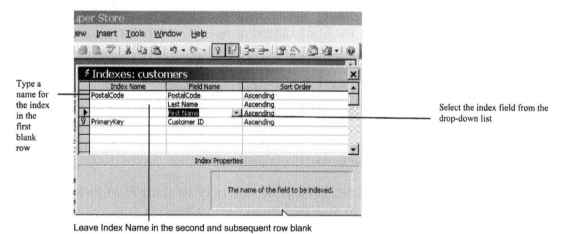

Type a name for the index in the first blank row

Select the index field from the drop-down list

Leave Index Name in the second and subsequent row blank

Viewing and Editing Indexes

You can see the indexed fields in a table by opening the indexes window in the Design view.

1. Open the Table in the **Design view.**

2.   Click on the Index button 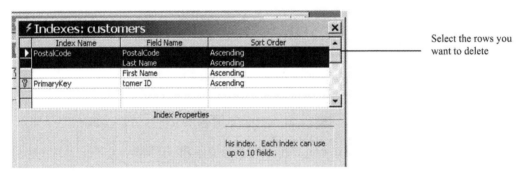 on the Tool bar, or click on the View Menu and select Indexes. Microsoft Access displays the Indexes Window.

3.   Make the changes you want and click on the save button to save the changes.

Deleting an Index

1.   Open the table in the **Design view**.

2.   Click on the **Index** button on the **Toolbar**. The Indexes window appears.

3.   Select the row or rows containing the index you want to delete.

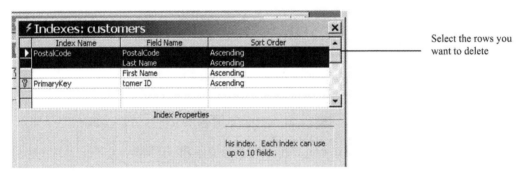

4.   Press the **Delete** key to delete the index. This will delete the index not the field from the table.

Smart Tags Property

Smart tags appear as short cut menus with a list of actions to choose from. They are time saving tags attach to fields or control in Microsoft Office to perform specific actions. They save time because clicking on any of options displayed will open the program relating to the option without clicking on the Start button or opening the program the usual way.

Example

For example in Microsoft Access 2003, if a field or control has a smart tag attached it, you can activate the field or control to display a list of action you can perform with the field. You can then select from the actions displayed to open the program relating to the field without going to Start, Program, Program name. For example clicking on **send Mail** from the list of actions will open the e-mail program.

Smart tags can be attach to a field in a table, query or to controls in forms and reports. The smart tag property is use to attached smart tags to fields or controls.

Attaching Smart Tags to a field in a table

You can attach a smart tag to a field in a table; for example, you can add a smart tag to an e-mail field in the customer table and make it easier and quicker to send e-mails to companies without opening the mail program.

1.   Open the table in **Design View**

2.   Select the field you want to add the smart tag to.

3.   Click the Build ... button in the Smart Tags property box.

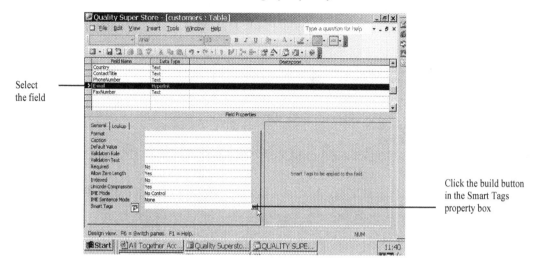

Microsoft Access displays the Smart Tags dialog box.

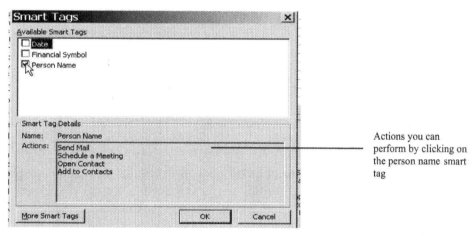

The Smart Tag dialog box

4.   Select from the available smart tags list. For example select **Person Name** smart tag. The details of the Smart Tag and the action you can perform with them are displayed in the lower window of the Smart Tag Detail box. The actions vary depending on the smart tag you choose.

5.   Click **Ok**.

You can view the result of applying a smart tag to a field in datasheet view.

To view the results of applying a smart tag to field, first open the table in datasheet view.

Open the table in datasheet view. When you open the table in datasheet view you will see small triangular shapes displayed next to the field you attached the smart tag to. Hovering the mouse over the field will display the smart tags icon .

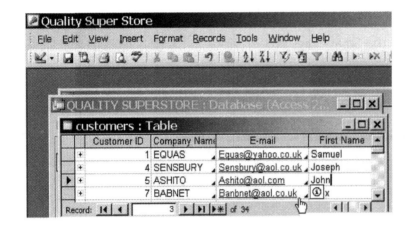

Click the smart tag icon to display a list of actions you can perform with the smart tag.

List of actions you can perform with the smart tag.

To send an email to the customer whose record you have selected click on the down arrow next to the smart tag icon, and select **Send Mail** from the list of options displayed. The e-mail program is displayed with the e-mail of the selected customer displayed in the e-mail box. Enter the message and send the e-mail to your customer.

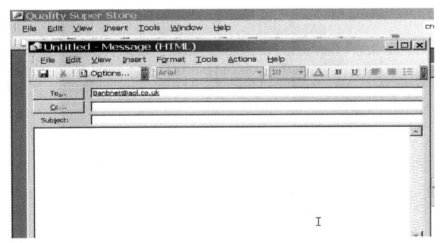

Microsoft Outlook is open with the e-mail address of the selected customer displayed.

Chapter

7

RELATIONSHIPS IN ACCESS DATABASE

One of the strength of a Relational Database Management System like Access is its ability to relate data from separate tables through a common field. Microsoft Access stores information about each subject in separate tables and combines the information through the relationships between the tables to create forms, reports and queries.

Relationships work by matching data from common fields in two tables. For example, the **customers** table is related to the orders table by the common field (Customer Id). Suppose you want to find the total number of orders placed by each customer, you will need to match information from the customers table with the **orders** table. The Customer Id field in the **customers** table is matched with similar Customers Id field in the **orders** table. Microsoft Access uses the relationships existing between the tables to find associated information. For example Microsoft Access will use the Customer Id of a particular customer field to find all the orders placed by that customer.

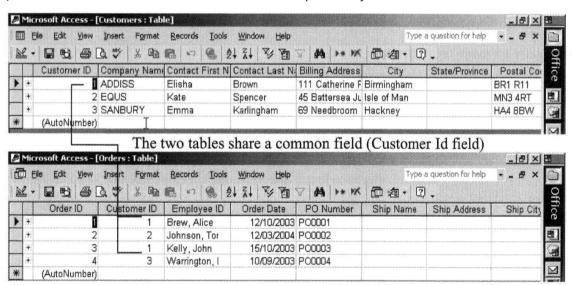

From the two tables you can tell that the Elisha Brown with a Customer Id 1 placed two orders one on the 15/10/03 and the other one 10/10/03 by matching the Customer Id field in both tables.

You can also pull information from two tables using the relationship that exist between the tables to produce a report, for example the Order Analysis Report shown below is a combination of information from the Orders table and the customers table..

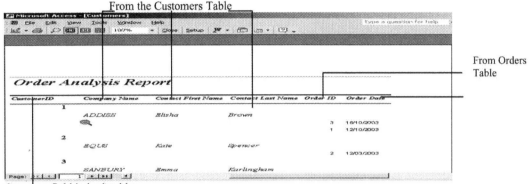

Setting up a relationship

To set up a relationship between two tables, you add one table's primary key to the other table, so that both tables have a common field. But how do you determine which table's primary key to use.

Determining which table's primary key to use

Before you can determine which table's primary key to use, you need to know the type of relationship that exists between the tables.

There are three types of relationships between tables. They are the

- One-to-many relationships

- Many-to-many relationships

- One-to-One relationships.

Types of Relationships

One-to-Many Relationship

The most common type of relationship is the one-to-many relationship. In a **One-to-many** type of relationship a record in table A has more than one related records in the other table B. An example of this type of relationship is the customers' table and the orders table.

To set up a One-to-many relationship, you add the primary key from the one-side of the relationship to the many side of the relationship.

Example

For example to set up the relationship between the **customers'** table and the **orders** table, you add the primary key (Customers Id) from the customers' table (the one-side of the relationship) to the Orders table (many side of the relationship). In practical terms, you will add a Customer Id field to the orders table.

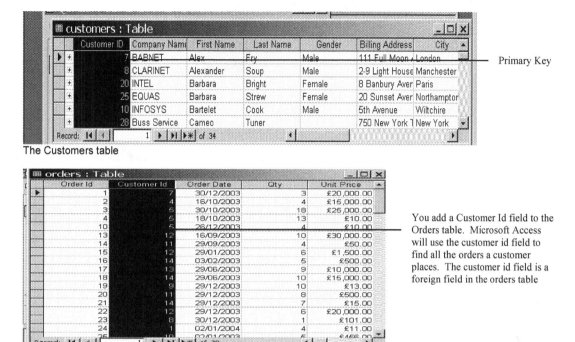

Primary Key

The Customers table

You add a Customer Id field to the Orders table. Microsoft Access will use the customer id field to find all the orders a customer places. The customer id field is a foreign field in the orders table

The Orders table

Many-to-Many Relationship

This type of relationship is complex and very difficult to implement. In this type of relationship a record in Table A can have many matching records in Table B, and a record in Table B can have many matching records in Table A. An example of this type of relationship is the employee and skills table. An employee can have many skills, and the same skills can be found in several employees.

Another example of a many-to-many relationship is the products and orders table. An order may consist of many different products as illustrated below.

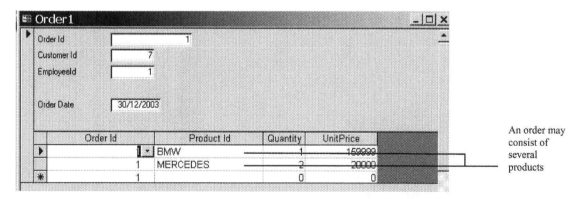

An order may consist of several products

Each product can be ordered many times, therefore a product can appear many times in the order table. This indicates that there is a many-to-many relationship between the order table and the products table. To enter the different products ordered in the same order table will mean repeating the order id field.

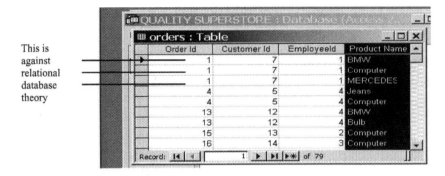

This is against relational database theory, which states that each row must be uniquely identified by a primary key, and there should not be any duplicate row.

A way around this problem is to create a third table known as a junction table and add the primary key from the Order table and products table to this table. The combination of the two primary keys from the order table and products table becomes the primary key for the third table.

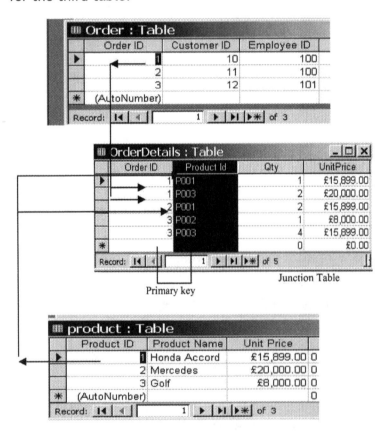

Primary key

Junction Table

The order table and the product table now have a one-to-many relationship with the orderDetails table. A many-to-many relationship is in fact a two one-to-many relationship combined together in a third table.

Setting up the relationship for the third table

To set the relationship for the third table the OrderDetails table, you add the primary keys from both the order table and products table to the OrderDetails table.

One-to-one Relationship

In a one-to-one relationship, each record in table A can have one matching record in Table B and each record in Table B can have only one matching record in table A. This type of relationship is a rare type of relationship, because in most cases the information can be combined into one table, but sometimes because of redundancy and security reasons the information is broken down into two tables. Suppose a retailer decides to annually reward managers by giving them bonuses every year. Keeping all the fields together in the employees table will results in most records having empty fields. This is because not all the employees are managers; it is therefore advisable in a situation like this to separate the table into two separate tables, i.e. **Employees** and **Managers** table. The Employees table will store data on all employees and the Managers table will store data about managers. The Managers table has a one to one relationship with the Employees table because every manager is also an employee.

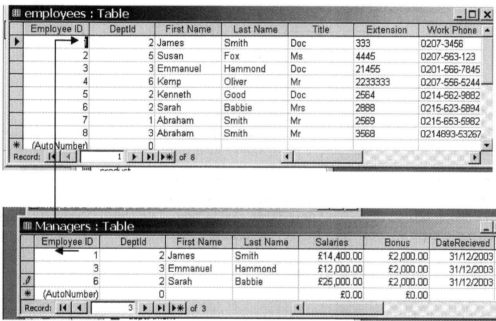

Each record in the managers table has a matching record in the employee table.

Setting up a primary key for a one-to-one relationship

You can create a one-to-one relationship if both the fields have a primary key. You can match the employee id in the Employee table to the Employee id field in the Managers table or vice versa to create a one-to-one relationship.

Creating A Relationship

In simple terms creating relationship means matching the primary key of a primary table with a related field in a related table. The matching field(s) quite often has the same name in both tables. Follow the steps below to create a relationship.

1. Close all tables.

2. In the Database window, click on **Tools** then select **Relationship** from the Tools Menu or click on the **Relationships** button on the Toolbar. If you haven't defined any relationship yet, the Show Table Dialog box will be displayed.

3. If this dialog box is not displayed, then click on the **Show Table** button on the tool bar or Select **Show Table** from the **Relationships menu.**

4. Select the table or query you want to use to create the relationship from the Table/Query box and then click the **Add** Button. Repeat this step until you have added all the tables.

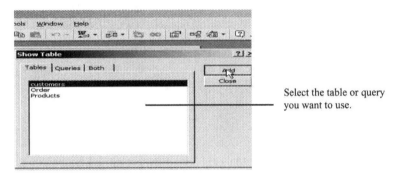

Select the table or query you want to use.

The show Table dialog box

> Tip: To select more than one table or query at a time, hold down the Ctrl key and click each table you want to add.

5. When you have finish selecting all the tables click on the **close** button on the **Show Table** dialog box to close the **Show Table dialog box**.   Microsoft Access displays the Relationship window with the selected tables displayed in the window.

The Relationship Window with the selected tables

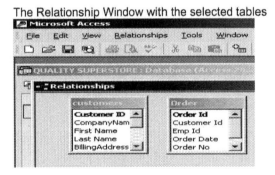

For the Customers and Order tables, the **Primary Table** is the Customers table and the **Related Table** is the Order table.

6. Click the field in the **Primary Table** you want to use to link the related table and drag it to the Related Table. To drag more than one field, press the **Ctrl** key and select the fields and drag to the Related Table. Quite often it is the primary key of the Primary Table, which is drag onto a similar field in the Related Table known as the foreign key. In our example, the **Customer Id** field is the primary key in the Customer Table and a foreign key in the Order Table. So you drag the

Customer Id field from the **Customer Table** to the **Customer Id** field in the **Order Table**.

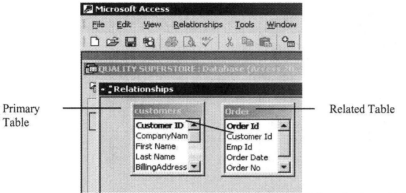

Drag the Customer Id field from the Customer Table to the Order Table

Microsoft Access displays a dialog box

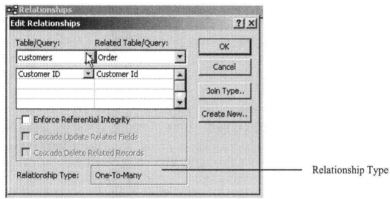

The Edit Relationships dialog box

7. Check the field names displayed in the **Edit Relationship** dialog box. You can change the fields if the fields selected are not the fields you want to use to create the relationship. The relationship type is displayed at the bottom of the Edit Relationship dialog box.

8. You can choose to enforce Referential Integrity by clicking on **Enforce Referential Integrity** options and choosing from the options displayed under Enforce Integrity options. (see Referential Integrity for explanation about the different options).

9. Click on the **Create** button to create the Relationship. A relationship will be created with a line running through the tables with the relationship.

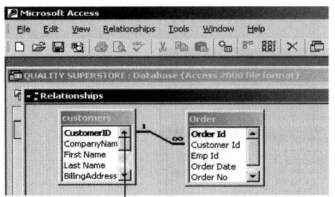

A Relationship is created between the Customer Table and the Order Table

10. Repeat steps 3-9 to create other relationships for your database. When you finish creating all your relationships, click the **close icon** on the relationship window to close the relationship window. Microsoft Access asks you if you want to save the relationship you have created. Click **Yes** to save the relationship.

    Note: Not only can you create relationships between tables, you can also create relationships between tables and queries.

Referential Integrity

Referential Integrity is a means of ensuring validity between related records. Microsoft Access uses Referential Integrity rules to control the entering, updating and deleting of records. This rules prevents you from accidentally deleting records in the related table if corresponding records exist in the primary table and also ensures that records entered in the related table have corresponding matching field in the primary table.

Conditions for enforcing the rules

The following conditions must be met before you can enforce Referential Integrity.

- Matching field from the primary table should be a primary key or should have a unique index.

- The Related fields should have the same data type.

- The relationship type should be clearly defined i.e. one-to-many, one-to-one. The relationship type cannot be indeterminate.

To enforce this rule you must click the check box next to the **Enforce Referential** Integrity in the **Edit Relationships** window.

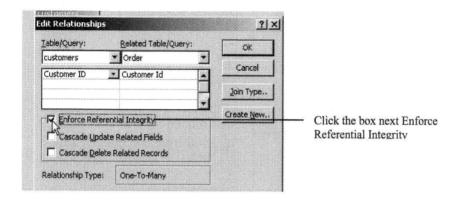

When you decide to enforce Referential Integrity, you must observe the following rules.

- You cannot enter a value in the foreign key field in the related table if that value does not exist in the primary key field of the primary table.

- You cannot delete a record from the primary table if matching records exist in a related table. For example you cannot delete a customer's record if matching records exist in the order table.

- You cannot change a primary key value in the primary table, if that record has related records.

Microsoft Access will inform you when you break the rules by displaying an error message and will not allow you to make the changes.

Referential Integrity Options

When you decide to enforce Referential Integrity, Microsoft Access presents you with two options, which determine how you delete and update records. These options are Cascade Update and Cascade Delete

Cascade Update Related Fields: When this option is selected, anytime you change the primary key of a record in the primary table, Microsoft Access automatically changes the primary key to the new value in all related records. All records in the related table are updated to reflect the changes in the primary key field, except for autonumber field(s).

Cascade Delete Related Records: When you select this option anytime you delete a record from the primary table, Microsoft Access will automatically delete records in the related table. For example if you delete John Smith's record from the Customer's table, all orders placed by John Smith are automatically deleted from the orders table.

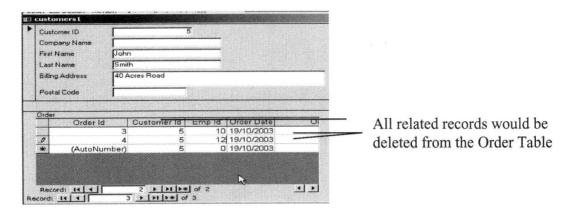

All related records would be deleted from the Order Table

Viewing Existing Relationship

1.   Switch to the Database Window.

2.   Click the **Relationship** button on the toolbar. You can view all the relationship in the database or view the relationship defined for a particular table.

3.   To view all the relationships defined in the database, Click on **Show All Relationship** button ▣ on the toolbar.

4.   To view only the relationships for a particular table

5.   Select the table and Click on the **Show Direct Relationships** ▣ button on the toolbar.

Editing an existing relationship

1.   Close all tables.

2.   Switch to the **Database window**.

3.   Click on the **Relationship** button ▣ on the toolbar.

4.   Double click on the **relationship line** for the relationship you want to edit.

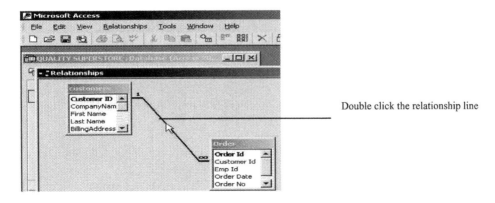

Double click the relationship line

Microsoft displays the **Edit Relationship Dialog box.**

5. Edit the relationship, click and select the options you want.

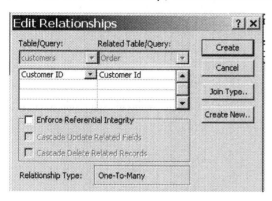

6. Click **Ok**.

Deleting a relationship

1. Switch to the Database Window.

2. Click on the **Relationship** button 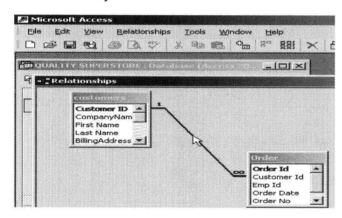 on the toolbar.

3. Click the **Relationship line** for the relationship you want to delete and click press the **Delete** key.

Chapter

ADDING AND EDITING DATA

After you have designed your tables, you can add and edit data to your table.   You may need to edit data to update information when conditions change, or when information becomes available or to correct inaccurate information.

Example

You can edit data in a table in Datasheet view. The following table shows the Order table in Datasheet view.

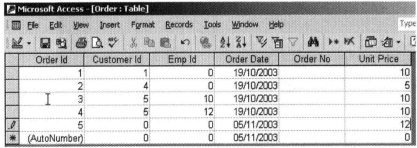

The Order table in a datasheet view

Adding and Editing Data in the Datasheet View

Adding Records

You can add data to a blank record in the datasheet view. The datasheet has a blank record where you can enter new records. The blank record is marked by an * in the record selector (to the left of the record).

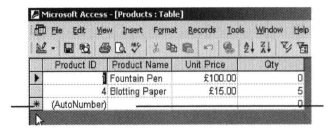

New Record   Blank Record

To Add Records in the datasheet view

1. In the Database window, select **Tables** under **Object**s and double click the table you want to open in the datasheet view.

The table is opened in the datasheet view. Alternatively, you can also select the Datasheet View from the View Menu if you are in the design view or any other view.

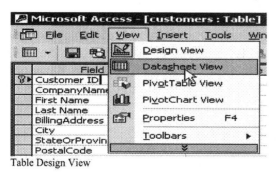

Table Design View

2. Click the **New record** button on the toolbar.

Tip If a table contains an **Autonumber** field, the field will initially display **Autonumber** , press the **Tab** key to move to the next field and start entering the information. Microsoft Access will automatically fill this field with a value when you start entering data in the other field.

3. Type a value in each field and press the Tab key to move to the next field.

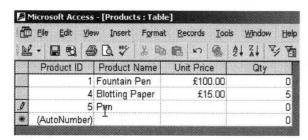

3. Press the tab key when you come to the end of the record to move to the next record. Microsoft Access saves the record when you move to the next record.

Tip To enter the current date, Press the **Ctrl** Key +;.

Editing a field

1. Select the contents of the field you want to change.

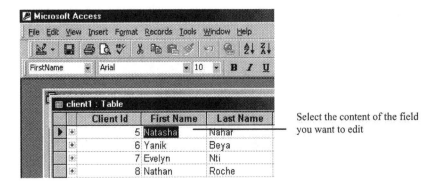

Select the content of the field you want to edit

2. Type the new value in the field. The characters you typed into the field replace the content of the field. You can also edit a field by clicking inside the field with the mouse. An insertion point appears in the field, use the **Backspace** or the **Delete** key to make changes to the field. Press the **ESC** key to cancel changes to the current field.

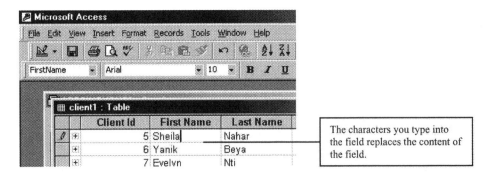

The characters you type into the field replaces the content of the field.

Saving Data

Microsoft Access automatically saves changes you make to your record as soon as you move to another record. You can also save changes to a record by clicking on the Save button 🖫 on the toolbar.

Data Validation

When you enter data or make changes to a field or record in a table, Microsoft Access checks the validity of the data you have entered in the field and alerts you if the value you have entered is not allowed. Microsoft Access checks the data as you try to move out of a field or try to save a record. You can undo the changes or enter a valid data into the field or record. Microsoft Access will do the following validation checks on your data.

- Data Type validation: Microsoft Access will check if the value you have entered matches the data type for the field.

• Input Mask: Microsoft Access will check if the value you have entered meets the input mask set for the field.

• Field Size: Microsoft Access will check the size of the data you have entered with the field size of the field.

• The Required Value: Microsoft Access will check whether or not data is required in that field and you have left the field blank.

• Validation Rule: Microsoft Access will check if the data you have entered breaks the validation rule set in the Validation Rule Property.

• Primary key check: Microsoft Access checks whether or not you have entered a duplicate value in the primary key field.

Selecting a field or Records

Before you can move, copy or delete a field or record you must select the field or record.

Selecting a field

1. Position the mouse where you want to start the selection.

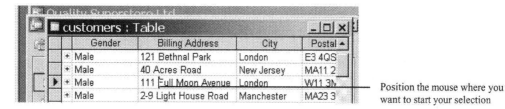
Position the mouse where you want to start your selection

2. Drag the mouse across to the desired position.

Drag across to the desired position

To select an entire field

1. Click the left border of the field. The border changes to the + Plus sign.

2. Click inside the field with the mouse. The whole content of the field is selected.

Mouse changes to a positive sign.

Selecting Record

1.   Click the **Record selector** (the box on the left-side of a record) next to the record you want to select. The entire record is selected.

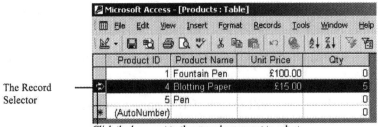

The Record
Selector

Click the box next to the record you want to select

Note: To select all the records in a table, you can choose **Select All Records** from the **Edit Menu.**

You can select several adjoining records by dragging the mouse through their record selectors.

You can select several columns in datasheet view by just clicking the field name at the top of the column. To select multiple columns, click the field name at the top of the column, and then press the shift key and click the field name at the top of another column. You can also drag the mouse pointer through the field names.

Deleting a Record

Deleting a record will permanently remove the record from you database. For example you may decide to delete records of products, which are no longer available.

To Delete a Record

1.   Select the record(s) you want to delete.

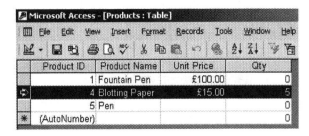

2.   From the **Edit Menu**, select **Delete** or press the **Delete** key or click the Delete Record button on the toolbar.

The delete dialog box appears informing you about the number of records you are about to delete and warning you that you won't be able to undo the delete operation.

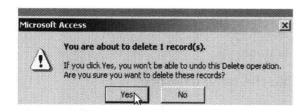

3. Click **Yes** to permanently delete the record.

Copy or move records in a datasheet

You can use the **copy** and **cut** buttons to copy or move records in your datasheet and then use the **paste** button to paste the record in another location. Follow the steps below to copy and move records in your datasheet.

Copy records in a datasheet

1. Open the table in **datasheet view.**

2. Select the record(s) you want to copy.

3. Click on the **Copy** toolbar button.

4. Perform any of the following actions.

   - **To paste the records you have copied within the same datasheet:**

     Position the mouse where you want to paste the records in the datasheet.

   - **To paste the records in another datasheet**

     Open the datasheet you want to paste the records into and position the mouse where you want to paste the records in the datasheet..

     Re-arrange the columns of the datasheet to match the order of the data you want to copy or move.

     You can either replace existing records or append the records at end of a datasheet.

5. Perform any of the following actions

   - **To replace existing records with the records you copied,**

     Select the records you want to replace and then click on the **Paste** tool button on the toolbar.

   - **To append the records to the end of the datasheet,**

     Choose **Paste Append** from the **Edit Menu.**

Move records in a datasheet

1. Select the record(s) you want to move.

2.   Click on the on the **Cut** ♨ button on the toolbar.

3.   Perform any of the following actions.

   - **To paste the records within the same datasheet**

     Position the mouse where you want to paste the records in the datasheet.

   - **To paste the records in another datasheet**

     Open the datasheet you want to paste the records into and position the mouse where you want to paste the records in the datasheet.

     Re-arrange the columns of the datasheet to match the order of the data you want to move.

     You can either replace existing records or append the records at end of a datasheet.

4.   Perform any of the following actions

   - **To replace existing records with the records you cut:**

     Select the records you want to replace and then click on the **Paste** tool button 📋 on the toolbar.

   - **To append the records to the end of the datasheet,**

     Choose **Paste Append** from the **Edit Menu.**

Navigating Between fields and records

You can move between fields and records in a datasheet view.

Navigating Between Fields

1.   Press the **Tab** key to move to the next field.

2.   Use the **Shift + Tab** key to move to the previous field.

Navigating between records

You can use the navigational buttons at the bottom of a table in a datasheet view to move quickly between the records.

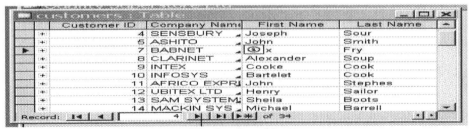

Navigational button

The Navigational buttons

	First Record		Previous Record
	Record Number		Next Record
	Last Record		New Record

Record: 14 | 4 | 4 | ▶ | ▶I | ▶＊| of 34   Total Number of Records in the table

Example

To move to the Next Record in the table, click on the ▶ button on the Navigational toolbar.

82

CUSTOMIZING A TABLE IN DATASHEET VIEW

Microsoft Access provides several ways you can change the layout of a datasheet. For example you can change the width of columns or row height and rearrange the order of the columns. You can also change the font, font color, line color or the gridlines. These changes affect the layout of the table and have no impact on the structure of the table or query. When you save the table, Microsoft Access saves changes to the layout of the datasheet.

Changing the Column Width

You can change the width of a column if the field values do not fit into the columns and appears truncated or if the field is too wide. You may also like to reduce the size of a column to view information in another column.

To change the width of a column

1. Open the table in **Datasheet View**.

2. Position the mouse pointer at the right edge of the column you want to resize.

3. Drag the column to the desired size. Dragging to the left to decrease the size of the column or dragging to the right to increase the size of the column.

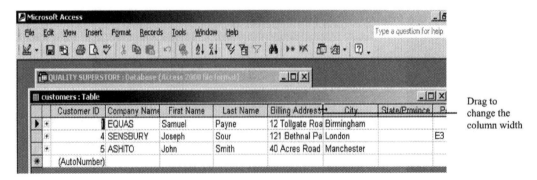

You can double-click the right edge of the column heading to automatically adjust the column width so that it displays all the data contained within a column.

Changing row height

If you don't want to adjust the column width to display the full content of a field you can adjust the row height. Adjusting the row height will display the content of a field in more than one row and improve the presentation of your data in the datasheet view.

To change the row height of a datasheet

1. Open the table in **Datasheet View**

2. Position the mouse pointer between two rows on the left side of the field or row selector.

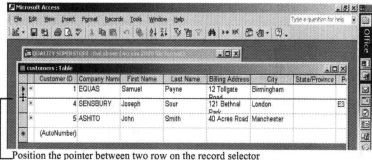

Position the pointer between two row on the record selector

3. Drag the row to the desired size. Drag up to decrease the size of the row or drag down to increase the size of the row.

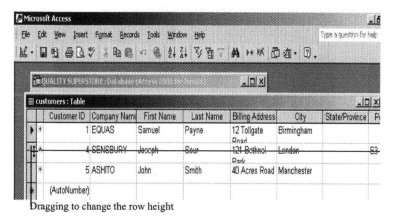

Dragging to change the row height

Formatting a datasheet

Microsoft Access provides a formatting tool for formatting datasheet. If this tool is not displayed, you can display it by following the instructions below.

1. Click on the **View Menu** and select **Toolbar**, then select **Formatting Datasheet** from the submenu.

   The formatting toolbar appears

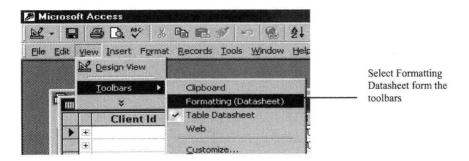

Select Formatting
Datasheet form the
toolbars

Changing the font of a datasheet

1. Open the table in **Datasheet View.**

2. Click on the **Format** Menu and select **Font.**

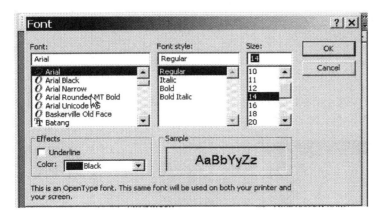

3. Select the **Font**, **Font style** and **Size** from the boxes labelled **Font, Font style and Size** respectively.

4. To apply a different colour to your datasheet, click the down arrow next to the box labelled **Color** under **Effects** and select a colour from the list.

5. Click on **Ok.**

    The font, font style, size and colour you selected are applied to your datasheet.

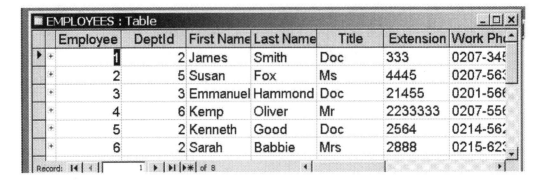

Formatting a datasheet with gridlines

You can apply both horizontal and vertical gridlines or only horizontal, vertical or none at all to the datasheet.

Example

Follow the steps below to customize a datasheet so that it displays horizontal gridlines only.

1. Open the datasheet you want to apply the horizontal gridlines.

2. Click on the down-arrow next to the gridlines tool ⊞▾ on the Datasheet formatting toolbar and select **Horizontal gridline** from the Datasheet formatting toolbar.

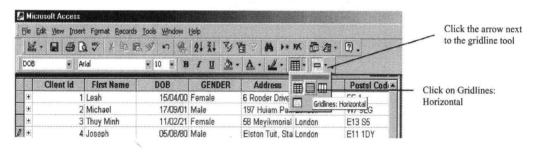

The result of applying horizontal gridlines is displayed below.

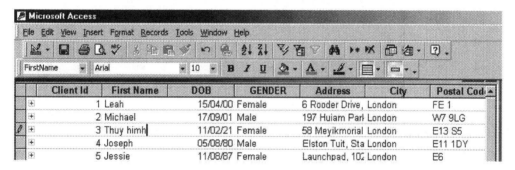

Adding Special Design Effects

You can make your datasheet more attractive by adding special design effects to it. For example you can add a 3 Dimensional effect to your datasheet. Follow the steps below to add a 3D effect to your datasheet.

1. Open the table in **Datasheet view**.

2. Click on the **Format Menu** and choose **Datasheet**.

    The **Datasheet Formatting Dialog** box appears.

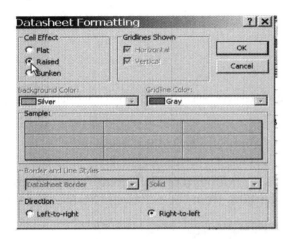

3. Click on **Raised or Sunken** in the box labelled **Cell Effect**.

4. Click on **Ok**.

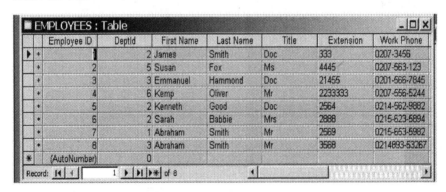

Rearranging columns

The columns in the datasheet view are arranged in the order in which they appear in design view. You can rearrange the columns in the datasheet view in any order you want. Rearranging the columns will not affect the order the fields are displayed in design view.

Rearrange columns

Example

Suppose you want to contact your customers by telephone about your new promotion. It would be easier if the telephone number field is next to the customer name field but because the fields are several columns apart you will have to scroll to the right to find each customer's telephone number and scroll back to the left again. Moving the telephone number field close to the customer name field will make your work easier and your task quicker to accomplish.

Moving a column

1. Open the table in **Datasheet View.**

2. Select the column you want to move by clicking the field selector.

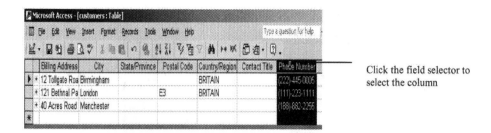

Click the field selector to select the column

3. Click and hold down the field selector again and drag the column to the position you want.

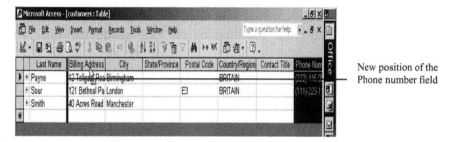

New position of the Phone number field

Hiding and showing columns

Hide a column

Hiding columns removes columns from view. You can hide columns when you do not want to work with them, so you can move quickly and easily through the datasheet.

Example

If you have four fields between the Name and the Phone Number fields of your database, you could hide the fields so that Phone Number field appears next to the Name field. When you use the tab key to move between the fields in the datasheet view, the cursor moves to the next visible column.

To hide a column in a datasheet view

1. Open the table in **Datasheet View.**

2. Select the column(s) you want to hide by clicking the field selector.

3. Select **Hide Columns** from the **Format menu.**

   The column you selected disappears from the datasheet and the columns to right shift to the left of the columns you have hidden.

Unhide Columns

To show hidden columns

1. Open the table in **Datasheet View.**

2. Click the **Format menu**, and then click **Show columns.**

The Unhide Columns dialog box appears.

Click the box next to column name to display the column

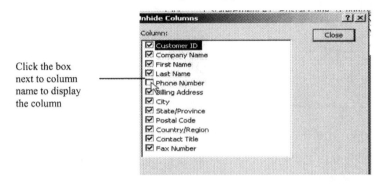

3. Select the column(s) you want to show by clicking inside the box next to the column name.

4. Click the **Close** button.

Freezing and Unfreezing Columns

When working with a table with many fields, you may decide to freeze certain fields so that they are always visible as you scroll through the table. Microsoft Access displays frozen columns on the left side of a datasheet and they remain visible as you scroll across the table. This is useful for working with tables with many fields.

Freeze a column

To freeze a column in a datasheet

1. Open the table in **Datasheet View.**

2. Select the column(s) you want to freeze by clicking its field selector. You can select more than one column by holding down the shift key and clicking the columns you want to select.

3. From the **Format** menu, click **Freeze Columns.**

    You will notice that as you scroll through the table to view columns that are on the right side of the datasheet and previously not visible, the frozen columns remain in view.

To unfreeze all columns

1. Open the table in **Datasheet View.**

2. From the **Format Menu,** click **Unfreeze All columns.**

Saving or cancelling your Datasheet changes

When you close the datasheet, Microsoft Access asks you whether you want to save changes you have made to the layout. Click **Yes** to save the changes or **No** to discard any changes you have made to the layout of your datasheet.

Chapter

FORMS

A form is a database object, which provides an easy way to enter, edit and view data in your database.

The layout of Microsoft Access forms is just like any form you use in your day-to-day transaction. A form offers a more convenient layout for entering, updating and viewing the information in your database.

A form also provides an efficient and accurate way of entering data. For example if you need to enter more complex transaction, which may entail entering information into separate, related tables. You can use a form to combine fields from all the tables into one form. This will save you time and reduce errors.

Creating a form

There are three ways of creating a form in Microsoft Access. These are

*   By using AutoForms

*   With the form Wizard

*   Creating a form in Design View

Creating a form using the AutoForm

The quickest and easiest way to create a form is to use the AutoForm Wizard. This method creates a form without any questions and displays all the fields in the underlying table or query.

1.   In the **Database window**, Click **Forms** under **Objects**.

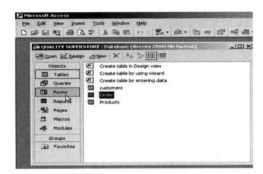

2.   Click **New** on the database toolbar.

Microsoft Access presents you with the **New Form** dialog box,

3.   Select one of the Autoform options from the available list.

AutoForm columnar: creates a form with each field appearing on a separate line with labels on the left.

AutoForm Tabular creates a form similar to a table.

Autoform Datasheet creates a form that resembles a datasheet.   **AutoForm Pivot Table** creates a form in pivot table view.

AutoForm Pivot Chart creates a form in pivot chart view.

4.   Click the drop down arrow next to **choose the table or query where the object's data comes from** and select a table or query.

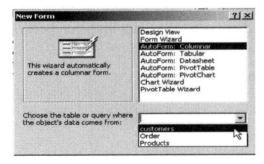

5.   Click **Ok.** Microsoft Access displays the form.

Creating a form with the form Wizard

1. In the **Database window**, click **Forms** under **Objects**.

2. Click on the **New** button on the database window toolbar.

3. The New form dialog box appears on the screen. Click on the **Form Wizard.**

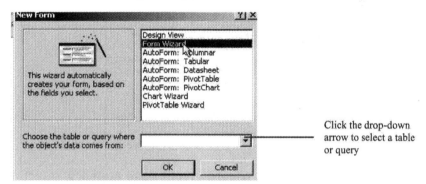

4. Click the drop down arrow next to **choose the table or query where the object's data comes from** and select a table or query.

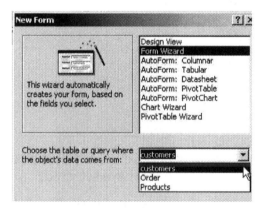

5. Click a field in the **Available Fields list** that you want to include on the form and then click the > button to move the field to the **Selected Fields list.** Repeat this step until you have included all the fields you want to include in your form. You can click on >> button to move all the fields quickly to the **Selected Fields** list. You can remove a field from the **selected fields** by click the field and clicking the < button.

    If you want to include fields from another table or query, repeat step 4 & 5 to choose another table or query and move the fields to the **selected fields list.**

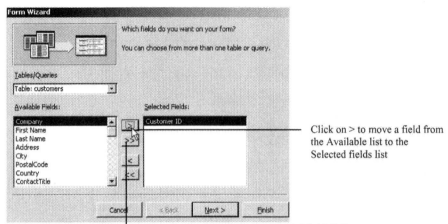

Click on > to move a field from
the Available list to the
Selected fields list

Click on >> to move all the fields from the Available list to the Selected fields list

6. Click **Next** to continue. The **Form Wizard layout page appears**, select any of the layouts from the form layout dialog box. The preview area on the left side of the dialog box displays what the form would look like with the option you select.

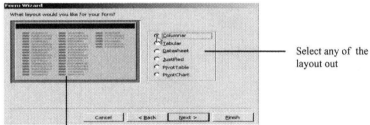

Select any of the
layout out

The preview area displays the option you select

7. Click **Next**. The **form Wizard Style Page** appears. Select any of the styles from the list. The preview area will display the style you have selected.

8. Click **Next** to continue. Microsoft Access displays a title dialog box and suggests the name of the table as the title for the form. You can accept the suggested title or enter a title for the form in the text box.

9. Click the **Finish** button. The form appears on the screen displaying the first customer record.

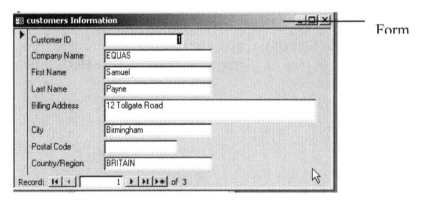

Form

Creating a form in the Design View

1. In the Database window, click on **Forms** under **Objects.**

2. Click on the **New** button. The New form dialog box appears.

3. Click on **Design View** from the options listed in the New Form Dialog box.

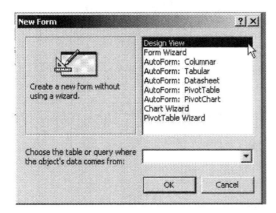

4. Click the drop down arrow next to **choose the table or query where the object's data comes from** and select a table or query.

    Note: Leave this box empty if you are creating a form to be used as a switchboard to open other forms or reports.

5. Click **Ok.** Microsoft Access displays a blank canvas in design view. A field list appears on the screen. If the **field list** is not displayed, click on the **field list tool** button on the toolbar to display the field list. You can then move the fields you want anywhere on to the canvas.

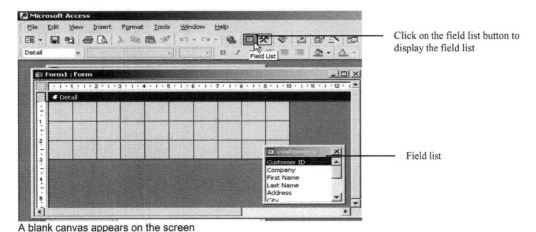

A blank canvas appears on the screen

Adding a new Record to a form

To enter data in a form, you need to open the form in **Form View.**

1. Open the form in **Form View.**

    If the form is already open; switch to **Form View.** If not,

In the **Database Window**, under **Objects,** click on **Forms** and select the form you want to add new records to.

Click on the **Open** button on the toolbar to open the form in **Form View.**

2.   Click the New record 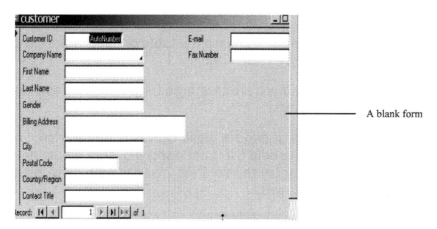 button on the toolbar.

A blank form

A blank form appears on screen.

3.   Click inside the first field you want to enter data into and start typing data into that field, press the TAB key to move to the next field.

If you want to move to the previous field, Press **Shift +Tab.**

Tip   If a form contains an **Autonumber** field, the field will initially display **Autonumber** , press the **Tab** key to move to the next field and start entering the information. Microsoft Access will automatically fill this field with a value when you start entering data in the other field.

4.   When you come to the end of the record i.e. the last field, press the **TAB** key to move to a new blank record.

Navigating through records

You can navigate through records in a form in order to review or edit information. Microsoft Access provides navigational buttons at the bottom of a form to help you to quickly move between records.

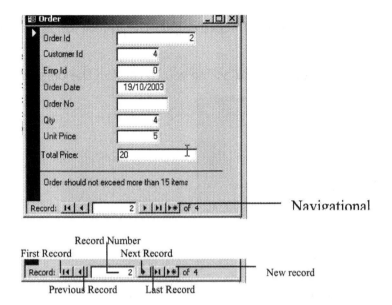

Use the navigational button to move to any record.

To move to specific record

1. Position the mouse over the number of the **current record.**

2. Type the number of the record you want to move to and then press the **Enter key.**

Editing records in a form

You can replace the content of a field or insert additional text in a field.

To replace the content of a field

1. Use the mouse to select the contents of the field you want to replace.

2. Type the new value for the field. The new value replaces the content of the field.

To insert additional text in a field

1. Position the mouse in the field where you want to insert the text.

    Press the Backspace key to correct any errors.

2. Type the text.

    To cancel any editing in the current field, press the **Esc key.** To cancel changes in the entire record, press the **Esc key again** before you move out of the field.

Deleting records in a form

1. Open the form in **Form View.**

2. Select the records you want to delete.

3.   From the **Edit** Menu, Choose **Delete Record** or click the **Delete Record** ![toolbar button icon] toolbar button.

4.   Microsoft Access displays a dialog box asking you to confirm the deletion.

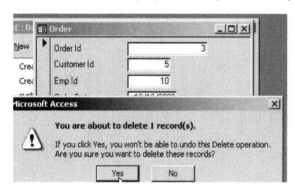

5.   Click **Yes** to delete the record. Once you confirm the deletion the record is permanently deleted.

Working with forms in different views

Microsoft Access provides 3 different ways in which you can view forms. They are as follows:

Design view: In design view, you can create a new form or make changes to the design of the form in design view.

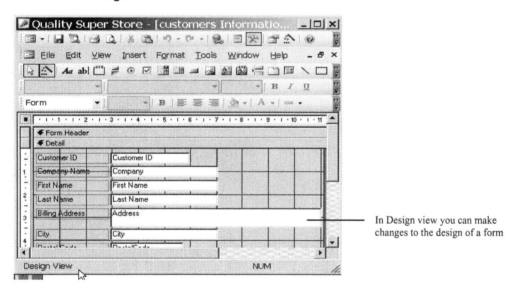

In Design view you can make changes to the design of a form

Datasheet view: you can view a form in datasheet view. In the datasheet view data is displayed in rows and columns.

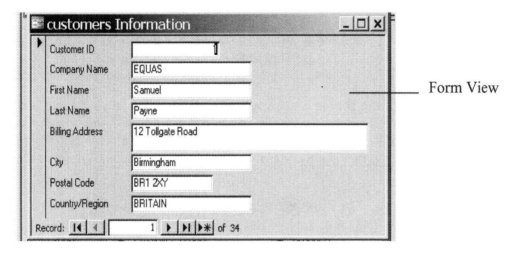

A Form in Datasheet view

Form View: In a form view the records are displayed like a normal form and you can view one record at a time.

Form View

Switching between different views

You can switch between the different views in a form by using the view ![view button] button on the toolbar. Follow the steps below to switch between the different views in a form.

1.   Click on the **View** ![view button] button on the toolbar.

2.   Click the down arrow next to the **View** button to select the view you want from the drop-down list. For example to switch to Design view, select **Design View** from the drop-down list displayed.

Chapter

ADDING CONTROLS TO A FORM

When you create a form in Design view, Microsoft Access presents you with a blank canvas and gives you the flexibility of putting the controls anywhere you want on the form.

Controls are the elements of a form that enables you to display fields from your table. For example you can have a text box control, which displays the employee names from the employee table. Controls can also display labels, lines or information that is not stored in the database. For example you can use a control to display calculated values or create titles on your form.

There are three types of controls. They are as follows:

*   Bound

*   Unbound

*   Calculated Control

Bound control

A control, whose source of data is from a field in a table or query.

Unbound control

A Control, whose source of data is not from a table or a query. Unbounded controls are used to display lines and pictures on your form.

Calculated control

A calculated control is a control, whose source of data is from an expression.

Example

For example the source of data for the control **Total Price** is from an expression. You can create a calculated control **Total Price**, which calculates the total price of items sold. You specify the expression for calculating the Total Price in the control source property box. For example you specify the expression = [UnitPrice]*[Qty] in the **Total Price** control's source property.

Example

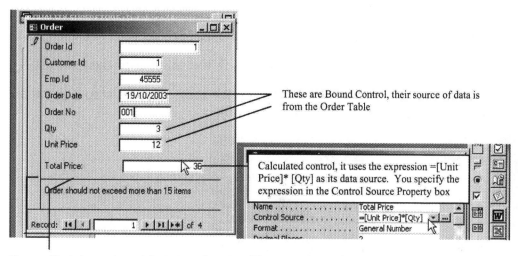

These are Bound Control, their source of data is from the Order Table

Calculated control, it uses the expression =[Unit Price]* [Qty] as its data source. You specify the expression in the Control Source Property box

Lines and Label are unbound Control and they do not have any source of data

Adding a bound Text Box Control to your form

1. Open the table in **Design View**.

2. Display the field list if the field list is not displayed. To display the field list, click the field list button or choose **Field list** from the **View menu**.

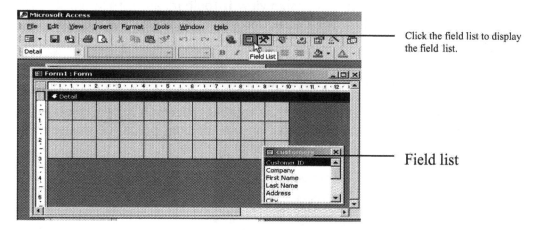

Click the field list to display the field list.

Field list

3. Select the field or fields you want to add to your form from the field list.

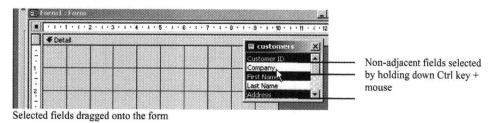

Non-adjacent fields selected by holding down Ctrl key + mouse

Selected fields dragged onto the form

- To select one field, click the field.

- To select a block of fields, click the first field and then hold down the shift key and click the last field.

- To select non-adjacent fields hold down the **Ctrl Key** as you click each field.

- To select all the fields on a list, double click the title bar of the field list.

3. Drag the field or fields from the Field list on the form. Repeat step 2 if you are dragging the fields one at a time on to the form.

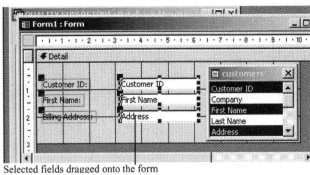

Selected fields dragged onto the form

Creating Unbound or Calculated Controls

Unbound or calculated controls are created using the Toolbox.   The toolbox can also be used to create all types of controls on your form. By default Microsoft Access displays the toolbox when you open a form in Design view if toolbars are turned on. If the toolbox is not displayed, you can follow the instruction below to display the toolbox.

Displaying the Toolbox

1. From the **View menu**, Choose **Toolbox**.

    Or click the toolbox button on the toolbar. Microsoft Access displays the toolbox. To display the name of the tool on the toolbox, place the mouse over the tool. Microsoft Access displays the name of the tool.

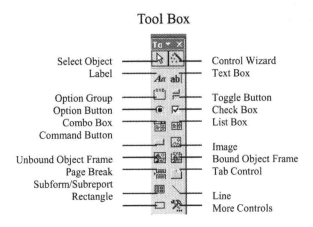

Tool Box

To create an unbound control

Open the form in **Design View**.

1. Click the **Text Box** tool in the toolbox.

2. Drag the Text box to the form. Microsoft Access displays a text box with a label. You can change the label by double-clicking the label and typing the label you want inside the label box.

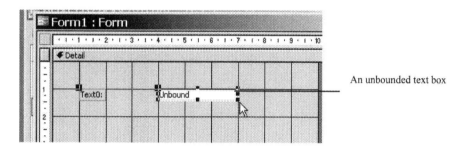

An unbounded text box

To create a calculated text box

Open the form in Design View.

1. Click the **Text Box** tool in the toolbox.

2. Drag the **Text box** to the form. Microsoft Access displays a text box with a label. You can change the label by double-clicking the label and typing the label you want inside the label box.

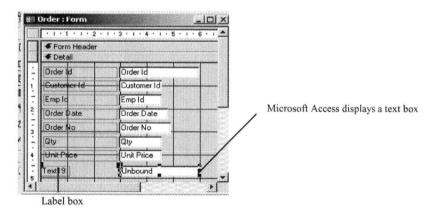

Microsoft Access displays a text box

Label box

3. Move the mouse pointer inside the text box and type the expression. An expression begins with an equal sign (=).

    Example to find the Value of goods sold (Total Price), you need to multiply the Unit Price by the Qty field, type an equal sign (=) followed by an expression that calculates the Total Price.

    =[Unit Price]*Qty.

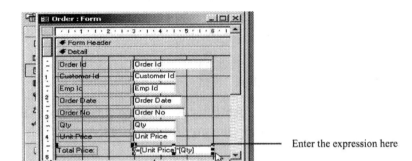

Enter the expression here

4.   Press Enter when you finish.

Creating a label

If the toolbox is not displayed, choose **Toolbox** from the **View Menu**

or

Click the toolbox button.

1.   Click the label tool to create a label.

2.   Click on the form where you want the label to appear.

3.   Type the text for the label.

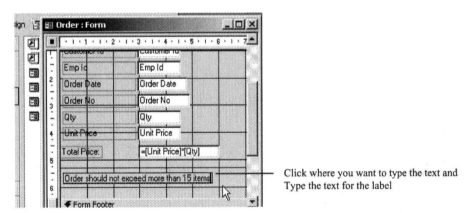

Click where you want to type the text and
Type the text for the label

4.   Press **Enter** when you finish typing.

Setting Control Properties

A bound control in a form inherits certain properties like the **Format, DecimalPlaces, Input Mask** and **StatusBar Text** property from its underlying table or query. For example if you create the Order Date field on a form by dragging the Order date field from the field list, Microsoft Access automatically sets the Format property and Input for the text box control to the value in the table.

You can change the settings of any inherited properties in the control property sheet. Changing the setting of a control doesn't affect the setting of that property in the underlying table or query, however, if you change an inherited property of a fields property (in the table) that has a controls bound to it, Microsoft Access gives you the opportunity to update all the controls that depends on the field.

If you change the field properties for property settings like DefaultValue, ValidationRule and Validation Text in a table, these changes will be enforced in the form whether or not they were created before you created the form.

Changing the Properties of a control

You can change the properties of a control by using the Property Sheet.

Example

For example when you initially created the **Order Date** field, the Order date was displayed in the following format, 12/12/03. To improve the presentation of your form or report, you may decide to display the date as follows i.e. 12-Dec-2003. If you want the Order Date control to be displayed in the following format i.e. 12-Dec-2003, you can change the **Order Date** control's **Format** property in the property sheet. Follow the steps below to change the property of a control.

To change the properties of an existing control

1. Double-click the control. (You can select more than one control by holding down the Shift Key and then clicking each control).

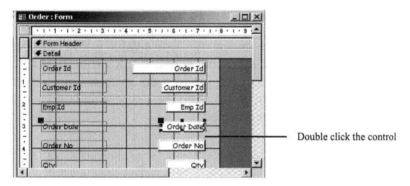

Double click the control

Microsoft displays the property sheet.

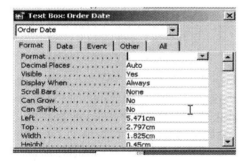

The property sheet is divided into five tabs. Each tab displays properties of a specific category. For example

- **All Properties** displays all the properties

- **Data Properties** displays properties relating to the data displayed in the control for example the control source, default value and the validation rule.

- **Event Properties** displays a macro or an event procedure. Microsoft Access executes this macro or event procedure when an event occurs. For example you can specify what event to execute in the **On Click** property in the property box.

- **Format Properties** displays properties relating to the Format or appearance of a control, for example the Format property displays the width, height and visible property of a control.

- **Other Properties** displays other characteristics of a control, which cannot be categorized into Data, Event or Format Property i.e. Name, Tab Order and Tab Stop.

2. Select a category by clicking on a tab. For example click on the **Format** tab.

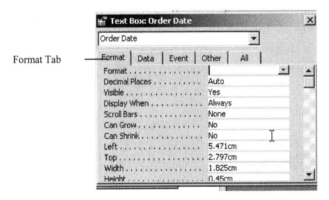

Format Tab

3. Click inside the property box to set the property. Type a value inside the property box you want to change. Where a down arrow appears, click the down arrow to display a list of settings and select from the list of settings displayed, where the **Build** button appears, click on the button to open the Expression Builder and use the Expression Builder to enter the expression.

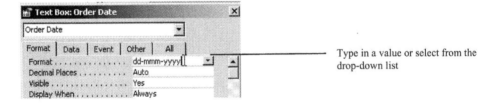

Type in a value or select from the drop-down list

Validating or restricting data entry in a form

It is very easy to make mistakes when entering data into a form. By validating data or restricting the values entered into a text box or control you ensure that correct information is entered, and users get immediate feedback about the data they have entered. Some of the ways in which you can validate or restrict data entered in a form is by using the validation Rule and Validation Text Properties, DefaultValue Property, InputMask property and Locking the field.

DefaultValue is a value that is automatically entered into a field when a new record is created.

Example

For example in the Order Entry form, you can set the DefaultValue Property of the Order Date control to current date, i.e. =[Date]. Users can either accept this value or enter another date into this field. Follow the instructions below to set the default value property of the Order Date.

Open the Order Entry form in **Design** view

1.   Double-click the **Order Date** control. The property sheet is displayed.

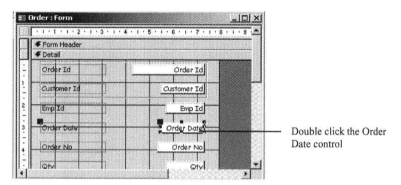

Double click the Order
Date control

2.   Set the **DefaultValue** property to the current date.

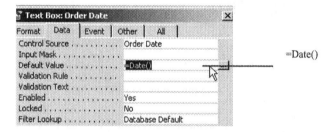

=Date()

Validation Rule and Validation Text Properties

The **ValidationRule** and **Validation Text** Properties checks the data you have entered and provide immediate feedback in the Validation Text Property. For example on our Order Entry Form, we could restrict the Qty field to values greater than 0. Double-click the control and type the Validation Rule in the ValidationRule Property box and the Validation Text in the Validation Text Property. In Form View if a user types a value less than 1 in the quantity field the validation text is displayed.

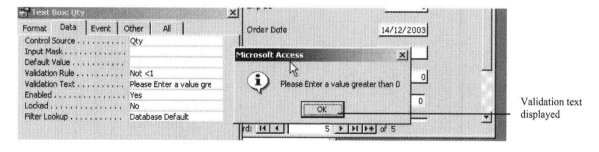

Validation text
displayed

Input Mask Property

An Input Mask Property is a mask or template that enables users to enter data in the correct format. It is useful for entering telephone numbers, faxes and date format. You can use parentheses, spaces, hyphens and slashes to display data. To change the Input Mask of a control, double-click the control and type the input format in the Input Mask.

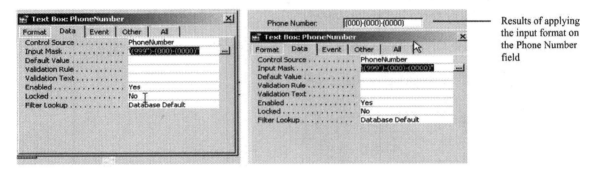

Results of applying the input format on the Phone Number field

Disabling a control

Disabling a control will dim the control and prevent it from receiving focus. This is useful for fields you don't want users to change for example primary key fields. To disable a control, double-click the control and set its **Enabled** property to **No**.

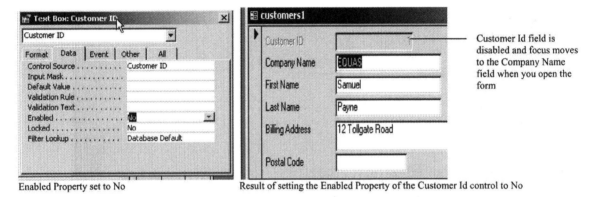

Customer Id field is disabled and focus moves to the Company Name field when you open the form

Enabled Property set to No

Result of setting the Enabled Property of the Customer Id control to No

Locking a control

Locking a control will make the content readable, but users may not be able to change the content of a field. To lock a control, double-click the control and set its **Lock** Property to **Yes**.

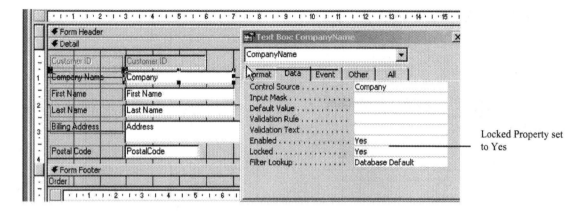

Changing the Tab Order

The Tab Key is used to move from one control to the other during data entry. The tab order controls the order in which the cursor moves through fields in a form when you press the Tab and Shift Tab keys. The order in which the tab moves from one control to the other is the tab order. When you first create a form, the tab order is from top to bottom.

Example

You may want to change the tab order if you re-arrange the controls in your form or report. Microsoft Access will not automatically change the tab order to reflect the re-arrangements. You will have to change the Tab Order manually to reflect the changes.

Another instance when you may want to change the Tab Order is when you add a new control to the form. Microsoft Access automatically places the control at the end of the tab order. This may not be the order you want to navigate through the control in your form. Follow the steps below to change the Tab Order.

1. Open the form in **Design View**.

2. Choose **Tab Order** from the **View Menu**.

    Microsoft Access displays the **Tab Order Dialog** box.

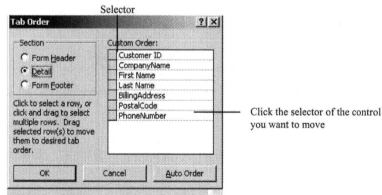

The Tab Order dialog box

3. Click the **Selector** for the control name you want to move.

4. Click the selector again and drag the control name to the desired location.

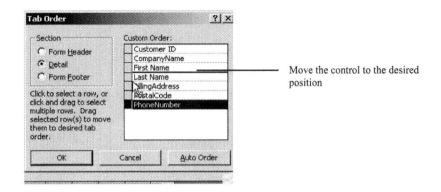

Move the control to the desired position

5.   Click **Ok**.

Forms Sections

A Form has five sections. Each Section has a specific purpose.

*   **Form header**: A form header is used to display the title of a form. A form header is displayed at the top of a form in form view and at the top of the first page when the form is printed.

*   **Page header:** A page header is used to display information such as column headings or any information you want printed at the top of every page. A page header appears only in printed forms.

*   **Detail section:** The detail section of a form displays records.

*   **Page footer**: Page footer displays information like the page number, date or any other information you may want at the bottom of every page. Page footer appears only in printed forms.

*   **Form footer:** A form footer displays information like command buttons, instructions for using the form. A form footer appears at the bottom of the screen or at the last page when printed.

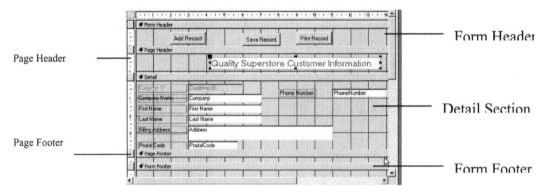

Resizing a form

You may find that the height or width of a section is not big to contain the information you want to display in that section. You can increase the height or width of a section.

To change the size of a section

1. Open the form in **Design View**.

2. Follow the instructions below to make the necessary adjustments

    To change the height of a section

    Place the pointer on the bottom border of the section and drag the pointer up or down to increase or decrease the section.

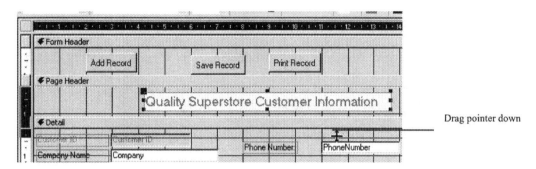

Drag pointer down

To change the width of a section

Place the pointer to the right border of the section and drag the pointer to the right or left.

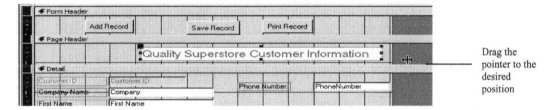

Drag the pointer to the desired position

Setting Section Properties

A form's section determines the appearance and behavior of a form.   Follow the instructions below to set the section property for a form.

1. Open the form in **Design view**.

2. Double-click the section selector to open the property sheet.

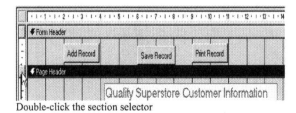

Double-click the section selector

3. Select the tab that relates to the property you want to change.

4. Click the property you want to set and type a value or expression or choose from a drop-down list if applicable.

Setting Form properties

Like a Section, a form has also got properties. A form's property determines the appearance and behavior of the form.

1. Open the form in **Design view**.

2. Double-click the **form selector** to display the property sheet.

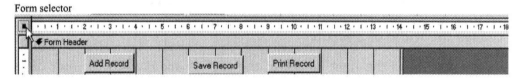

3. Choose the tab that relates to the property you want to change.

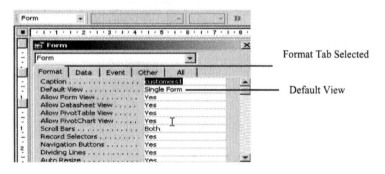

4. Click the property you want to set and type a value or expression or choose from the drop-down list if applicable.

Setting the Default View for a form

The **Default View** of a form determines the open view of a form. The **Default View** property has three different views.

- **Single Form** The Single form view is the default view. Records are displayed one at a time.

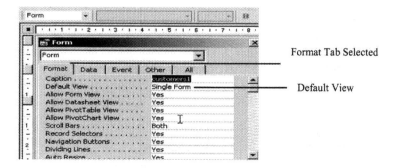

Format Tab Selected

Default View

- **Continuous** form Displays multiple or several records on the screen.

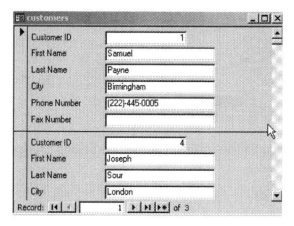

- **Datasheet:** Displays the fields in a form in rows and columns. Is usually used to display subforms.

Order Id	Customer	Emp Id	Order Date	Order No	Qty	Unit Price	Total Price
1	1	45555	19/10/2003	001	3	12	36
2	4	0	19/10/2003		4	5	20
3	5	10	19/10/2003		18	10	180
4	5	12	19/10/2003		13	10	130
(AutoNumber)	0	0	15/12/2003		0	0	0

Customizing a form to serve the purpose you want to use it for

Forms are mainly use to enter, edit or view data. You can customize a form so that when it opens it is ready to be used for the purpose it is design for. For example you can customize a form so it can be used purposely for viewing data only, users cannot make changes to the data.

Customizing a form so users can add, edit or delete records

You can use a form's property sheet to customize a form so that users can be allowed or disallowed to add, edit or delete records.

Example

Some users can cause havoc to your data if you give them too much freedom. For example some users can delete very important information from your database. It is therefore important to control users' action by setting the **Allow Addition, Allow Edits, AllowDeletions** property to the desired value.

Customizing a form so users can add records

1.   Open the form in **Design View.**

2.   Double-click the **form selector** to open the property sheet.

3.   Click on the **Allow Additions** property and click on **Yes.**

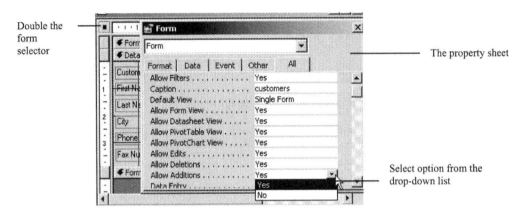

To prevent users from adding records to the form set **Allow Additions** property to **No.**

Customizing a form so users can edit records

1.   Open the form in **Design View.**

2.   Double-click the form selector to open the property sheet.

3.   Click on the **Allow Edits** property and select **Yes.**

    To prevent users from editing records click on **No.**

Customizing a form so users can delete records

1.   Open the form in **Design View.**

2.   Double-click the form selector to open the property sheet.

3.   Click on the **AllowDeletions** property and click on **Yes.**

    To prevent users from deleting records select **No.**

Make a form a Data Entry Only form

1.   Open the form in Design View.

2.   Double-click the form selector to open the property sheet.

3.   Set the **DataEntry** property to **Yes.**

Make a form Read-Only

1.   Open the form in **Design View.**

2. Double-click the **Form Selector** to open the property sheet.

3. Click inside the **Allow Edits** property box and select **No.**

4. Click inside the **Allow Deletions** property box and select **No.**

5. Click inside the **Allow Additions** property box and select **No.**

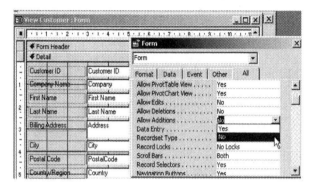

Chapter

IMPROVING THE APPEARANCE AND LAYOUT OF YOUR FORM

Using the wizard to create a form is easy, but quite often the form that the wizard creates is not very attractive. You can improve the appearance of your form by moving and resizing the control, adding colour, adding special fonts, changing the font sizes and adding lines and using other formats to formatting the form.

Moving Controls

After you have created a form with the wizard, you can move controls around to improve the layout of your form.

Move a control and its label together

1. Click the **control** or its **label**.

    Microsoft Access displays a selection handle around the control. You can select several controls by holding down the Shift key as you click each control.

    Selection handle around the control

2. Move the mouse towards the edges of control or its label, the pointer changes to an open hand.

    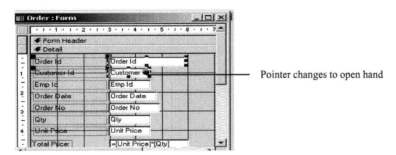
    Pointer changes to open hand

3. Click and hold down the mouse as you drag the control to its new position.

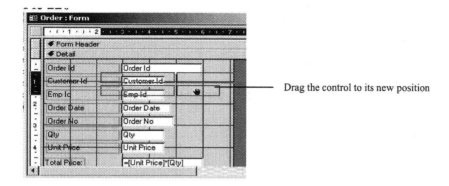

Drag the control to its new position

To move a control and its label independently

1.   Click the **control** or its **label**.

2.   Position the mouse pointer over the selection handle at the top left. The mouse changes to a pointing finger.

Mouse changes to a pointing finger

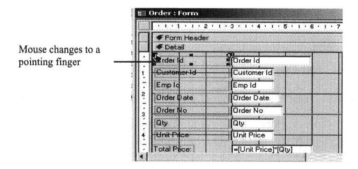

3.   Drag the mouse to the new position.

Resizing a Control

Resizing a control involves reducing or enlarging the size of the control. You can enlarge a control so it can display more information. You can reduce the size of a control to reduce the amount of extra spaces left after displaying the content of a control.

1.   Click the **control** you want to resize. You can select more than one control by holding the **shift key** and **clicking** each control. A selection handle appears around the control.

2.   Point to the **sizing handles** so that the pointer turns into a double-headed arrow.

Sizing handle changes to a double

3.   Drag the sizing arrow to the length you want and release the mouse button.

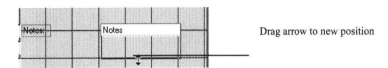

Drag arrow to new position

The results of moving, resizing and aligning a control

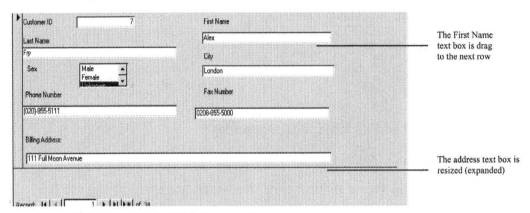

The First Name text box is drag to the next row

The address text box is resized (expanded)

The results of moving, resizing the fields in the customer form

Changing the fonts and font size

1. Select the **control**(s). You can use **Ctrl +A** to select all of the fonts.

2. Select the font name, font size from the **Font** and **Font size** boxes on the toolbar.

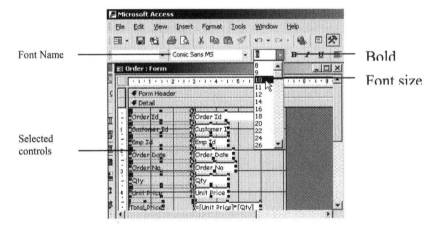

Font Name

Bold

Font size

Selected controls

Aligning text within a control

You can improve the appearance of your forms and reports if the controls are neatly aligned.

1. Select the **control** for which you want to align the text.

2. Click one of the **alignment** buttons on the toolbar or right click the control and select align and then click on the alignment you. For example if you choose **Align** and then **Left** all selected controls will be align left.

Alignment buttons

Alternatively, From the **Format Menu**, Choose **Align** and select the alignment you want from the submenu.

right aligning controls

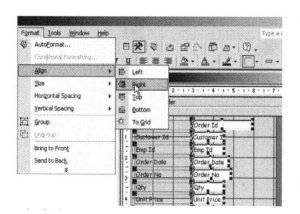
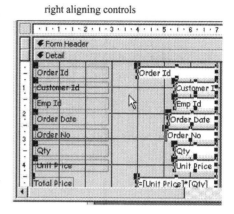

To change the horizontal spacing between a group of control

You can further improve your form by changing the horizontal and vertical spacing.

1. Select the **control**.

2. From the **format Menu**, Click on **Horizontal Spacing** and select the **horizontal spacing** you want from the submenu.

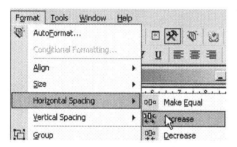

To change the vertical spacing between a group of control

1. Select the **control**.

2. From the **format Menu**, Click on **Vertical Spacing** and select the Vertical spacing you want from the submenu.

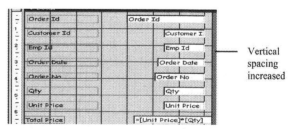

Vertical spacing increased

Adding Special Effects to the design of your form

Adding Rectangles

1. Click the **Rectangle** tool in the toolbox

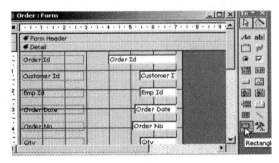

2. Point to a place on the form where you want to position the upper-left corner of the rectangle.

3. Click and drag the pointer to draw a rectangle the size you want.

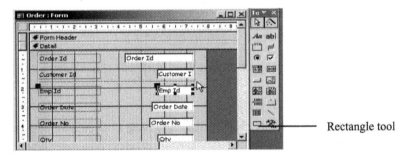

Rectangle tool

Drawing a line

1. Click the Line tool from the toolbox.

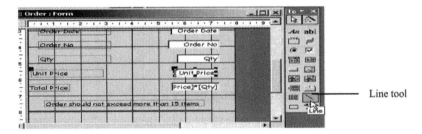

Line tool

2. Point to a place on the form where you want to start drawing the line.

3. Click and drag the pointer to a line size you want.

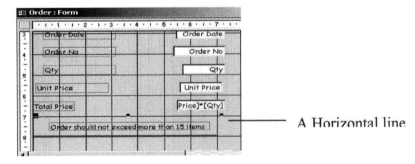

A Horizontal line

Creating a three dimensional effect

1. Select the **control(s)**.

2. Choose **Palette** from the **View menu** or click the palette button on the toolbar.

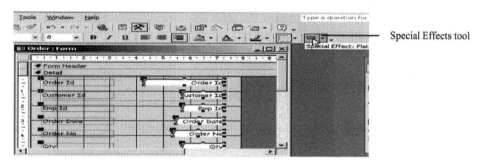

Special Effects tool

3. Select the look you want from the palette.

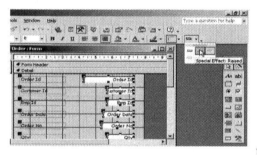
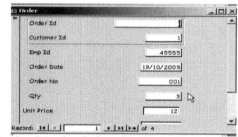

Results of applying the raised special effects on the Order form

Adding Background Color to your form

1. Select the **controls** you want to add the background colours.

2. Click the arrow next to the Fill/Back Colour tool on the toolbar.

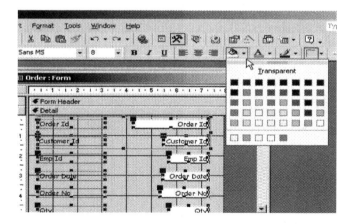

3. Select the background colour you want to apply from the palette.

Changing the color of the text

1. Select the **controls** that contain the text you want to change.

2. Click the **arrow** next to the Font/Fore Colour.

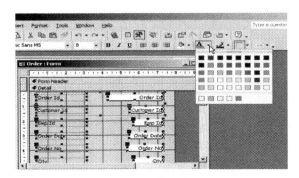

3. Select the **colour** you want to apply from the palette.

Chapter

CUSTOMISING YOUR FORM WITH CONTROLS AND COMMAND BUTTON

You can use special data entry controls to give your form a more professional look and make it easy to use. For example you can provide users with a list to choose from and use command buttons to open related forms.

Creating a List Box or a Combo Box

It is quicker and easier for users to select from a list than to type values into a text box. A list also reduces the chances of entering wrong information into a text box. Users can select a list of choices from a list box and combo box.

A **list box** is a fixed list of values you can choose from. A list box is displayed at all times. A list box is appropriate if choices available for a particular field on a form are fixed and hardly changes. For example in the gender field on the customer form you have a limited choice of entering Male or Female or Unknown. It is most unlikely that these values may change. You can use a list box to enter the values.

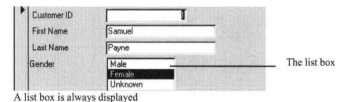

The list box

A list box is always displayed

A **Combo box** is similar to the list box except that users can type in new values. A combo box is used in anticipation that a new value may be added to the list in future. For example in the Employee table, you could use a combo box to create the department field in anticipation that when a new department is created users can type in the new value to add the value to the existing values in the list.

The values in a combo box is not displayed until the arrow is click

Creating a List Box or Combo Box with a Wizard

You can create a list box with a wizard or without a wizard.

Using a wizard to create a list box or combo box

1. Open the form in **Design View**.

2. Click the **Control Wizard** tool on the toolbar to select the **Control Wizard**. When the Control Wizard is selected it is highlighted.

3. Click the **List Box** or **Combo Box** button in the toolbox.

4. Click on the form where you want to place the **List Box** or **Combo box** button.

    The List Box or Combo Box Wizard dialog box is displayed on the screen

5. In the wizard first dialog box, click the button labelled **I will type in the values that I want.** Then click **Next**

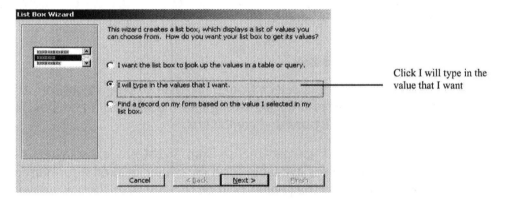

Click I will type in the value that I want

6. Type in the values for your list. Use the Tab Key to move to the next row. Then click **Next**.

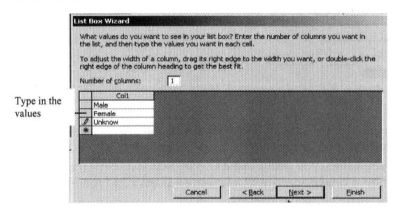

Type in the values

7. Click on **Store that value in this field,** and choose which field should receive the data from the drop-down list. Select the Gender field. Then click **Next**.

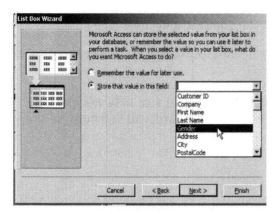

8. Type the title that you want to appear for the Control.

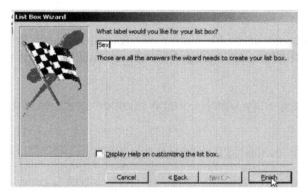

9. Click **Finish.** In step 3 if you selected a list box, a list box is created and displayed on your form.

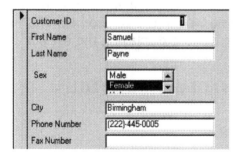

Creating a List Box or Combo Box without a Wizard

1. Open the form in design view.

2. In the toolbox, click the **Control Wizard tool** so that it is **not** highlighted.

3. Click the **List Box** or **Combo Box** button in the toolbox.

4. Create a bound control by displaying the field list (click the field list button on the toolbar) and selecting a field in the field list and dragging it to the form.

    Or create an unbound control by

Clicking the **Text Box** ![icon] tool in the toolbox and

Dragging the Text box to the form. Microsoft Access displays a text box with a label.

5.   Set the properties for the list or combo box in the **property sheet**. When you create a List Box or Combo Box without a Wizard you set most of the properties yourself.

Examples of Data Properties

Control Source is used to specify the data that would appear in a control

Row Source Type is used to specify where the row data comes from i.e. (table or query, list of values, or list of field names).

Row Source is used to specify how to get data for each row. You can use the Row Source Type and Row Source property to tell Microsoft Access how to get data for a list or combo box.

Bound Column Use this property to specify which column number specifies data for the Control Source.

Limit To List used to specify whether or not to limit users to values in list.

Default Value used to specify the default value assigned to the Control Source when you create a new record in form view.

AutoExpand You can use the AutoExpand property to specify whether Microsoft Access automatically fills the text box portion of a combo box with a value from the combo box list that matches the characters you enter as you type in the combo box. This makes you quickly enter an existing value in a combo box without displaying the list box portion of the combo box.

Column Count specifies the number of columns to display in a combo box.

Setting the properties for a List Box or Combo Box

1.   Double-click the control to open the property sheet.

2.   In the **RowSourceType** property box select **Table/Query** to show values from a table or query.

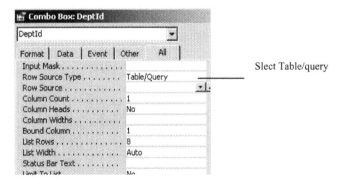

3. In the **RowSource** property box select or perform any of the following option.

- Select a **Table/Query** containing the values or field names that you want to appear in the list box.

- Type a list of fixed values and separate each field with semi-column (;).

- Type an SQL statement.

In this example we want to type an SQL statement in the **RowSource** property box therefore we choose the third option. SQL means Structured Query Language. You need to be familiar with the SQL language before you can use it. We want to use an SQL query to display the Dept Id field and the Department Name and order the fields displayed by the department's name. So type the following SQL statement in the **RowSource** property.

SELECT DISTINCTROW Department.DeptId, Department.DeptName FROM Department ORDER BY Department.DeptName;

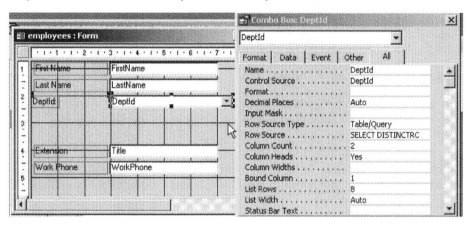

4. Click the **ColumnCount** property box and type the number of columns you want to display. In this example we want to display two columns the i.e. **department Id** and the **department name**.

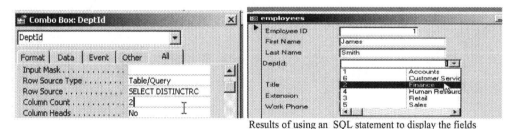

Results of using an SQL statement to display the fields

Restricting users to a list

Combo boxes uses less space on a form and provides flexibility for users, users can select a value from a list or enter new values. In some situations you can take advantage of the fact that a combo box will use less space and use a combo box in your form to display a list of choices, and then limit the values in the combo box to values in a list.

Example

For example you could use a combo box to display a list of department codes and prevent users from entering new values by limiting users to values in the list.

Restricting users to values on the list

To prevent users from entering a value that is not in the department table we set the **Limit to List** property of the DeptId to **Yes.** This will prevent users from entering values that are not in the department table.

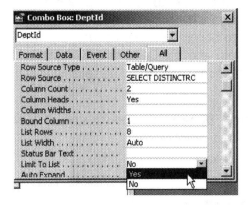

A Combo box that accepts new values

You can also create combo boxes that allow users to enter new values. For example on our employees form we can create the Title field using a combo box that would accept new values.

In **Design View** create a bound field from the Title Field in the employee table using a combo box by following the steps for creating a combo box without a wizard and set the following properties.

Properties	Values
Row Source Type	**Value List**
Row Source	Enter "**Mr; Ms; Mrs**"
Limit To List	**No**

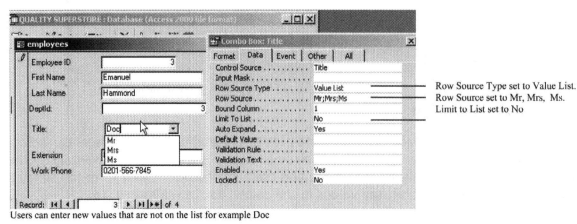

Users can enter new values that are not on the list for example Doc

Creating Check boxes, Option Buttons and toggle Buttons

Check boxes, Option buttons and toggle buttons are used to set Yes/No values.   When selected they indicate a **Yes** or **True** value.   When deselected or cleared they indicate a No or False value.

Creating a Check Box

Example

In our Order form, we can include a check box to show whether or not an order has been shipped.   The check box is bound to the Order Shipped field.

1.   Open the form in **Design view.**

2.   Click the Check Box tool ⬚ in toolbox.

3.   In the field list, select the Order Shipped field.

4.   Drag the Order Shipped field to the Order form.

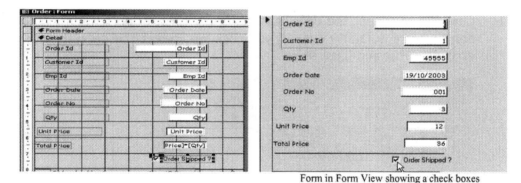

Form in Form View showing a check boxes

5.   Click the label and change its name to **Order Shipped?**

Creating an Option Group

An **Option Group** is a group of options for a field enclosed in a frame. It provides users with a set of options or alternatives from which users can choose. An Option Group is useful if you have few choices for a field entry. The group of options, enclosed in the frame, can be represented, by option buttons;, toggle buttons or check buttons.

Example

In the Order Tracking System, orders are made by post, by telephone, text message or fax. We can create an option group for the **Order By** field with the four options and users will click an option rather than rather than type in values such as by post, by telephone etc.

Creating an Option Group with a wizard

1.   Open the form in **Design View** .

2.   Click the **Control Wizards** 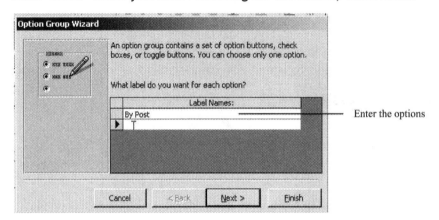 button in the toolbox to select it.

3.   Click the Option group button in the toolbox.

4.   Drag your mouse pointer on your form where you want the option group to appear. When you release the mouse button, the wizard starts.

5.   Enter the labels you want for each button. Use the **Tab key** to move to the next field. When you finish entering all the labels, click **Next**.

Enter the options

6.   Click **Yes** to Accept the default value or click **No, I don't want a default** if you don't want a default value. If you click Yes, select the default value from the drop-down list and Click **Next**.

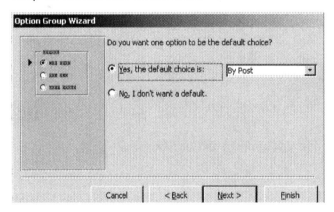

7.   Microsoft Access presents you with the options and their values. Accept the default values and click Next.

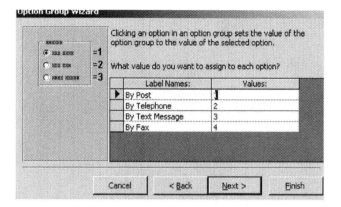

8. Click **Store the value in this field,** and choose which field the data will be stored into from the drop-down list. Select **OrderedBy.** Click **Next.**

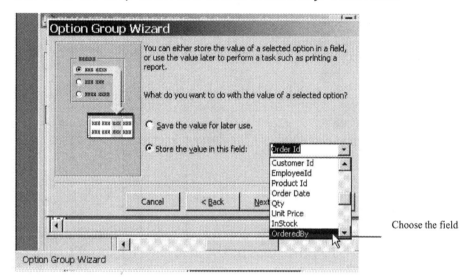

Choose the field

9. Select the type of control you want (i.e. option button, check box or toggle button). Then select a style and click **Next.**

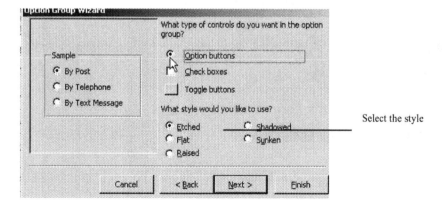

Select the style

10. Enter a name or caption for the **Option** Group. For example enter Order By. Then click **Finish.**

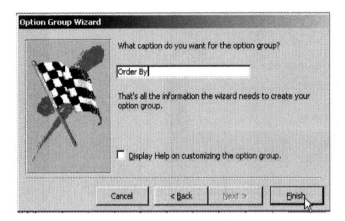

You can add a frame to the options in **Design view.**

To see the results, open the form in form view.

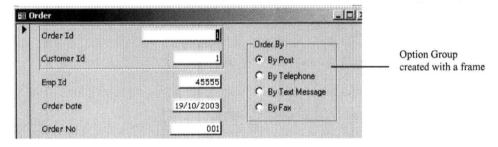

Option Group created with a frame

Change a control from one type to another

You can change a control to another type of control. For example you can change a **Check Box** to an **Option Button.** Follow the steps below to change a control to another type of control.

1. Open the form in **Design view.**

2. Click the control you want to change to select it.

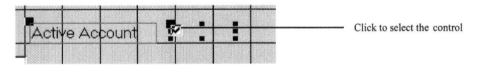

Click to select the control

3. Select **Change To** from the **Format Menu.**

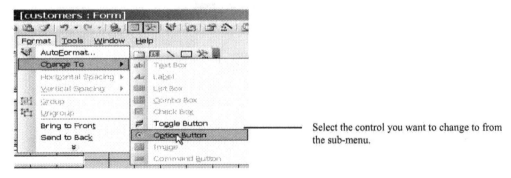

Select the control you want to change to from the sub-menu.

4. Select the type of control you want to change to from the sub-menu.

   Note: The type of control highlighted in the Sub-menu depends on type of control selected.

5. Open the form in Form View to see the results of the changes you have made.

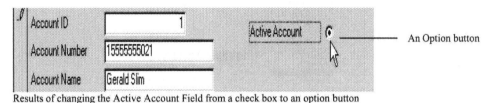

Results of changing the Active Account Field from a check box to an option button

Creating Command Buttons

Command buttons are buttons used to perform actions. They provide an easy way of performing a task by simply clicking on them. For example on the Customers form you can use a command button to open orders placed by a customer by just clicking the Orders button.

To make the command buttons functional, you have to write a macro or Access Basic event procedure and attached them to the command button's **OnClick** property.

You can create a command button by using the command button wizard or by creating the command button from scratch. When you use the command button wizard to create a command button, Microsoft Access provides you with a wide selection of pre-designed command Button. Microsoft Access also creates an event procedure, an Access Basic procedure that runs when an event occurs on the form. However, when you create a command button on your own (from scratch), you will have to create your own Access Basic event procedure and attached it on the button's **Onclick** property.

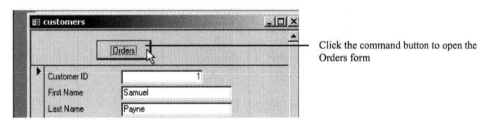

Click the command button to open the Orders form

To create a command button with a Wizard

1. Open the form in **Design view**.

2. Select the Control Wizards 🔲 button in the toolbox.

3. Click the **Command button** 🔲 in the toolbox.

4. Click on the form where you want the command button to appear.

5. Microsoft Access opens the command button wizard dialog box.   Click on the Categories box and select an action from the Actions box. For example to open the customers form click on the **Forms Operations** categories and select **Open form** from the actions box. Click **Next.**

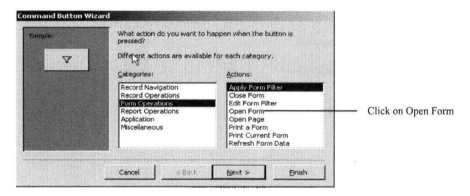

Click on Open Form

6. The subsequent screens depend on the action chosen. In our example we chose **Open Form** so the wizard presents us with a list of forms to choose from. Select the form you want to open and click **Next** to continue.

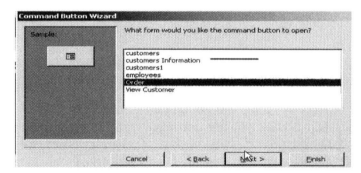

7. Click on **Open the form and find specific data to display.** Click **Next.**

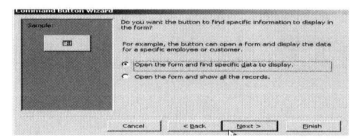

8. Select the matching fields from the **Customers box** and **Orders box**, then click on <-> button.

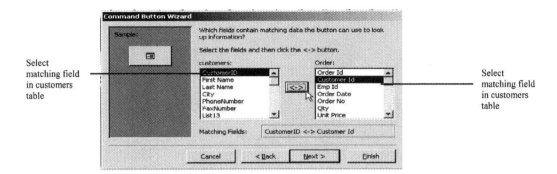

Select matching field in customers table

Select matching field in customers table

9. Choose **Text or Picture** for the button. If you choose text enter the text you want the command button to display. If you choose picture select a picture from the list. Click **Next** to continue.

10 Type a meaningful name for the button and click **Finish.**

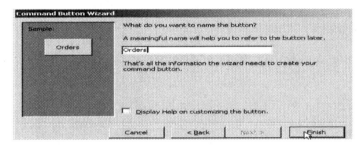

11. The button appears on the form. Clicking the button will open the Orders form and display Orders placed by the customer.

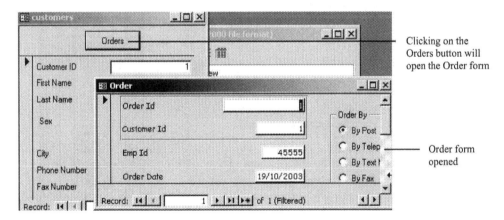

Clicking on the Orders button will open the Order form

Order form opened

Creating a Command Button Without a Wizard

In this example you will create a command button without a wizard to open the payment form.

Example

Suppose you want to create a command button that will open the payment form. Follow the steps below to create a command button without a wizard.

1.   Open the form in **Design view.**

2.   Deselect the **Control Wizards** 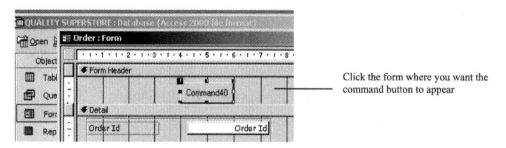 tools in the toolbox. Make sure it is not highlighted.

3.   Click the **Command Button tool** on the toolbox.

4.   Click the form where you want to place the command button. Microsoft Access adds the control to the form.

Click the form where you want the command button to appear

5.   Double-click the command button to open the property sheet for the command button.

6.   Select the **OnClick** property. Click the **Build button** to create a new macro or event procedure or enter the name or select the macro or event procedure from the drop-down list

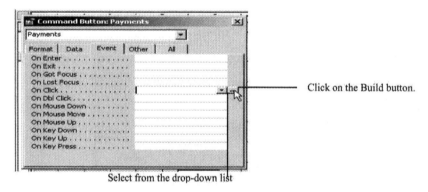

Click on the Build button.

Select from the drop-down list

7.   When you click on the **Build button,** Microsoft Access presents you with options to choose a Builder. Select any of the options. For example you can choose the Macro Builder to build a macro for your command button. In this example choose the Macro Builder.

The **Save As** dialog box appears. Name the Macro Payments

Microsoft Access presents you with the Macro dialog box.

8. Select an **action** from the drop-down list in the **Action** column.

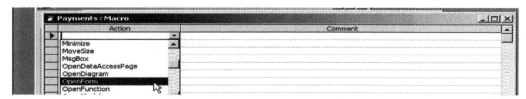

9. When you select an action, the Action Arguments box appears. Select the form name from the drop-down list box.

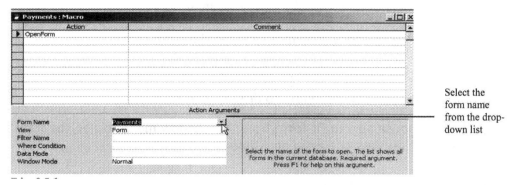

Select the form name from the drop-down list

10. Close and save the macro dialog box. After you close the macro box, Microsoft Access inserts the name of the macro in the **On-Click** property.

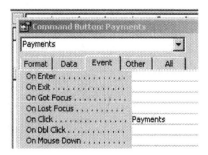

11. Enter a name in the property name box. To display a text on the command button, enter a text in the caption box. To display a picture on the command button, click the picture property box and type the path and file name of the picture.

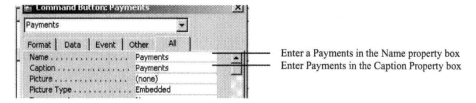

Enter a Payments in the Name property box
Enter Payments in the Caption Property box

Creating a form with multiple pages

In certain situations a form may be more than one page long. This makes the controls on the form unable to fit into one screen. You can use a **Page Break** or a **Tab Control** to separate the pages and make them fit into one screen or different pages.

A **Page Break** is used to mark the beginning of a new screen on a form with multiple pages. A page break is active in **Form view** only and the **Default View** property of a form should be set to **Single** form. In **Form View** the **Page Down key** and **Page Up Key** is used to move between the different pages.

A **Tab Control** is used to display the different pages on separate tabs. The content of each page is displayed on a tab. You can switch between pages by clicking the different tabs.

To add a page break to a form

1.   Open the form in **Design View.**

2.   Click the Page Break tool ▤ on the toolbox.

3.   Click the form where you want to place the page break.

     A dotted line appears on the left border of the form to indicate a page break.

4.   Open the form in **Form View** to display your form.

     Select **choose size to fit form** from the Window menu to size the form's window so that it displays one page at a time.

To add a Tab Control to a form

1.   Open the form in **Design View.**

2.   Click the **Tab Control** ⊡ tool in the toolbox.

3.   Click on the form where you want the tab to be position. A Tab appears on the form with two pages labelled Page 1 and Page 2.

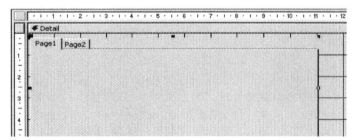

4.   Click the tab page you want to add controls to.

5.   Click the **field list tool** ▣ and select the controls you want to add to the form. You can also add any type of control to the form except another tab control.

6. Double-click the Tab header and change the name and caption for each tab in the property sheet.

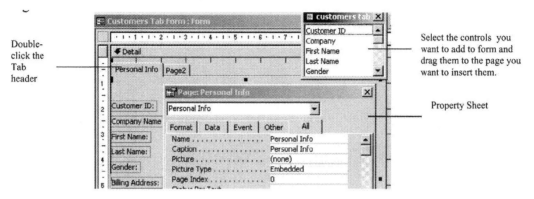

Double-click the Tab header

Select the controls you want to add to form and drag them to the page you want to insert them.

Property Sheet

12. Switch to **Form View** to view the form.

Select **choose size to fit form** from the **Window** menu to size the form's window so that it displays one page at a time.

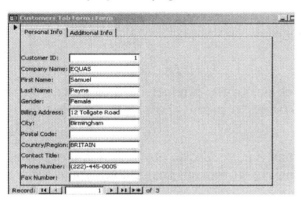

Chapter

14

ADDING GRAPHICS TO FORMS

You can add pictures and objects to a form to make the form more professional and attractive. Microsoft Access provides two objects type you can add to your form. They are the **bound** and **unbound** object types.

A **bound** object is a picture, which is stored in a field in a table, as you move from record to record in a form the picture changes.

Example

For example you can add a bound object to the product form to display the picture of each product. As you move from record to record the picture changes to display the different products in your database.

An **Unbound** object is an object, which is not bound to any field in a table. The object is stored in the design of the form. The object remains the same as you move from record to record.

Example

An example of an unbound picture is a company's logo on a form. As you move through the records in a form the company's logo remains the same.

Add a bound object frame

1.   Create a field in the product table, and set its field data type to OLE Object.

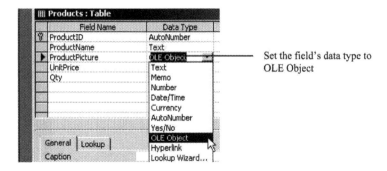

Set the field's data type to OLE Object

3.   Open the form or report in **Design view.**

4. Choose field list from the **View menu** or (click the field list button on the toolbar).

5. Drag the field that stores the OLE object to the form or report. Microsoft Access creates an object frame bound to that field.

After you have created the object frame in **design view**, you need to switch to form view to embed or link the object.

To create an embedded object in a bound object frame

1. Open the form in **Form view** and select the record you want to add an object to.

2. Click on the bound object frame to select it.

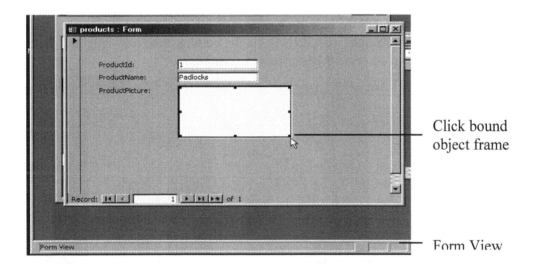

Click bound object frame

Form View

3. Click on the **Insert menu** and select **Object**.

4. If you want to create a new object, select the **Create New** option. In the **Object Type** list, select the type of object you want to embed.

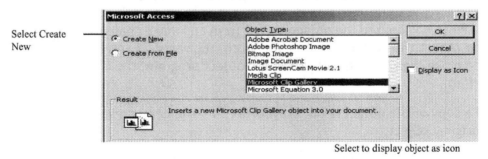

Select Create New

Select to display object as icon

5. If you want to display the object as an icon instead of displaying the object itself, select the **Display as Icon** check box.

6. Choose **OK**. Microsoft Access opens the object's application.

7. Create the object by using the application that you selected in step 4.

8. Click **Ok** to exit from the application or Choose **Exit** from the **File menu** of the object application to return to Microsoft Access. The object is added to your form.

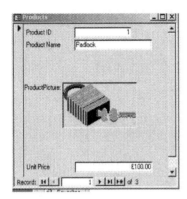

9. Follow steps 2-8 to continue adding different objects to your records. When you finish adding the objects, scroll through the records and you will see that as you move from record to record the pictures changes.

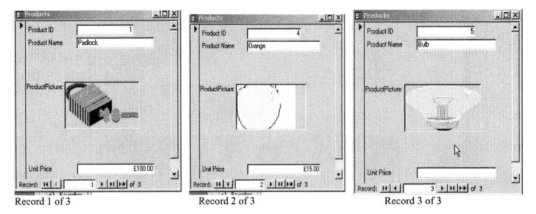

Record 1 of 3   Record 2 of 3   Record 3 of 3

To embed or link an existing object in an unbound object frame

If you have already created and saved an object, for example you have created a company logo and saved it somewhere on disk, you can embed or link it to an unbound object frame. When you **embed** the object in your form and make changes to the object on your form the object will only change on your form, however, if you **link** the object to your form and make changes to the object in the object program, the changes will be reflected in your form.

Embed a copy of the object is put on your form.   The copy on your form is independent of the original object.

Link Microsoft Access maintains a link to the source object and any changes is immediately reflected in your form.

1. Open a form or report in **Design view**.

2. Click the **unbound Object Frame** tool in the toolbox.

3. Click on the form where you want to add the unbound object frame.

   The Insert Object dialog box is displayed on your screen.

4. Select **Create from File** button.

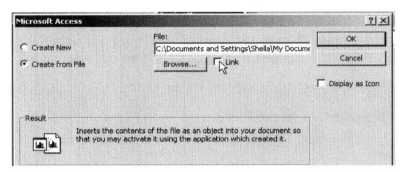

5. Type the name and path of the file that contains the object you want to embed or link in the **File** box or choose the **Browse** button to browse and select the file that contains the object you want.

6. Click the **Link** box, if you want to link the object. If you don't want to link the object, leave the Link box blank.

7. Click **Ok**.

   Microsoft Access inserts the object to form. The object i.e. the company logo remains the same as you move from record to record.

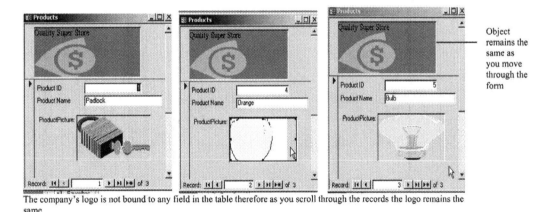

The company's logo is not bound to any field in the table therefore as you scroll through the records the logo remains the same

Resizing an object

You may notice that when you insert an object to the object frame, the object doesn't always fit perfectly into the frame. You may want to adjust the object frame so that the picture or object is displayed perfectly within its frame. You can adjust the object frame by changing its Size Mode property in the property sheet.

To make the object fit its frame

1. Open the form in **Design View**.

2. Select the **object frame**.

3. Click the **Properties** button on the toolbar to display the property sheet.

4. Select any of the options from the **Size Mode** property drop-down list. You can set the **Size Mode** property to **Clip, Stretch or Zoom.**

    Clip displays the picture at its actual size. If the picture is larger than the size of the control the part of the picture or object will be cut off.

    Stretch displays the object to fit the size of the frame.

    Zoom Adjust the object to fit the frame.

Chapter

TO FIND SPECIFIC VALUES IN A FIELD

Scrolling through records can be time consuming when you have a large database. You can easily locate specific records or find specific values in a field with the Find command. As you add more records to your database, the size of your database increases and you can no longer quickly find data or records by scrolling through the database. You can use the Find command to quickly find records in your database. When you use Find to locate records, Microsoft Access finds and highlights the first occurrence of the data. You can continue to search for more records by clicking **Next**. Follow the steps below to find records in your database.

Finding a record

1. In **Form** or **datasheet view** select the field you want to search.

Click inside the field you want to search

2. Click on **Find** from the **Edit** menu or click the **Find** 🔍 button on the toolbar. The **Find** dialog box is displayed.

3. In the **Find what box,** type the value you want to find. If you are not sure of what you are looking for, you can use wild characters. For example, use * to match any number of characters you are not sure of.

Wildcard Character

	Character	Example
*	Match any number of characters	Al* will return Alex, Alexis and Alexander
?	Match any single character	Ale? Will return Alec and Alex in the same position as the ?
#	Matches any single numeric digit	#th will return 4th or 6th, 1## will return 100th in the same position as the #

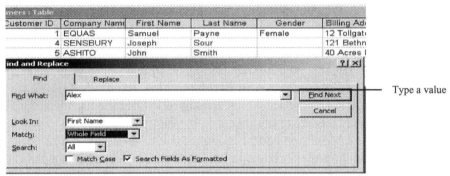

Type a value

The find dialog box

4. The **Look In** box contains the field you want to search. You can accept the default value or click the drop-down list to select the table if you want to search the entire table.

5. In the **Match box** select any of the following from the drop-down list.

    Whole Field finds data based on the whole text you have typed. For example if you type in "Alex" Access will find "Alex" and not "Alexander"

    Start Field finds fields that begin with the specified field "Alex" will find "Alexis", "Alexander" and also "Alex".

    Any Part of the field will find data that contains the specified text. For example if you type in "Al" the search will find any data that contains Al for example "Alex", "Alexis", "Always" "Wald" etc.

6. Click on the **Search box** and select from the drop-down list. The default selection is **All** which searches all records. **Down** will search forward and **Up** will search backwards only from the current record.

7. If you want to match the case of the text you are searching, click the **Match Case** box. This will limit the search to entries that are the same case. For example if you type in ALEX, the search will only find "ALEX" and not "alex"

8. Click on **Find Next.** The first match is displayed. You may have to move the **Find dialog box** to a new position to see the record.

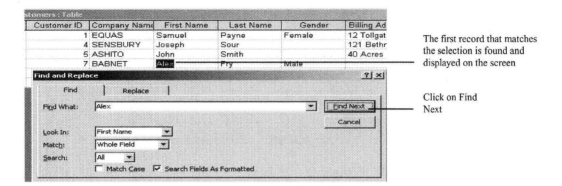

The first record that matches the selection is found and displayed on the screen

Click on Find Next

9. To find the next occurrence, Click **Find Next** again. If Microsoft Access can't find any more occurrence of the text, it displays a message telling you that the search item cannot be found. Click on **Ok** to clear the message.

10. Click on **Cancel** to close the **Find** dialog box.

Using the Replace Feature

You can change the content of a field in all or some of your records. You can use the Replace feature in Microsoft Access to find and replace the same data in several places. The Find and Replace feature is almost the same except that with the Replace feature, you can replace the found text with another text. For example you could replace all occurrence of **Cooke** with **Cook**.

1. Click the field you want to search and replace text on.

2. Select **Replace** from the **Edit menu.** The find and replace dialog box is displayed on your screen.

3. Type the text you want to find in the **Find What** text box.

4. In the **Replace With box** type the replacement text.

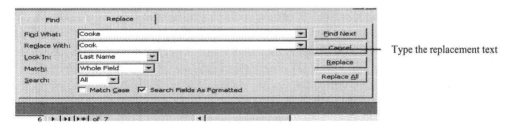

Type the replacement text

5. Set any other options you want to use in the **Find and Replace** dialog box.

6. Click on the **Find Next** button.

   Microsoft Access moves to the first occurrence of the text and selects it. You may have to move the **Find and Replace dialog box** to a new position to see the record with the selected text.

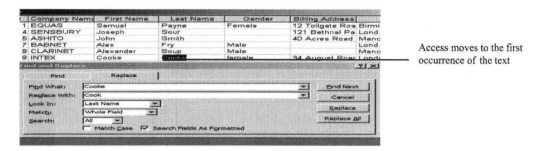

Access moves to the first occurrence of the text

7.   To replace all occurrence of the text with the replacement text all at once click on the **Replace All** button.

To replace each occurrence of the text one at a time click on the **Replace** button and click on **Find Next** to continue.

If you do not want to replace the selected text, choose **Find Next**.

8.   If you chose to replace the text one at a time, continue replacing the text until you come to the end of the search. At the end of the search Microsoft Access displays the following message.

9.   Click on **Ok** to finish the search.

10. Click on Cancel to exit the **Find and Replace** dialog box.

Sorting Data

Sorting data is about organising data in a meaningful way. Another way of organising your data so you can quickly retrieve the information you want is by sorting. Sorting helps you to organise your data in a particular order. For example you can sort your data to display the customers names by Last Name and then First Name. You can sort records in a table or form in ascending or descending order. In a form you can sort records by one field at a time and in a datasheet you can sort more than one field at a time. When you sort data by more than one field at a time Microsoft Access sorts the data from left to right. For example in the example below Microsoft Access will sort the records first by Last Name and then by First Name.

To sort records by one field

1.   Click the field you want to sort by.

2.   Click the **Sort Ascending**  or **Sort Descending** button on the toolbar.

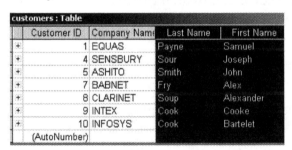

Click the field you want to sort

The records appear sorted by date

The records appears sorted by Order Date

To sort records by more than one field

1. Select the fields you want to sort. The fields should be placed side by side in the order you want to sort them.

2. Click the **Sort Ascending** or **Sort Descending** button on the toolbar.

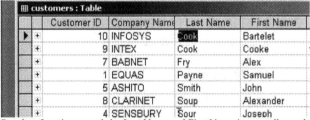

Results of sorting records by Last Name and First Name in ascending order

Filtering Records

A filter provides a subset of the data in your table or form. A filter separates records in a table, form, or query that meet certain criteria. As you may have seen the **Find** command is only useful for finding specific records. If you want to focus on more records for example if you want to focus on customers who bought jeans so you can sell related products to them, you may have to use the filter command to get the subset of data that you want.

There are different ways you can filter the data in your tables or form. For example you can filter by selection, by form, Filter Excluding Selection or perform an advanced filter.

Filter by selection

1. Open the table in **Datasheet view**.

2. Click the data you want to use to filter the records.

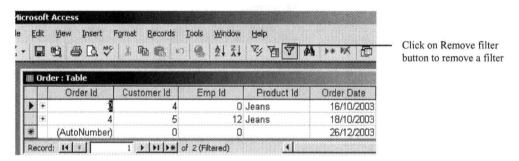

Click on Remove filter button to remove a filter

3. Click the **Filter by selection** tool in the toolbar or click on **Filter by Selection** from the **Records Menu**.

    Microsoft Access filters the data and retrieves data that meets the criteria you specified. You can use the results of your search to target customers for example you can use the results of the search to sell jeans related products to customers who bought jeans.

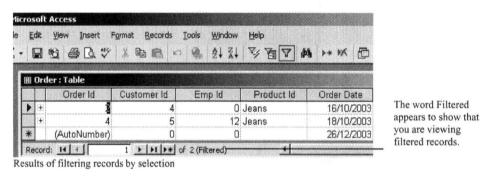

The word Filtered appears to show that you are viewing filtered records.

Results of filtering records by selection

To remove the filter, Click on **Remove Filter** from the Records menu or click the **Remove/Apply filter** button on the toolbar.

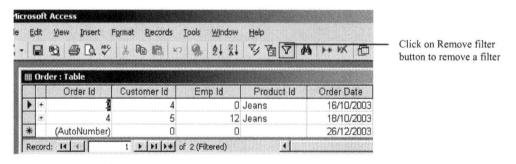

Click on Remove filter button to remove a filter

Filter by Excluding Selection

In certain situations it is easier to filter a datasheet by specifying the records that you do not want to see. Filtering by excluding a selected value enables you to hide records that you do not want to see.

Example

For example you may want to filter the products table to exclude all product records in computers. In a situation like this, the best option is the **Filter Excluding Selection**. When performing **Filter Excluding Selection**, you select the value you do not want to see i.e. computers from a relevant cell (product name column). Then select **Filter** from the **Records Menu** and then **Filter Excluding selection** from the submenu. This will display all records except the records with the value you selected.

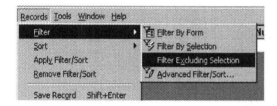

Filtering by forms

You can apply the filter by forms command to a table as well as to a form. **Filter by forms** is useful if you want to filter by more than one field. Follow the instructions below to apply filter to your form.

1. Open a table or form. Choose **Records, Filter by Form**, or click **filter by form button** on the toolbar. The Filter by form window is displayed on your screen. This window displays a single blank form in the same format as one of the records.

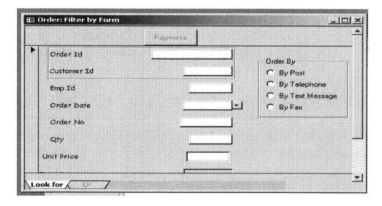

2. Click the field you want to set your criteria on. For example to filter for orders for a particular day click the Order Date field and select an entry in that field.

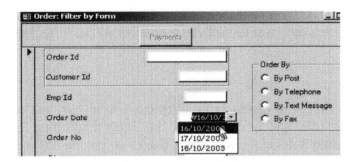

3. You can enter as many criteria as you want. For example you could also select the Emp Id field and select an employee to find out how many orders a particular employee took for 16/10/03.

4. Click the **Apply Filter** ![icon] button on the toolbar. The filtered data appears on the screen. The number of records filtered appears at the bottom of the screen.

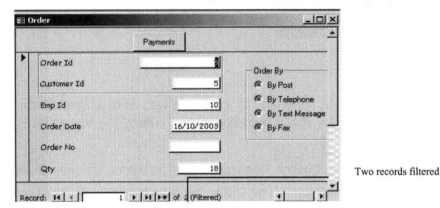

Two records filtered

5. Click the **Filter by form** button. Your criteria are still displayed. When you enter a criteria on a form they are saved as a form property until you replaced them.

    Suppose you decide to find the orders taken by this particular employee on 16/10/03 or 17/10/03 you can add an additional criteria using the **Or tab** to find this data.

6. Click on the **Or tab** to add another criteria to your form. Another **Or Tab** is displayed when you click the **Or tab.**   The **Or tab** is similar to the **Look for tab.** It displays the same blank fields as the **Look For** Tab. You can enter or select values in the same way you entered values in the **Look For** Tab. Enter a criteria in the field(s)

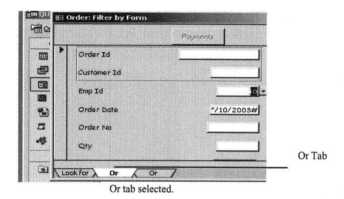

Or tab selected.

7. Click the **Apply filter** button. Microsoft Access displays the results of your filter.

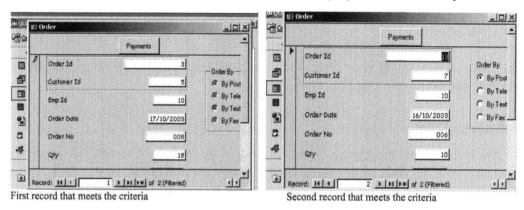

First record that meets the criteria   Second record that meets the criteria

8. To remove the filter, click on **Apply/Remove filter** button on the toolbar.

9. Close the Orders form.

Saving Your Filtered Data as a Query

You can save the results of your filtered data as a query and use it as you would use a query. Follow the steps below.

To save a filter as a query

1. Open the Filter in **Filter by Form view.**

2. Select the **File, Save As Query.**

    The Save **as Query** dialog box appears on your screen.

3. Type a name and click **ok.** Access saves the filter.

Filtering with Expression

Rather than entering a value in the fields, you can type an expression containing a comparison operator. Examples of comparison operators you can use are <, >, =, <=, >= or <>.

Example

You can use **Filtering with expression** to find orders with Unit Price less than £10.   For example you could enter a comparison operator in the Unit Price column to find Orders with Unit price less than £10.

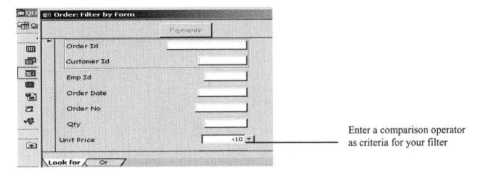

Enter a comparison operator
as criteria for your filter

To clear an entry

To clear all entries in your filter, Click on the Clear Grid ☒ button on the toolbar or click **Clear Grid** from the **Edit Menu.**

Advanced Filter

In the previous examples the results of your filter were not sorted. If you want to filter and sort your records at the same time you can use advanced filter. This type of filter is similar to a query in that it displays a window similar to the query design view and gives you an opportunity to sort your results. The difference between the advanced filter and a query is that with the advanced filter you can only work with fields within the current table. With a query you can work with fields from more than one table.

To perform an advanced filter

1.   Open the table in **Datasheet view.**

2.   Select **Filter** from the **Records Menu** and then click **Advanced Filter/Sort** from the sub-menu. Microsoft Access opens the Advanced Filter window.

3.   Click and drag the fields you want to use for your criteria from the table to the grid.

4.   Specify the criteria and sort order under the fields you have included in the filter.

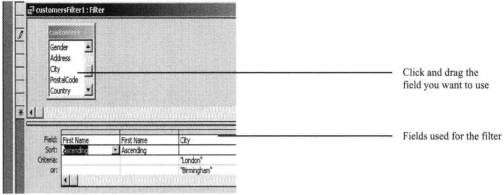

Click and drag the field you want to use

Fields used for the filter

Grid showing the fields for the criteria

5. Click **Apply Filter/Sort** from the **Filter Menu** to view your filtered data.

Criteria set to London or Birmingham

Results of setting the criteria to London or Birmingham

6. To remove the filter, Click **Remove Filter.** Close the table.

Chapter

QUERIES

A Query is a database object, which enables you to ask questions about the data stored in your database. A query can enable you to view, update and analyse data in your database. Microsoft Access provides different types of queries to help you analyse the information in your database. The following are some of the different types of queries that Microsoft Access provides.

Functions of a query

- A query will help you to extract information from your database.

- Allow you to perform calculations in your data.

- You can use queries as source of data for forms, reports, graphs and other queries

- Make changes to data in your tables.

Difference between a query and a filter

- You can query more than one table at a time.

- Create calculated fields with a query.

- Summarize and group data

- Choose the fields to display in your query.

Example

You can create a query that retrieves customers who haven't placed any orders during the year and offer them discounts or promotional items to encourage them to buy more. You create the query and include the **customers' names** and **telephone numbers** and sort the list by **Order Date** in ascending order.

Types of queries

Select Query is the most commonly used query. You can use a select query to retrieve data from more than one table, group and summarize the data and perform calculations on the data.

Parameter query is a type of query that prompts you for information such as the criteria to use to retrieve the information you want.

Crosstab query is a type of query that summarises the information in your database in rows and columns in spreadsheet like format for easier analysis. The information in a crosstab query is grouped on the left side of the datasheet and across the top of the datasheet. You can use results of a crosstab query to compare values and see trends in your data. It can be used to create reports and graph.

Action query is a type of query, which makes changes to many records in just one operation. There are different types of Action queries they are

- **Delete query** deletes a group of records from one or more tables.

- **Append query** is a type of query which add records from one or more tables to the end of one or more tables. Useful for adding records to history table.

- **Update query** is a type of query, which makes changes to one or more tables.

- **Make-table** is a type of query, which creates a new table from all or part of the data in one or more tables. Useful for creating backup copy of a table.

There is also the **SQL Query**. This type of query uses the Structured Query Language to query, change and analyse information in your database. SQL Query is beyond the scope of this book.

Creating a Query

Like most database objects you can create a query with a query wizard or without a query wizard. If you are using data from more than two tables to create your query, then you must create the relationship before starting to create the query. Refer to the chapter for creating relationship between tables.

Creating a Select Query with a wizard

The easiest way to create a query is with the Query wizard. When you create a query with the query wizard the wizard can perform calculations like sum, average, count etc., however, you may not be able to set criteria for retrieving the records or sort the records. This way of creating a query is useful for viewing all the information in your database, and not for specific information. Follow the instructions below to create a select query.

1. In the **Database window**, click the **Queries** tab under **Objects** and then click **New.**

The **New query** dialog box appears.

2. Click on **Simple Query Wizard** and click **Ok.**

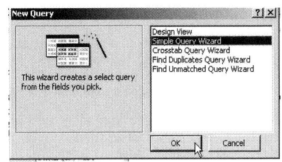

The **Simple Query Wizard** dialog box appears.

3. Choose the table you want to base your query on from the **Tables/Query** drop-down list

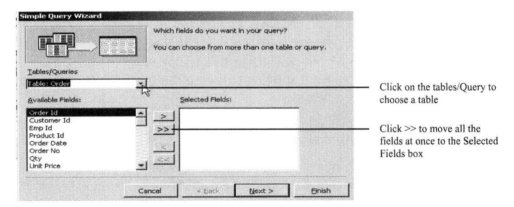

4. Click a field name in the **Available fields** list, and then click the > button to move it to the **Selected Fields** list. Repeat this process to move all the fields you want to include in your query. You can move all the fields at once by clicking the **>>** button, when you finish selecting and moving the fields, click **Next.**

5. (Optional) if you are basing your query on more than one table, select another table and move the fields you want to include in the query by following step 4. When you finish click **Next** to continue.

6. Accept the default option of showing every field of record and click **Next.**

7. Enter a title for the query when ask **what title do you want for your query?**

8. Click on **Finish** to view the query results.

CustomerId, Order Date, Qty and Unit Price are from the Order Table

CustomerId	Order Date	First Name	Last Name	Billing Address	Qty	Unit Price
1	17/10/2003	Samuel	Payne	12 Tollgate Roa	3	12
4	16/10/2003	Joseph	Sour	121 Bethnal Pa	4	5
5	17/10/2003	John	Smith	40 Acres Road	18	10
5	18/10/2003	John	Smith	40 Acres Road	13	10
5	26/12/2003	John	Smith	40 Acres Road	4	10
7	16/10/2003	Alex	Fry		10	4

Record: 1 of 6

First Name, Last Name and Billing Address are from the Customer table

Creating a Select Query without a wizard

1. In the **Database window**, click the **Queries** tab under **Objects** and then click **New.**

    The New Query dialog box appears.

2. Click **Design View** in the **New Query** dialog box and then click **Ok.**

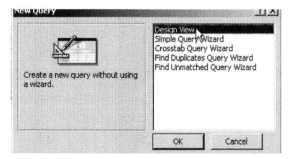

    The **Show Table** dialog box appears displaying all the tables in the database.

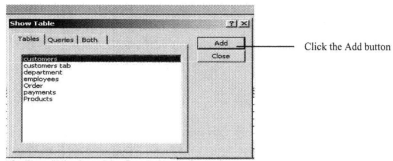

    Click the Add button

The Show dialog box with a list of tables in the database

3. Click the table you want to include in your query and then click the **Add** button. The table appears in the **Query Window** displaying all the fields in the table. Repeat step 3 to add more tables to your query. If a relationship exists between the tables you have selected, Microsoft Access shows the relationship between the tables.

4. Click the **Close** button when you finish adding the tables. The Query Design view window opens.

5. Add fields to the Query.

Adding Fields to a Query

There are several methods you can add fields to a Query. Some of the methods are as follows:

First Method

1. Click in the **Table** box in the lower part of the grid and select a table from the drop-down list.

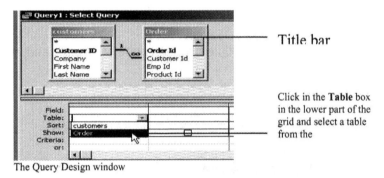

The Query Design window

2. Click in the **Field** box to open the drop-down list for the field and select a field. The fields displayed depend on the table you selected in step 1.

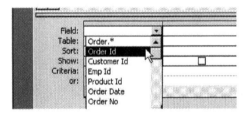

3. Click on the **Tab** key to move to the next column. Repeat steps 1 & 2 until you have finish selecting all the fields you want to use for your data.

Second Method

1. Drag the field from the **field list** to a cell in the **Field Row** of the QBE grid.

    To select a block of fields, select the first field you want to include, hold down the **Shift Key** and click the last field and then drag to a cell in the Field row. To add more than one field at a time, hold down the **Ctrl Key** and click the fields you want to add; and then drag the group to a cell in the Field row.

Third Method

The third method is to double-click the field name in the field list.

Fourth Method

1. Double-click the title bar of the field list.

2. With the mouse pointing to any of the fields selected in the field list, drag the fields to the grid.

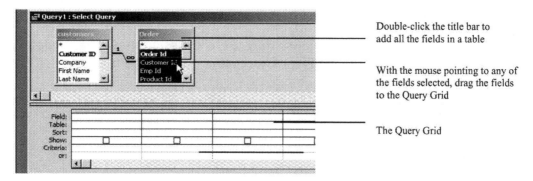

Double-click the title bar to add all the fields in a table

With the mouse pointing to any of the fields selected, drag the fields to the Query Grid

The Query Grid

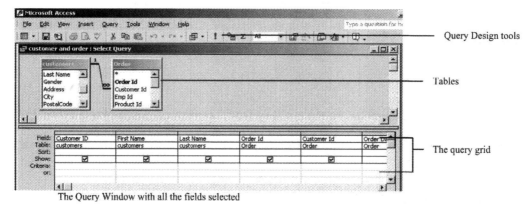

Query Design tools

Tables

The query grid

The Query Window with all the fields selected

6. Click the **Run** button ![Run button] on the toolbar to see the results of your query.

Customer ID	First Name	Last Name	City	Order Id	Order.Custome	Order Date
7	Alex	Fry	London	1	7	17/10/20
7	Alex	Fry	London	13	7	16/10/20
11	John	Stephes	Accra	14	11	29/12/20
12	Henry	Sailor	Los Angeles	15	12	29/12/20
13	Sheila	Boots	Lisbon	17	13	29/12/20
14	Michael	Barrell	Ontario	16	14	29/12/20
14	Michael	Barrell	Ontario	18	14	29/12/20

Record: I◄ ◄ | 1 | ►I ►I ►* of 11

The results of running the query

Saving a Query

1. From the **File Menu,** click on **Save** or click on the **Save** tool on the toolbar. Microsoft Access presents you with the **Save As** dialog box, Enter a name for your query and click **Ok.**

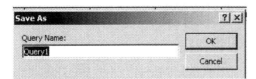

Exploring the different views in a Query window

A query has five different views: they are the **Design view**, **Datasheet view**, **SQL view**, **Pivot Table** view and **Pivot Chart view**. You will be using the first three views for most of your queries.

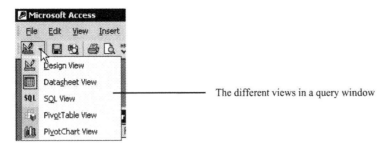

The different views in a query window

The Design View

The **Design view** is used to create a query from scratch or customize an existing query. In the Database window, clicking the **Design view** will display the query in design view.

The query is displayed in design view.

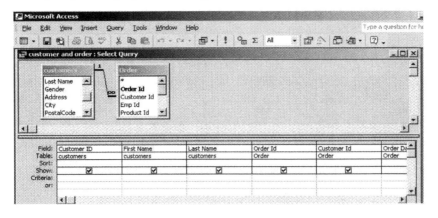

The Datasheet view

The Datasheet view is used to view the results of a query in the design window.

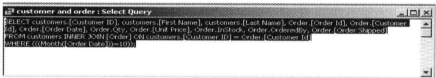

The results of clicking the datasheet view button

The SQL view

The SQL view is used to view or enter SQL statement to create or change a query.

SELECT customers.[Customer ID], customers.[First Name], customers.[Last Name], Order.[Order Id], Order.[Customer Id], Order.[Order Date], Order.Qty, Order.[Unit Price], Order.InStock, Order.OrderedBy, Order.[Order Shipped] FROM customers INNER JOIN [Order] ON customers.[Customer ID] = Order.[Customer Id] WHERE (((Month([Order Date]))=10));

The SQL view of the customer and order query

Switching between view

Switching view is useful particularly when you are working with a complex query with multiple criteria. You can toggle between design view and datasheet view to see if the query is doing what you want it to do before making further changes.

1. Click the down arrow next to the view button  to select a different view.

Opening a query

Opening a query from the Database Window

You can view or open an existing query from the database window by clicking on the open button on the toolbar.

1. In the **Database window,** click the **Query** object and click the query you want to view.

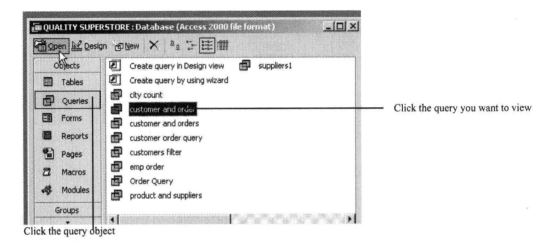

Click the query you want to view

Click the query object

2. Click on **open** button on the toolbar to open the selected query. The query opens in datasheet view.

Click open

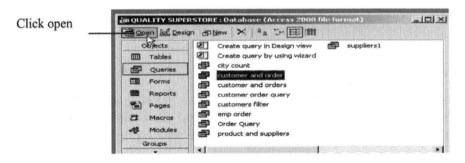

Opening a query in Design view from the Database window

1. In the **Database window**, click the query object and click the query you want to view.

2. Click the Design button on the toolbar to open the selected query in design view. The query opens in design view.

CUSTOMISING A QUERY

You can customize a query in many ways, for example you can add a field, delete a field, move and resize columns in a query.

Adding a column to a query

You may decide that you need an additional column to create a new field in the query. For example you may decide to add a new field to calculate the number of items (No of items). Follow the steps below to add a column to a query.

1. Open the query in **Design view**.

2. Click to the left of the column where you want to add a new column.

3. From the **Insert Menu** click on **Column.**

Inserting a field

1. Open the query in **Design view**.

2. From the **field list,** select the field you want to insert.

3. Drag the field from the list to a column in the grid.

Deleting a field

1. Select the field you want to delete, by pointing the mouse above the field name. The mouse changes to a pointer.

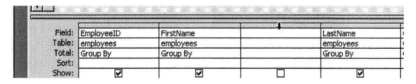

2. Click inside the field to select the field.

Field:	EmployeeID	FirstName		LastName	Order Id
Table:	employees	employees		employees	Order
Total:	Group By	Group By		Group By	Count
Sort:					
Show:	☑	☑	☐	☑	☑
Criteria:					

3.   Press the **Delete** key to delete the selected column.

Using the Asterisk in a QBE GRID

If you want to include all the fields in a table, you can use the asterisk in the QBE grid. To add an asterisk to a field column in the QBE grid, double-click the asterisk (*) at the top of the field list.

Excluding fields from the Query Results

By default all the fields selected during the creation of the query are displayed. You may for certain reasons not want to display all the fields in a query for example in the above query you may be interested in the customers and the orders they have placed not in their addresses. In this case you can exclude the address field from the query. Follow the steps below to exclude fields from the query,.

1.   In the Database Window, Click on **Queries** and then on select the query you want.

2.   Click on the **Design** button in the Database Window to open the query in Design view.

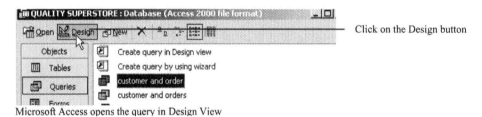
Click on the Design button

Microsoft Access opens the query in Design View

3.   Click inside the **show box** of the field you don't want to display to clear it.

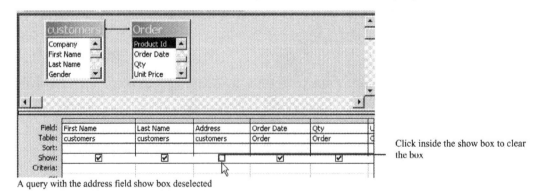
Click inside the show box to clear the box

A query with the address field show box deselected

When the query is run the address field will not show. All the fields with a checked box will be displayed.

Rearranging or moving a column

1. Select the field(s) you want to move by clicking above the column and selecting the field(s) as you did above.

2. Click inside the selected field and drag the field to a new position. As you move, the mouse changes to a rectangle as you move.

Click inside the selected field and drag the field

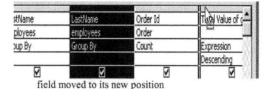
field moved to its new position

Add a table to a query

You may find that after you have designed a query, you may decide that you need additional information from another table. Follow the instructions below to add another table to your query.

1. Open the query in **Design view.**

2. Click on the **Show table** button on the toolbar. Microsoft Access displays the **Show table** dialog box. The **show table** dialog box contains all the tables and queries in the database.

3. Click the tab, which shows the object you want to work with. For example to work with tables, click the table tab to display all the tables.

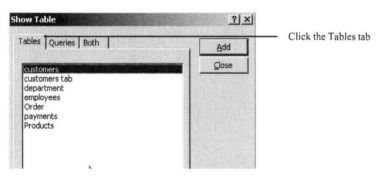
Click the Tables tab

4. Click to select the name of the object you want to add. For example to add the customers table to the query, click the customers table.

5. Click on **Add** to add the selected table. Repeat steps 3-5 to add more tables or queries to your query grid.

6. Click on **Close** to close the **Show table** dialog box. The object(s) you selected will be added to the grid.

Removing a table from a query

1. Open the query in **Design view.**

2. Select the table or query you want to remove by clicking inside the field list.

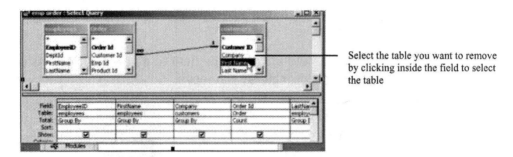

Select the table you want to remove by clicking inside the field to select the table

3. Press the **Delete key** to delete the table or query. Fields from the table or query that you drag to the **design grid** are removed from the grid.

Viewing and setting properties for queries

By default fields added to the QBE grid will inherit properties of the underlying table. The properties of a query will determine the behavior of the query itself and the properties of a field will determine the behavior of the field.

You can view and set properties for the fields in a query or for the query itself.

To view and set the properties of a field or query

1. Select the **field** or **query**. To select a field, click inside the cell in the field row. To select a query, click in the query window or anywhere outside the grid or field list.

    To select a field

Click inside field

click inside the field to select a field

To select a query

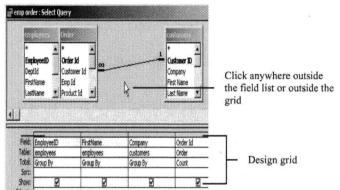

Click anywhere outside the field list or outside the grid

Design grid

Click anywhere outside the field list or outside the grid to select a query

2. Click on the **properties button** ⌐ on the toolbar. The properties dialog box is displayed.

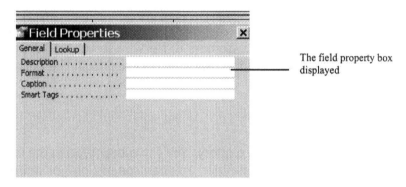

The field property box displayed

3. Set the property for the field or query. You may have to enter a value for a property or select from a drop-down list.

Showing unique values in a query

By default a query returns all the values that matches the criteria. Sometimes the results of a query may contain duplicate values. You can eliminate duplicate values by setting the unique values property for the query to **Yes** in the property box. Following the steps below to set the unique values property.

1. Select the query by clicking anywhere in the **query design view** outside the **field list** or the **design grid**.

2. Click on the properties button 🖼 on the toolbar. The property sheet is displayed.

3. Set the **unique values** property to **Yes.**

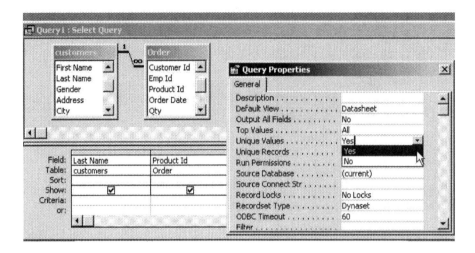

Adding Criteria to Your Query

To view specific records in your database, you must specify the criteria when you design your query. For example to target customers in Norway so you can send specific promotional material to them you must specify "Norway" as criteria in the country field. This will only retrieve customers in Norway.

Specifying the criteria

Expressions are used in specifying criteria for a query. You can either type in the expression directly into the grid or use the expression builder. You can specify one or more criteria to search for records.

To specify criteria directly into the grid

1. In Design view type the criteria or expression in the criteria cell for the field. For example if you want to extract customers with smith as their last name, enter "smith" in the criteria cell of the Last Name as shown below.

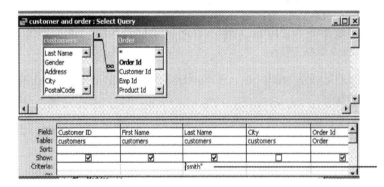

Enter the criteria directly underneath the field you want to use as your criteria.

Viewing your Query Results from Design View

1. Click on the **Run** button or Select **Run** from the **Query Menu**. You can also click on the **view** button on the toolbar.

To specify criteria for a field using the Expression Builder

1. Select the criteria cell in which you want to define an expression.

2. Click on the **Build** button on the toolbar.

    Microsoft Access displays the Expression Builder.

3. You can select any of the objects, functions or expressions displayed like folders on the lower left part of the builder to create your expression. You can also enter the expression directly into the expression builder. In our example, we are going to use the Built-In-Function to retrieve the orders for the today. Double-click the **Function Folder** and select the **Built-In-functions.** Different categories of built-in-functions are displayed.

4. Click on the **Date** function on the lower right box as indicated below and click on the **Paste** button to paste the date function.

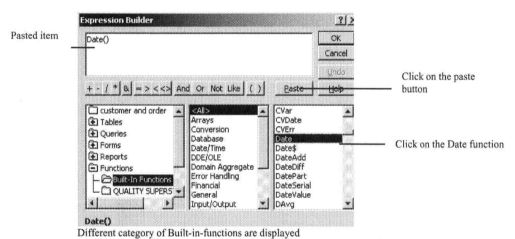

Different category of Built-in-functions are displayed

5. Click on the **ok** to close the Expression builder and return to your query.

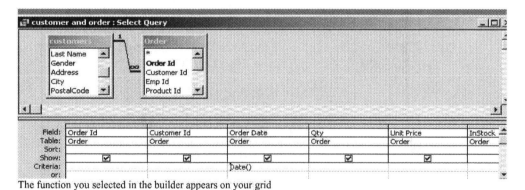

The function you selected in the builder appears on your grid

Comparison Operators

=	is equal to	<	is less than
>	is greater than	<=	is less than or equal to

>= is greater than or equal to   <>   Is not equal to

Examples of criteria you can use in your query

Expression	Results
12/10/2003	Exactly matches 12/10/2003
= 10	Exactly matches 10
<29/12/2003	Before 29/12/2003
<= 10	Less than 10 or equal to 10
<= 29/12/2003	29/12/2003 or before 29/12/2003
> 10	Greater than 10
>= 10	Greater than 10 or equal to 10
>= 29/12/2003	29/12/2003 or after 29/12/2003
<> 10	Not equal to 10
<> 29/12/2003	Not equal to 29/12/2003
<> New York	Not equal New York

Empty Fields

(Is Null)	Find records that do not contain data in the field
(Is Not Null)	Find records that contain data in the field

Between .And.

Between 5 And 200	Find values from 5 and 200
Between 10/10/2003 And	
29/12/2003	Find records with dates on and between10/10/2003 and 29/12/2003
N?ke	Will find Nike, Nuke and Nake
C*	Will find Cooke, Coke and Cow
*/12/2003	Will find all dates in December

Specifying more than one criteria

So far you have used one criteria to find records in your query. You may find out that in some situations using one criteria will not bring you the information you need. Microsoft Access allows for more than one criterion for searching information in your query. For example if you want to find suppliers in New York who sell computers, you will need to specify more than one criteria in order to retrieve the information you want. Use the following criteria to search for suppliers in New York who sell computers.

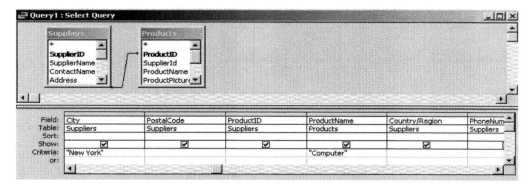

Selecting Records that contains values

As you may have realized by now, not all the fields in your table are complete. For example not all your suppliers may have e-mail address. You can use the expression Not Null or Is Not Null to search for fields that contain values and Null or Is Null to search for fields without values. For example to search the suppliers' table for suppliers without e-mail addresses you can use these criteria.

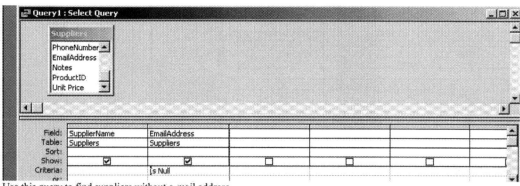

Use this query to find suppliers without e-mail address

To search for suppliers with e-mail addresses use the following query.

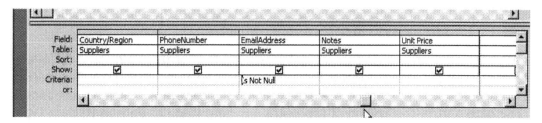

Using Or

You can use **Or** to find customers in New York or New Jersey. Enter New Jersey under the Criteria cell under city and enter New York under **Or** cell under city.

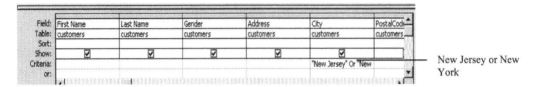

Or cell

Using One field to enter Or

You can also use one field to enter the criteria. For example you can enter New York Or New Jersey under the criteria field under cell.

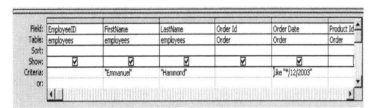

New Jersey or New York

Using And

Suppose you want to find out the orders taken by a particular employee for this month you could use the And Operator to find this information.

Field:	EmployeeID	FirstName	LastName	Order Id	Order Date	Product Id
Table:	employees	employees	employees	Order	Order	Order
Sort:						
Show:	☑	☑	☑	☑	☑	
Criteria:		"Emmanuel"	"Hammond"		like "*/12/2003"	
or:						

The query looks for an employee named Emmanuel Hammond and pulls out all the orders he has taken for the month. The */12/2003 will retrieve all the orders for the month.

Using the Date, Year and DatePart function

The **Date() function** returns the current date. When you use the **Date()** in your query, Microsoft Access returns the system date in your computer.

The **Date Part** function returns part of the date. The syntax for this function is **DatePart(datepart,date).** The arguments for this function are **datepart** and **date.** The **Datepart** of the argument represents the part of the date you want to return for example the month or year. The **date** part of the argument represent any field that has date as its data type. For example Order Date, Date of Birth, Date Hired etc.

Example

You may want to return the year, month or quarter of a date. "**m**" will return the (month of year), "**yyyy**" will return the year "**q**" will return the quarter as in a calendar quarter.

Example of Date() function

If today's date is the 30/12/2003 the Date() function will return all orders for this date

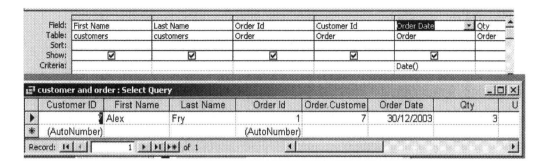

Another Example of DatePart function

To find out all the orders for the fourth quarter that is from October to December use the following expression in your query. Type the expression in the criteria row of the Order Date.

DatePart("q",[Order Date]) = 4

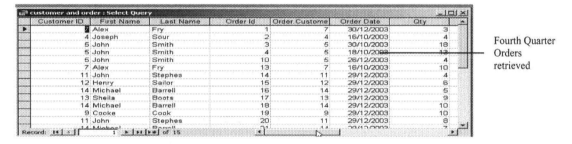

4 in the expression represent the fourth quarter.

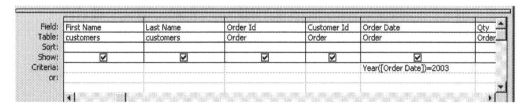

Fourth Quarter
Orders
retrieved

Year() function

The **Year()** function will return the year in an expression.

Example of Year() function

Suppose you want to find all your all orders for the year 2003. You can use the Year function to get this information. Use this function Year([Order Date]) = 2003

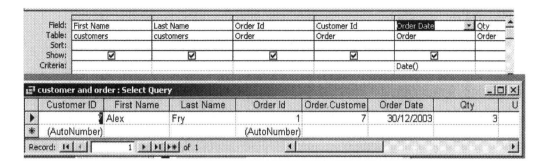

2003 in the expression represents the year you want to retrieve information on.

Month()

The **Month()** function is another type of date function. You can use **Month()** function in your query to return the month.

Example

You can also use the Month function to find the orders for a particular month.

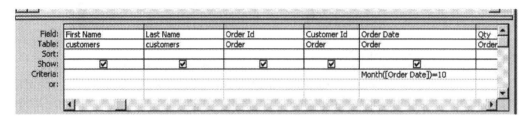

10 in the expression represent the month you want to retrieve information on.

175

Chapter

PERFORMING CALCULATIONS IN A QUERY

There are two ways you can perform calculations in a query: They are

- Using the predefined "Total" function
- Creating your own expressions for totals

Using predefined functions to calculate total

Microsoft Access provides the following functions you can use to perform calculations in your query.

Function	Purpose
Sum	To find the total values in a field
Avg	To find the average of values in a field
Min	To find the lowest value in a field
Max	To find the highest value in a field
Count	The number of values in a field (excluding fields with null values)
StDev	The standard deviation of values in a field
Var	The variance of values in a field
First	Displays the first matching value in the group
Last	Displays the last matching value in the group

Calculate Total on all records in a table

You may decide to find the total number of customers in your database. Create a query using the Customers table. Drag the **Customer Id** field to the query grid.

1. Click the **Total button** Σ on the toolbar. The total row is displayed.
2. Select **Count** in the Total cell under Customer Id.

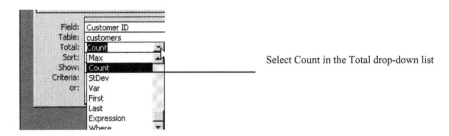

Select Count in the Total drop-down list

3. Click the **View** button on the toolbar to see the results of your query.

Calculating on a group of records

You can perform calculations on a particular group of records. For example you could decide to find out how many orders you have received from each city. Follow the steps below to perform calculation on a group of records.

To find the total for each group

1. Create a select query adding the **customers** and **order** table to the grid.

2. Drag the fields you want to use to perform the calculations to the grid. For example drag the **City** field from the Customers table to the Grid; drag the Order Id field in the Order Table to the grid.

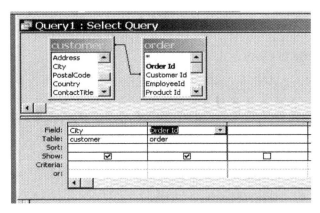

3. Click the Total button Σ on the toolbar.

    The total row is displayed, with **Group by** displayed in each Total cell.

Total
Field

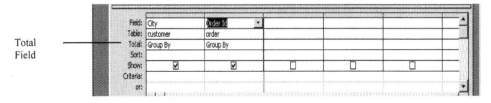

4. Leave the **Group by** in the Total cell of each field you want to group by. For example leave the Group by in the Total cell of city field.

5. For each field you want to perform calculation on, click the Total down arrow to select a function. To find the total number of orders, we need to count all the orders. Each order is uniquely identified by an order id. So we select the **Count function** in the Order Id field.

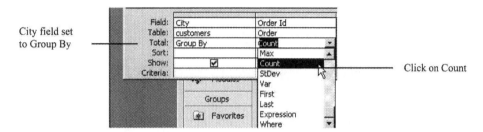

6. Click on the view button 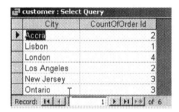 on the toolbar to view your query.

From the results of the query we can conclude that majority of our orders came from London.

Create a calculated field in a query

You can create a new field that displays the results of a calculation. For example you can create a new field that will display the **Total Price** of goods sold. This value is computed by multiplying the **Unit Price** by the **Qty**. To create a calculated field, click an empty field cell in the QBE grid and type an expression that will perform the calculation. When making reference to other fields in your calculation, you should enclose the field names in square brackets. For example, to multiply the Quantity field [Qty] by the Unit Price [Unit Price], type [Qty] *[Unit Price] in an empty Field cell.

To create a calculated field

1. Open the form in **Design View.**

2. In an empty column, type an expression in the field row. If the expression includes a field name, put a bracket around it. For example to calculate the **Total Price** of goods sold use this expression [Qty]*[UnitPrice]

3. Press the **Enter key** to move to another cell. Microsoft Access adds a default name to your expression. For example **Expr1 :[Qty]*[Unit Price].**

4. Double click **Expr1** to select it and give it a more descriptive name like **Total Price.**

Field:	EmployeeID	FirstName	LastName	Order Id	Total Price: [Qty]*[Unit Price] ▾
Table:	employees	employees	employees	Order	
Sort:					
Show:	☑	☑	☑	☑	☑
Criteria:					
or:					

Create a new field and enter an expression in the field

5. Click on the **view** [E ▾] button on the toolbar to view your query.

emp order : Select Query

	Employee ID	First Name	Last Name	Order Id	Total Price
▶	1	Susan	Fox	15	276
	2	Susan	Fox	19	130
	3	Emmanuel	Hammond	16	190
	4	Kemp	Oliver	17	99
	5	Kenneth	Good	14	200
	5	Kenneth	Good	18	520
*	(AutoNumber)			(AutoNumber)	

Using the & Operator to join text and fields

You can use the **&** operator to join text and fields into a single calculated field. Any text including blank spaces is usually enclosed in quotation marks.

Example

Assuming that the value for the first name field is Jane and the Last Name value is Smith, the calculated field below will display the results Jane Smith.

[First Name], & " " &[Last Name]

Group Query

You can evaluate each employee's performance by grouping the query on employee and summing up each employee's sales.

1. Click on the **Total button** [Σ] on the toolbar. Microsoft displays the Total row with group set to **Group by** for all the fields.

2. Change the **Total** cell in **Total price** field to **Sum** and the **Total** cell in **Order Id** field to **Count**. Change the label Total Price to **Total Value of Goods Sold**

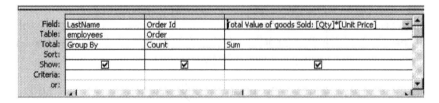

Field:	LastName	Order Id	Total Value of goods Sold: [Qty]*[Unit Price] ▾
Table:	employees	Order	
Total:	Group By	Count	Sum
Sort:			
Show:	☑	☑	☑
Criteria:			
or:			

3. Click on the View [E] button to view the results of your query.

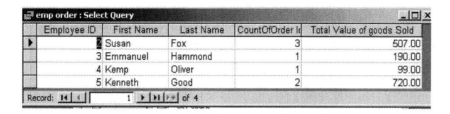

From this query you can tell that Susan Fox has taken more orders than her colleagues. Also the value of goods sold by Kenneth Good is higher than any of his colleagues.

Sorting your records

You may want to sort the results of your query so you can view it in a particular order. For example in the employee sales evaluation query, you may want to sort the results by Total value of goods sold.

Sorting a field in a query

1. Open the query in **Design view.**

2. Click in the sort row for the field you want to sort.

   A drop-down list appears.

3. Select the order you want to sort your records. **Ascending** sorts your records from lowest to highest i.e. from (0-9) and from (A-Z), **Descending** sorts from highest to lowest i.e. (9 to 0) and from (Z-A). In this example we want the results of query to be sorted by the total value of goods sold from the highest value to the lowest value so we select **Descending.**

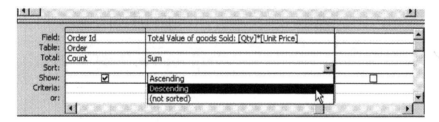

4. Click the **view** button on the toolbar to display the results of your query.

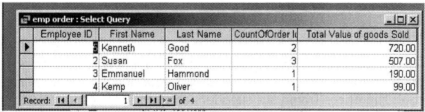

Results of sorting query by total value of goods sold

Using Top Values Queries

Microsoft Access 2003 provides an enhancement of its sort feature, which allows you to look at the highest and lowest values for a field in a query. For example you can use the

Top Values function to find the top values of a query. A retailer can use this feature to find the employee with highest sales. This information can be used during appraisals to motivate and reward employees. Follow the instructions below to find the highest and lowest values.

1. Create a query like the query displayed below.

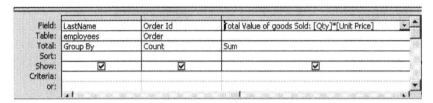

2. To find the highest values, sort the **Total Value of Goods Sold** in descending order.

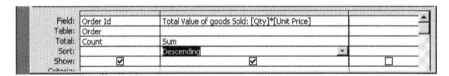

3. In the **Top Values** drop-down-list on the toolbar, select the number of top or bottom values that you want to view. For example if you want to find the top two highest value of goods sold, type 2 in the **Top Value** drop-down list.

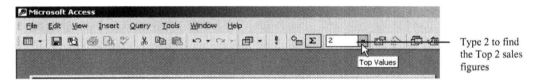

Type 2 to find the Top 2 sales figures

4. Click on the view button to view the results of your query.

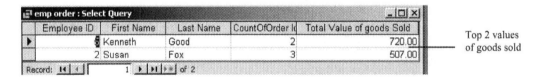

Top 2 values of goods sold

From the query results Kenneth has the highest sales figures followed by Susan. To find the employee with the lowest sales figure, change the sort order to Ascending and click on **1** in the **Top Values** drop-down list.

Another Example

Another area where you can apply the Top values to your query is comparing prices of your suppliers. In order to maximize profit you must get your goods from a cheaper source. You can extract all the prices from your suppliers and ask Microsoft Access to select the lowest price for you for a particular product.

For example to search for all the prices of computers from different suppliers use the query below. Enter Computer in the criteria cell as indicated below.

Field:	ProductID	ProductName	SupplierID	SupplierName	ContactName	Unit Price
Table:	Products	Products	Suppliers	Suppliers	Suppliers	Suppliers
Sort:						
Show:	☑	☑	☑	☑	☑	
Criteria:		"Computer"				
or:						

This will result in a list of all the suppliers for computer and their prices.

Product ID	Product Name	Supplier ID	Supplier Name	Contact Name	Unit Price
8 Computer		8 Schmes	Paul Schemes	700.00	
8 Computer		11 Malatan Ltd	Michael Alatan	599.99	
8 Computer		12 BERRIES	Stephen Marke	399.99	
8 Computer		13 Sea View	Peter Cave	500.00	

List of all computer suppliers and their prices

To select the lowest price, set the sorting field of Unit Price to **ascending**

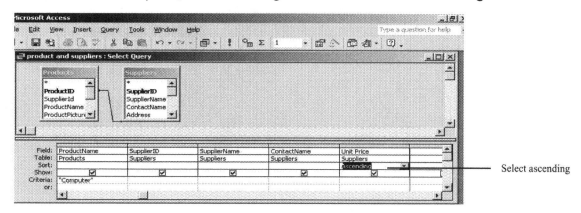

Select ascending

and change the Top Values button on the toolbar to **1** as indicated below.

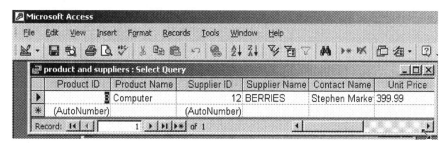

The cheapest price is from Berries as indicated in the query results below.

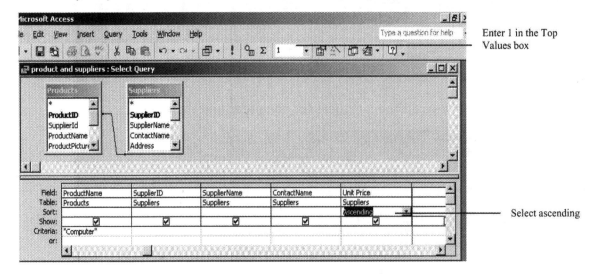

OTHER TYPES OF QUERIES

So far we have used Select query to locate information in our database. This chapter will discuss the other types of queries.

Parameter Query

A parameter query is a type of query that prompts you for criteria to run a query or a value you want to insert in a field. For example if you frequently run the same query but often change the criteria each time you run the query, you can create a parameter query that will prompt you for the different criteria. A parameter is a place holder that you can fill in when you run your query. When you create a parameter query, you don't have to change the criteria in the QUERY DESIGN grid, instead you are prompted for the criteria in the Parameter dialog box as indicated below. You can create a parameter query that can prompt you for more than one criteria.

Example of running a parameter query

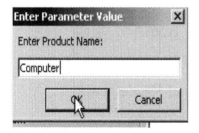

Microsoft prompts you for the criteria

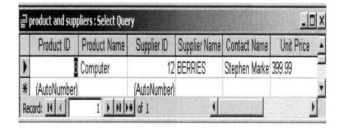

Results of running the query with the parameter

Creating a parameter query

1. Create a **query** without using a wizard. For example select **Query, New** and select **Design View.** A new query opens in design view with the **Show Table Dialog box.**

   Click and select the tables you want to use from the **Show Table Dialog box** and click on the **Close** box to close the **Show Table Dialog** box.

2. Drag the fields you want to use in your query to **Query Design Grid.**

3. Enter a prompt enclosed in square brackets in the **Criteria cell** for each cell you want to use as a parameter.

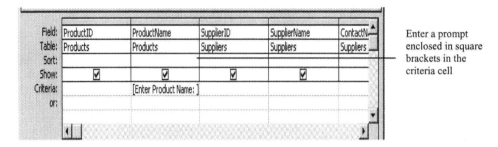

Enter a prompt enclosed in square brackets in the criteria cell

4. Run the query. Microsoft Access displays the Enter Parameter dialog box.

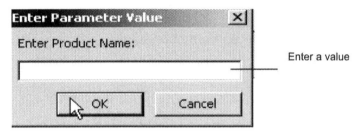

Enter a value

5. Enter a value and click **ok.** Data matching the criteria that you specified is retrieved and displayed in the query window.

Specifying the data type for a query parameter

In most cases you can create a parameter query without specifying a data type as in the above example and it will work perfectly well. However, in certain situations you must specify the data type for the parameter. For example you must specify the data type of the parameter if

- You are creating a parameter for a field with Yes/No data type.

- If your parameter query is a **crosstab** query or the underlying query for a cross tab.

- If the fields in your query comes from a table in an external SQL database.

Example of creating a data type for a query with a Yes/No data type

For example if you want to find out about orders you received which were out of stock you could use the parameter query to prompt you to find those orders. The **Instock** field in the Order table is a **Yes** or **No** field so in this case the data type for this field will have to be specified.

Specifying the data type of a query parameter

1. Create a **parameter query** using the **Order** and **Products** table.

2. Drag the Order Id, Product Id, ProductName, Order Date and Instock fields from the Order and Products tables to the **Grid** as indicated below.

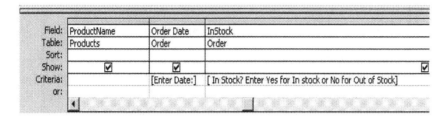

3. This **query** prompts you for more than one **criteria**. Enter a criteria in the **Order Date** and in the **Instock** field as indicated below.

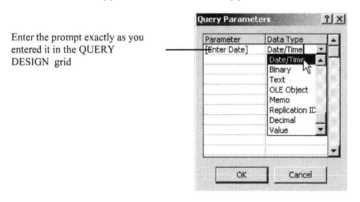

4. From the **Query Menu,** select **Parameters.** The **Query Parameters** dialog box is displayed.

5. Enter the prompt you entered in the **Query Design grid** of your parameter query and press tab to move to the data type box.

   Note enter the **prompt in the order they appear** in the Query Design grid. For example enter the first prompt first, followed by the next prompt.

6. Select a data type from the **Data type** column.

Enter the prompt exactly as you entered it in the QUERY DESIGN grid

Query Parameters		? X
Parameter	**Data Type**	
[Enter Date]	Date/Time	
	Date/Time	
	Binary	
	Text	
	OLE Object	
	Memo	
	Replication ID	
	Decimal	
	Value	

OK   Cancel

7. Repeat step 5&6 to continue adding parameters and selecting the data type. Enter the prompts in the parameter box in the same order they appear in the **QUERY DESIGN grid**. For example enter the order parameter first followed by the Instock parameter.

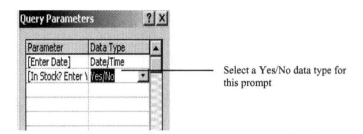

Select a Yes/No data type for
this prompt

8. When you finish entering the prompts, click **Ok** to close the **Query Parameters** dialog box.

9. Run the query by click the run button on the toolbar.

    Microsoft Access prompts you for the **Order date** and the **Instock** prompt. Enter a date for the **Order date** prompt and Enter "Yes" or "No" for the **Instock** prompt. For example to retrieve orders, which were out of stock Enter "No" in the Instock, **prompt**.

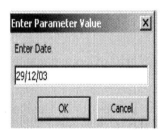
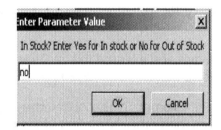

Microsoft Access retrieves the following orders, which are out of stock.

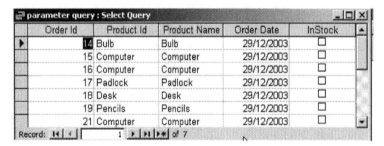

Crosstab Query

A **Crosstab** Query is a type of query that is used to present summarised information. You can use a Cross Tab information to group your data into two; one on the left side of the data sheet and the other group across the top. This will help you to compare performance of the two group of information. When designing a crosstab query, you must decide which fields to use for row headings, column headings, and summary values, and how you want to summarize the values. You can use functions like **Sum**, **Count**, and **Average** to perform totals or summary on the different group of information displayed in your cross tab results.

Example

To compare employees sales performance over the month you can use a cross tab query to group employees record on the left side of the datasheet and the monthly total sales for each employee across. You can easily compare and analyse employees' sales performance over the year.

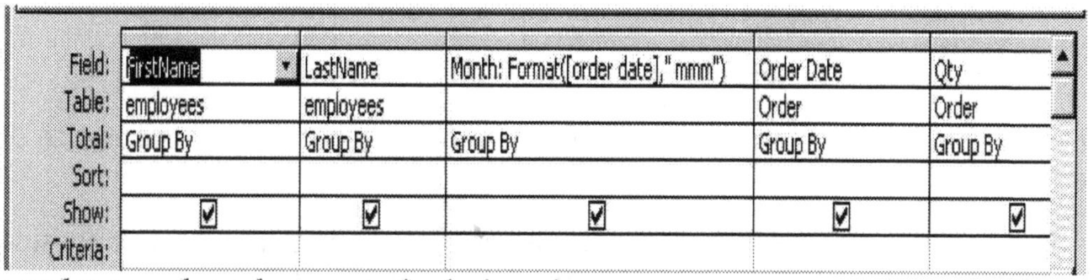

Field:	FirstName	LastName	Month: Format([order date]," mmm")	Order Date	Qty
Table:	employees	employees		Order	Order
Total:	Group By	Group By	Group By	Group By	Group By
Sort:					
Show:	☑	☑	☑	☑	☑
Criteria:					

employee order select query in design view

A select query showing Monthly sales figures for employees

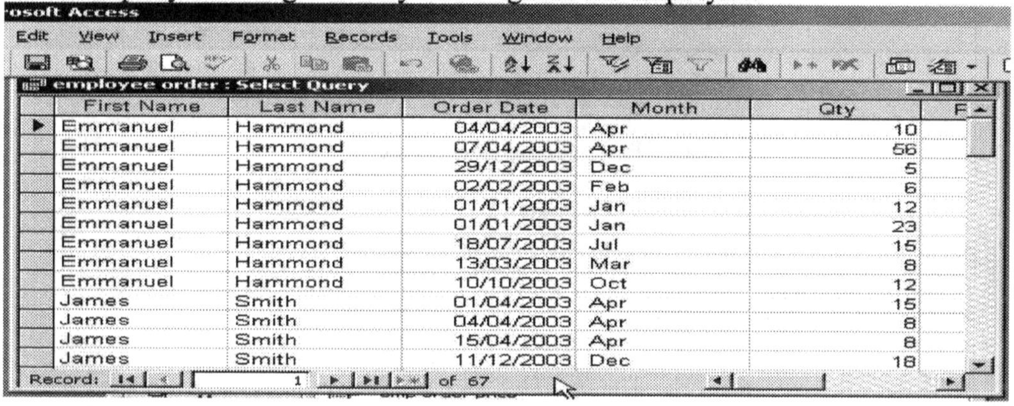

osoft Access

Edit   View   Insert   Format   Records   Tools   Window   Help

employee order : Select Query

First Name	Last Name	Order Date	Month	Qty	F
Emmanuel	Hammond	04/04/2003	Apr	10	
Emmanuel	Hammond	07/04/2003	Apr	56	
Emmanuel	Hammond	29/12/2003	Dec	5	
Emmanuel	Hammond	02/02/2003	Feb	6	
Emmanuel	Hammond	01/01/2003	Jan	12	
Emmanuel	Hammond	01/01/2003	Jan	23	
Emmanuel	Hammond	18/07/2003	Jul	15	
Emmanuel	Hammond	13/03/2003	Mar	8	
Emmanuel	Hammond	10/10/2003	Oct	12	
James	Smith	01/04/2003	Apr	15	
James	Smith	04/04/2003	Apr	8	
James	Smith	15/04/2003	Apr	8	
James	Smith	11/12/2003	Dec	18	

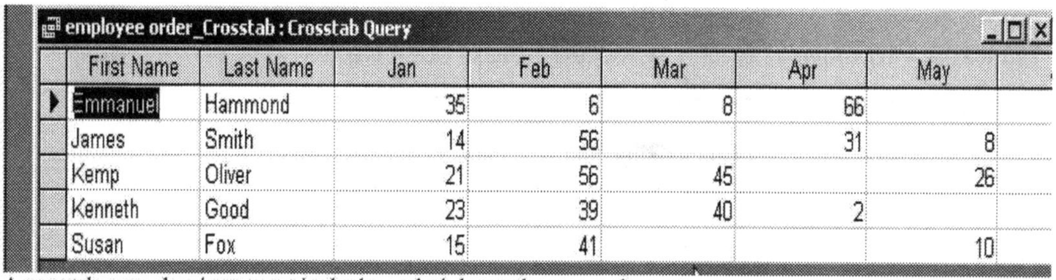

Record: 14 ◄ | 1 | ► ►I ►* | of 67

employee order_Crosstab : Crosstab Query

First Name	Last Name	Jan	Feb	Mar	Apr	May	
Emmanuel	Hammond	35	6	8	66		
James	Smith	14	56		31	8	
Kemp	Oliver	21	56	45		26	
Kenneth	Good	23	39	40	2		
Susan	Fox	15	41			10	

A cross tab query showing summarized sales analysis by employee over the year

When you compare the results of the two different queries displayed above, you will realize that it is easier to analyse the performance of employees using the cross tab query. With the Crosstab query, information is presented in a more compact form and easier to read and therefore analyse.

Creating a Crosstab Query with a Wizard

1.   In the **Database window,** click the **Queries button** under **Objects** and then click on **New.**

2.   Choose the **Crosstab Query Wizard** button in the **New Query** dialog box.

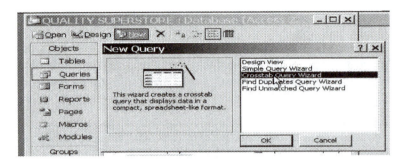

3. In the first dialog box, choose **table or query or both** depending on the source of data for the query you are creating.

    Tip: If you need to use fields from more than one table, first create a query using more than one table and use it as a query to create a crosstab query.

4. Select the table or query you want to use from the list of query or tables displayed. Click **Next**.

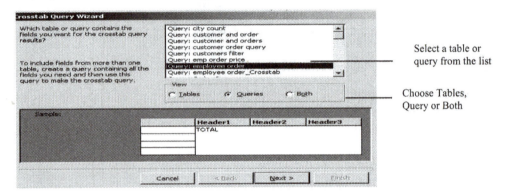

5. Select the fields you want to use as row headings from the **Available fields** and click the > to move it to the **selected fields.** Click **Next**.

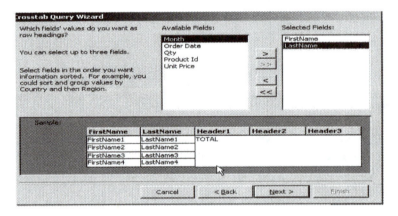

6. Select the field you want to use as column. We want to use the month field as column, so we select the **Month** field. Click **Next**.

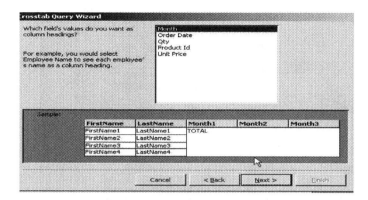

7. In the fields column select the field you want to use to calculate the intersection for each row and column and select the function you wan to use to do the calculation. For example we want to calculate the total orders each employee takes per month, therefore we select **Qty** in the fields box and **Sum** in the function box as indicated below. Click **Next**.

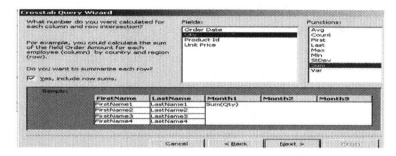

8. Enter a name for the query and decide whether or not you want to view the query or modify the query in design view. Click **Finish**.

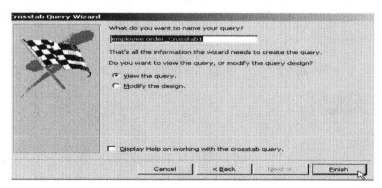

Creating a crosstab query without a Wizard

1. In the Database window, click the **Query button** and then choose the **New button.**

2. Choose the **Design View** in the **New Dialog box** and click **Ok.** The **Show Table** dialog box appears in **Query Design Window**.

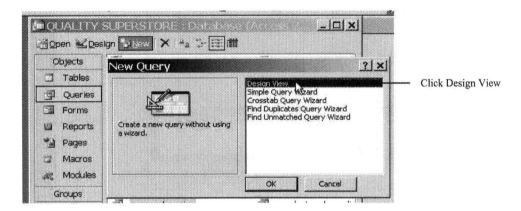

Click Design View

3. In the **Show Table** dialog box, choose the tab that displays the tables or query you want to work with.

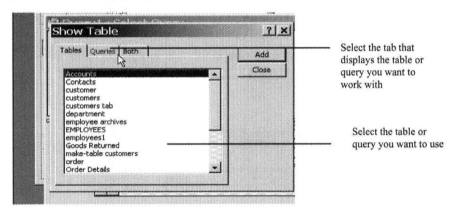

Select the tab that displays the table or query you want to work with

Select the table or query you want to use

4. Select the **table or query** and click the **Add** button to add the table or query to the **Query Design Window**. Repeat this step until you have added all the tables or query you want to include in this query. When you finish selecting all the objects you want to work with, click on the **Close** button.

5. Drag the fields to the Field row of the Query grid and specify the criteria.

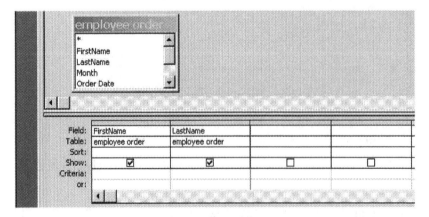

You can also enter expressions in the field row. For example we want to display the monthly sales as headings in the following format i.e. **Jan, Feb** etc. Therefore instead of selecting a field we enter an expression to display the column heading in the above format. Enter an expression field using the **Date Format** expression; for example enter.

Month: Format([Order Date],"mmm")

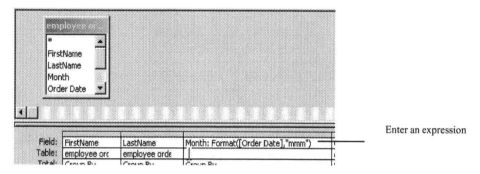

Enter an expression

6. From the **Query Menu,** choose **Crosstab** (or select Crosstab Query from the **Query Type** drop-down list on the toolbar). Microsoft Access displays the Total and Crosstab rows.

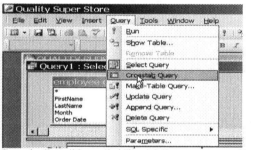

From the Query Menu select Crosstab Query   Or   Select Crosstab Query from the Query Type drop-down list

7. Click the **Crosstab** cell for the field name you want to use as the row heading, and then select **Row Heading** from the drop-down-list.

You can choose more than one row heading.

Click the Crosstab cell for the field name you want to use as row heading

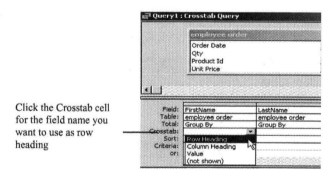

8. Click the **Crosstab cell** for the field name you want to use as the column heading, click the arrow, and then select **Column Heading** from the list. Note you can only choose one column heading. Click tab to move to the next field.

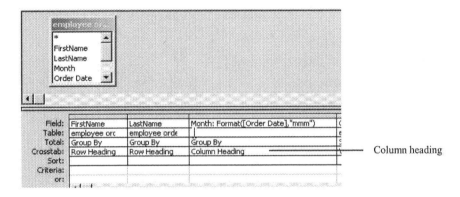

Column heading

9. Click the **Crosstab** cell for the field whose value you want to summarize, click the drop-down-list and select **Value** from the list.

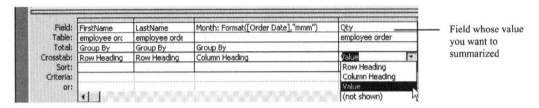

Field whose value you want to summarized

10. Click the total cell for this field whose value you want to summarize. A drop-down list appears. Click the type of aggregate function you want to use to summarize your data.

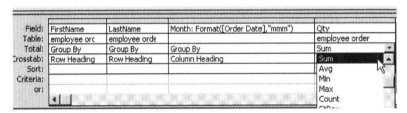

11. Specify any criteria you want to use.

12. Click the **view** [E] button on the toolbar to view the results of your query.

First Name	Last Name	Apr	Aug	Dec	Feb	Jan
Emmanuel	Hammond	66		5	6	35
James	Smith	31		24	56	14
Kemp	Oliver		56	9	56	21
Kenneth	Good	2		28	39	23
Susan	Fox		2	29	41	15

Record: |◄| ◄ | 1 | ► |►I|►*| of 5

Modifying your column Headings

By default Microsoft Access displays the column headings in alphabetical or numeric order. This may not be the order you want for your column headings. For example in the example above you may want to display your column headings in the following order Jan, Feb, March, April ...... Dec. You can make changes to the column headings in the **Column Headings** property in the property sheet.

To Modify the Column Headings

1. Open the query in **Design view** if is not open in design view.

2. Select the **Month** field used as the column headings.

3. Click the **Properties** button on the toolbar. Microsoft Access displays the query property sheet. Enter the months of the year as column heading in the order you want them to appear separated by a list separator i.e., or;. For example "Jan";"Feb"; ….. December

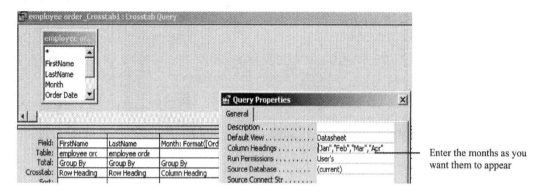

Enter the months as you want them to appear

4. Press Enter when you finish.

5. Click the view button to see the results of your query.

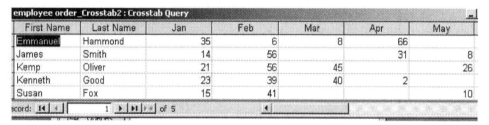

Action Query

An Action Query is a type of query that makes changes to your data in one operation. For example if you want to delete workers who have left the company, you can run one action query that removes all these workers. There are four types of action queries. They are **Make-Table Query**, **Delete Query**, **Append Query** and **Update Query**.

Make-Table

A **Make-Table Query** creates a new table from all or part of a table in one or more tables. A Make-Table is useful for

•   Making a back-up copy of a table.

•   Archiving information. For example you can keep a history table of all your customers.

•   Create a table to export to other Microsoft Access Database.

Example

Suppose you want to create another database i.e. **inventory database**. Some of the tables that the new database that you want to create may include Order, customers etc. to save time, instead of creating these tables from scratch you can create a **Make-Table** and export the tables to the inventory database.

Creating a Make-Table

1. Create a query by selecting the tables or queries that contain the fields you want to include in the new table.

2. From the **Query Menu**, click on **Make-Table** or click the **Query Type** 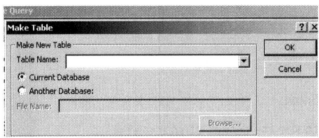 button on the toolbar and select **Make-Table Query**. Microsoft Access displays the **Make-Table** dialog box.

The Make-Table dialog box

3. Enter a name for the new table.

4. If the table is going to be saved in the current database select **Current**. If the table is going to be saved in another database, select **Another Database** and type the name of the database including the path if necessary. You can use the Browse button to locate the database where you want to store your table.

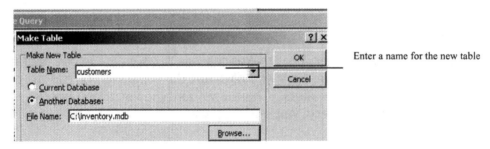

Enter a name for the new table

5. Click **Ok.**

6. Drag **all the fields** you want to include in the **new table** to the **Query Design grid** and set any criteria.

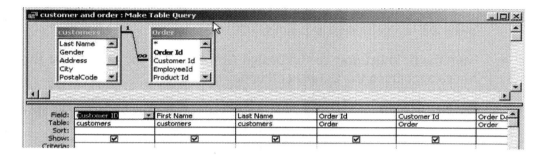

7. You can preview the results of a make-table query before you create the table. Click the **view** [image] button on the toolbar. If you want to make changes to the table, click the view [image] button again to return to the Query Design window and make the necessary changes.

8. With the query open in Design view, click on the run [image] button on the toolbar to run the query.

Delete Query

The Delete query is a type of query, which deletes a group of records from one or more tables. Once you delete the records with the **Delete** query you can't undo the operation again so you must be careful when using a Delete query. Sometimes running a delete query may delete records in related tables. For example deleting a record in a table with a one-to-many relationship with another table with the **referential integrity** set to **Cascade Delete**. Deleting a record on the one-side may result in deleting related records in the many side of the relationship. Deleting records can be dangerous, so always make a backup copy of your data before using the delete query.

Example

Suppose you decide to delete the records of employees who have left the company in the past year. You can create a **Delete query** to delete the records.

Creating a Delete Query

1. Create **a new query** and add the table you want to delete the data from to the query.

2. From the **Query Menu,** select **Delete Query.**

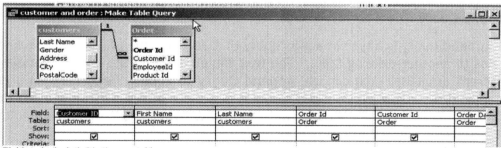

Fields to be included in the new table

3. Drag the (*) asterisk from the field list to the **Query Design Grid**. From appears in the **Delete cell** under this field.

4. From the **field list** drag to the **Design Grid** the field you want to set the criteria. Where appears in the **Delete cell** under this field.

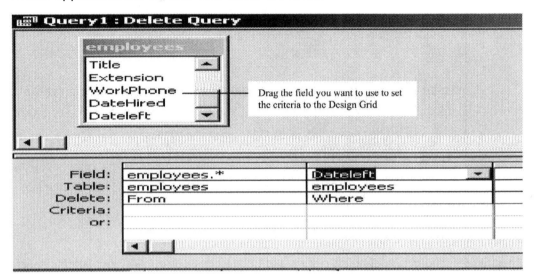

6. Type the criteria in the field you want to use as the criteria.

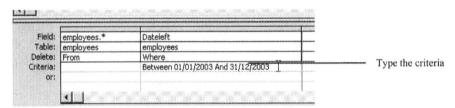

7. To preview the records that will be deleted, click on the **view** [E] button. The datasheet view will display records of employee who have left the company during the year 2003. To switch to the design view to make changes click the view [icon] button again.

8. Click the run [!] button on the toolbar to run the query and to delete the records that meet the criteria you have specified. Microsoft Access displays a message indicating how many records will be deleted.

Append Query

An **Append query** is a type of action query that adds a group of records from one or more tables to another existing table. The new table can be in the current database or in a different database. You can use **Append Query** to append fields base on a criteria or to append records when some of the fields in a table do not exist in another table. For example you could create a table called **past employees** and append the employees who leave the company for future reference.

Creating an append query

1. Create a query and add the tables or queries that contains the records you want to append to another table.

2. From the **Query Menu,** click on **Append Query.**

   Microsoft Access displays the Append Query dialog box.

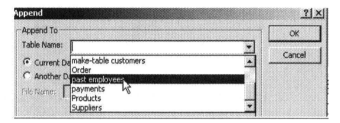

3. If the table you are appending records to, is in the current database, click **current** and select the table from the drop-down list. If the table is not in the current database click the button next to **Another Database** and enter the path where the table is stored alternatively click on the **Browse** button to locate the file.

4. Click **Ok.**

5. Drag all the fields you want to append to your table from the field list to the **Query Design grid.**

6. Enter the criteria in the criteria cell in the field you want to set the criteria on which the records will be appended.

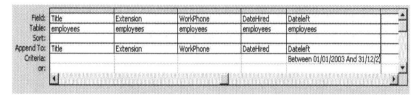

7. Click on the **Run** ![run button] button on the toolbar. Microsoft Access displays a message telling how many records will be appended

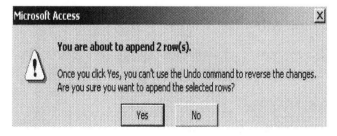

8. Click **Yes** to append the records.

Appending Records with Autonumber fields

By default Microsoft Access automatically increases the value of the autonumber field by one for each record that contains an autonumber field you add. When you append records to a table you can have Microsoft Access automatically increase the autonumber field or you can keep the values from the original table.

To have Microsoft Access automatically add counter, do not drag the **autonumber** field to the **Query Design** grid when you create the query. To keep the values from the original list, drag its autonumber field to the **Query Design grid** when you create the query.

Update Query

An Update Query is a type of query that makes overall changes to a group or records in one or more tables. For example you can use an **Update Query** to raise the salaries of staffs who have sold goods worth more than a £1000 during the year by 20%.

Creating an Update Query

1. Create a query and add the tables or queries that include the records you want to update.

2. From the **Query Menu,** click on **Update Query**.

3. Drag the fields(s) you want to update or for which you want to set a criteria from the field list to the Query Design grid.

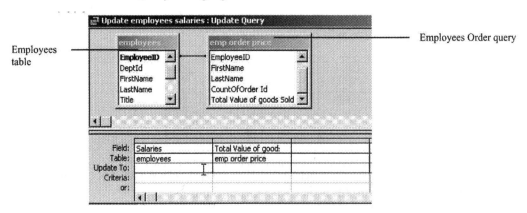

4. In the criteria cell enter the criteria.

5. In the **Update To** cell for the fields you want to update, enter the expression or value you want to use to change the fields.

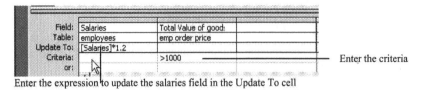

Enter the expression to update the salaries field in the Update To cell

6. To view the records that will be updated, click the view ![E] button on the toolbar. Click the view ![icon] button again to switch to the Query Design view.

7. Click the Run ![!] button to run the query and update your records.

Chapter

REPORTS

In Microsoft Access a report is used to present data in an organised and formatted way.

You can use a report to organise information in groups and to perform calculation. For example you can create a sales analysis report and organise the information by employees and also calculate overall sales total in a report.

Microsoft Access gives you the flexibility of designing a report the way you want and the opportunity to include text, labels, lines, boxes and pictures.

Creating a Report

There are three ways of creating a report. They are

- Using AutoReport

- With a Report Wizard

- Without a Report Wizard.

Creating a Report Using AutoReport

AutoReport is suitable for creating reports based on one table or a query. The AutoReport creates a preformatted report displaying all the fields and records in the underlying table or query. Follow the steps below to create a report using AutoReport.

1. In the Database Window, click **Reports** under **Objects.**

2. Click the **New** button under the Database window toolbar. The **New Report** dialog box appears.

3. In the **New** Report dialog box choose either

    - **AutoReport: Columnar :** each field appears on a separate line with a label to its left.

or

- **AutoReport Tabular** the fields are displayed by each other and the labels print once at the top of each page.

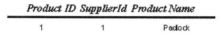

Product ID	SupplierId	Product Name
1	1	Padlock

4. Select the table or query you want to use from the drop-down list at the bottom of the **New Report** dialog box.

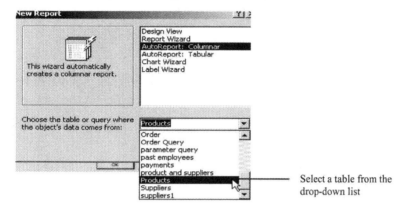

Select a table from the drop-down list

5. Click **Ok**.

The report appears in **Print Preview**.

Creating a Report With the Report Wizard

The report wizard is useful for creating reports based on one or more tables or query. If you are basing your report on more than one table, make sure the relationship between the tables is defined.

1. In the **Database Window,** click **Reports** under Objects.

2. Double-click **Create Report by using wizard.** The first page of the Report wizard appears.

Double-click Create a report by suing wizard

3. Select a table or query containing the fields you want to use from the **Table/Query** drop-down list in the first page of the Report wizard.

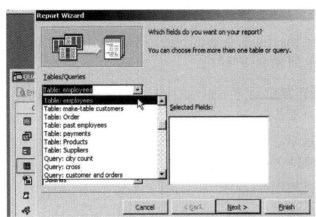

The first page of the Report Wizard

4.   Select a field from the **available fields** box and click **>** to move the field to the **selected fields** box.   Click on **>>** to move all the fields to the **selected fields** box.

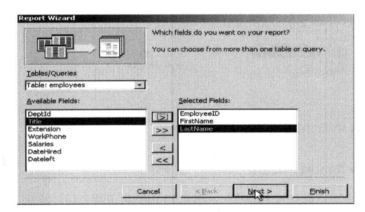

5.   Repeat step 3&4 if you want to include fields from another table or query.   If you are using more than one table in your report, the tables you choose should have relationships defined between them.   Click **Next** to continue.

6.   If you selected fields from more than one table in your report, Microsoft Access offers you the opportunity to choose the table you want to group data in your report on. Choose the table you want to group your data on and click **Next** to continue.

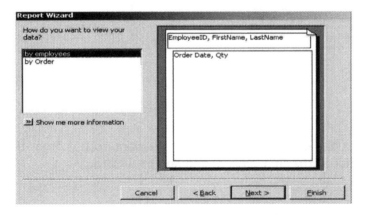

7. If you want the report to be grouped by any of the fields you selected for your report, click the field(s) and click the > button to move the field(s) to the report model on the right side of the page. Click on **Next** to continue.

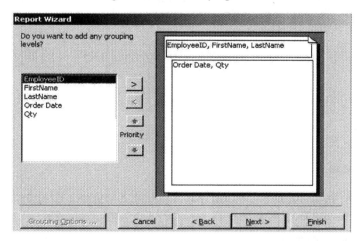

8. The **Report Sort Page** appears. By default the report sorts the report according to the groups you have selected, however you can choose an additional field which will be used to sort the report within the groups you have selected. Select the additional field you want to sort the report by and click **Next** to continue.

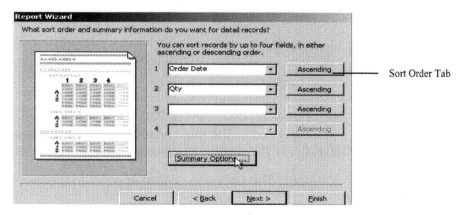

9. By default the Sort Order Tab is set to **Ascending.** You can change the sort order by clicking on the **Sort Order Tab.** If any of the fields that you have chosen to sort the data by is numeric, the Summary options button becomes available.

10. Repeat step 8&9 if you want to sort by another field.

11. If any of the fields you have chosen in step 9&10 contains numeric values, click the **Summary Options** button.

   The Summary Options button displays a list of the numeric field(s), each with Sum, Avg(Average), Min(Minimum) and Max(Maximum) check boxes. Click the function you want to apply to your field. Microsoft Access also gives you the option to choose whether or not you want detailed and summarized information or summary only. Select the Option you want in the **Show** box below. You can also calculate the percentage by clicking the **Calculate percent of total for sums**. Click **Ok** exit out of Summary Options.

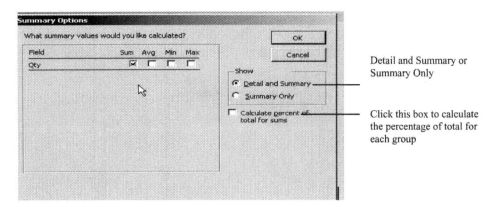

Detail and Summary or
Summary Only

Click this box to calculate
the percentage of total for
each group

12. Click Next to continue.

13. Choose a layout for your report. When you choose a layout, it appears in the preview window showing how the report will be laid out.

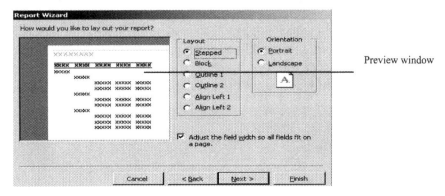

Preview window

14. Select the orientation for your report. Select **Portrait** or **Landscape. Portrait** presents your report vertically across the page or screen and **Landscape** presents your report horizontally across the page. Click **Next**.

15. Select a **Style** for your report. The style you choose appears in the preview. Click **Next** to continue.

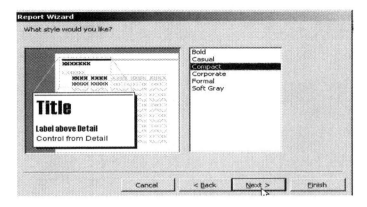

16. Enter a Name for your report and accept the default option **Preview the Report.**

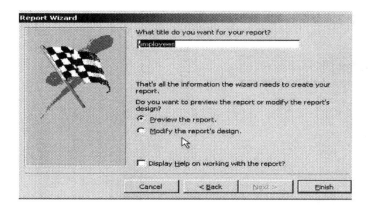

17. Click on the **Finish** button to see the report in Print Preview.

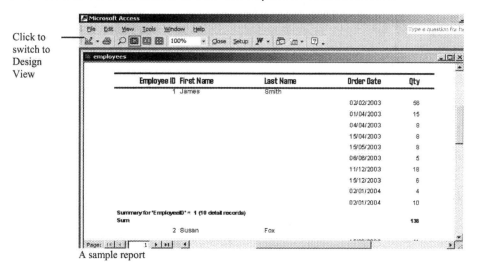

Click to switch to Design View

A sample report

18. To print the report, click on the **Printer** button on the toolbar.

Create a report without a wizard

1. In the Database window, click **Reports** Under **Objects.**

2. Click the **New** button on the Database window toolbar. The **New Report** dialog box appears.

3. Click **Design View** from the **New Report** dialog box.

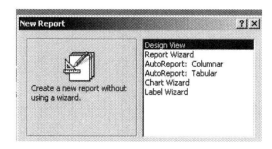

4. Click the table or query that contains the data you want to use for your report in the lower part of the **New Report** dialog box as indicated below.

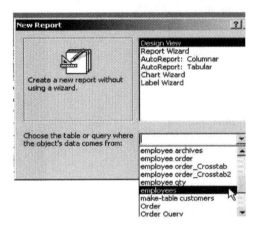

5. Click **Ok**.

Microsoft Access displays a blank report with a field list in design view.

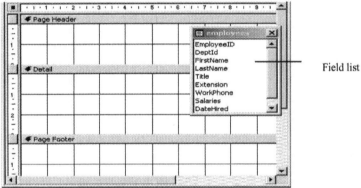

A blank report opens in design view

6. You can add controls from the field list and also create your own controls to perform calculation in your report. This will be discussed in the next chapter, **Customising a Report.**

Views in a Report

There are three views in the Report Window. They are the **Design View, the Print Preview** and the **Layout View.**

You can use the View ![button] button on the report toolbar to switch between different views.

The different views in the Report Window have different functions. For example

Design View: the design view in a report is used to create a report without a wizard or to make changes to the layout of a report.

Print Preview is used to check how the report will look like when printed.

Layout Preview: In this view Microsoft Access uses a few sample data to display the layout of the report.

Chapter

CUSTOMISING A REPORT

Microsoft Access is very flexible. It gives you the opportunity to modify the design of an existing report or a new blank report you have created. Modifying a report includes adding controls (both bound and unbound) to different section in the Design View, setting properties for the report, organising report into different section and formatting the report.

The **Report Design** View is similar to the Form Design View. Like a form, a report consists of various controls added to different sections in **Design View**. You can use the same techniques discussed in the chapter **"Customising a Form"** to customise a report. For full discussion of this topic, please refer to the chapter on **customising a form**.

Adding Controls to your report

You can add both **bound** and **unbound** controls to your report.

Bound control is a type of control whose source of data is from a table or query.

Unbound control is a type of control whose source of data is not from a table or query. Examples of **unbound** controls are **lines, labels, boxes** and **circles** and controls for **performing calculations** in a report. Calculated controls derive their values from expressions.

Adding bound Controls to a report

Open the report in **design view**, if the field list is not displayed, click **Field list** from the **View menu** to display the field list.

1. In **Report Design view** select the field(s) you want to place on the report.

    To select a field, click the field, to select a block of fields, click the first field you want to select and hold down the **Shift key** whilst selecting the last field, to select more than one field at a time, hold down the **Ctrl key** and click each field you want to select.

2. Drag the field(s) from the field list to the **Detail section** of the **Report Design View.** Each field you drag to the **Report Design view** has a label attached to it.

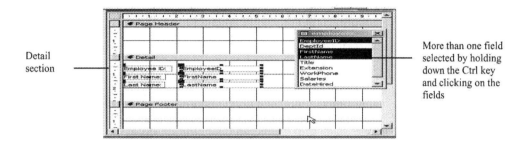

Detail section

More than one field selected by holding down the Ctrl key and clicking on the fields

The Toolbox

You can use the toolbox to add bound or unbound controls to your report. By default the toolbox is open when you open a report in design view. If the toolbox is not visible, click on the **View menu** and click on the **Toolbox** to display the toolbox. The toolbox can be position either horizontally or vertically by selecting it and dragging it to the position you want.

The toolbox in horizontal position

Adding bound control using the toolbar

1.   Open the report in **Design View.**

2.   Click the tool for the type of control you want to add to your report. For example click on the List box.

3.   Select the field from the **Field list** and drag it on to the report.

Adding an unbound control

An **unbound control** is created using the **Toolbox** in the **Report Design** view.

To add an unbound control using the toolbar

1.   Open the report in **Design View.**

2.   Click the toolbox for the type of control you want to add to your report. For example click on the List box.

3.   Click and drag on the report where you want to position the control.

Lines and boxes in a report

Suppose we want to make our report more attractive, we could add lines and add boxes to our report. Lines and boxes are unbound control.

Example

You can add lines and boxes to the Report Header of our report.

To add a line and a box to a report

1.   Click the line ![line tool] tool on the toolbox.

2.   Click the left corner on the report where you want to draw the line and drag the size of line you want to draw.

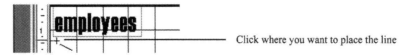

Click where you want to place the line

3.   Click the box ![box tool] tool on the toolbox.

4.   Click and drag the rectangle on the report to the size you want.

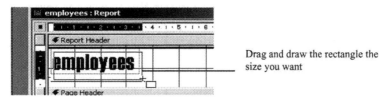

Drag and draw the rectangle the size you want

Calculated control

A calculate control is an unbound control used to calculate values. Microsoft Access uses expressions in the calculated control to calculate values.   An expression is a combination of operators (= - + * /), field names and functions. You can type an expression directly into the control or use the property sheet to enter the expression into the control.

To create a calculated control by typing the expression directly into the control, follow the steps below.

1.   Click the **Text box** ![ab tool] tool in the toolbox.

2.   Click and drag the text box to the report to create a text box.

     Microsoft Access automatically creates a label for the text box.

A text box is created

3.   Change the label by double-clicking in the label and replacing the text with your own text. For example type Length of Service.

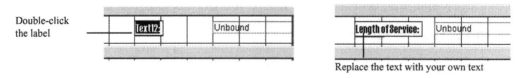

Double-click the label

Replace the text with your own text

4.   Click inside the text box (the text box is the box labelled Unbound).

5.   Type the formula you want to use for your calculation inside the box. An expression begins with an = sign. Type a equal to sign (=) followed by the expression.   For

example to calculate the length of service for an employee the datehired field is subtracted from the system date. Type the expression = (Date()-[Datehired])/ 365 into the text box. As a rule in Microsoft Access, all formulas begin with = sign and field names are enclosed in brackets []. You can also use the expression builder to enter expressions in a text box.

To create a calculated control by using the Property sheet

Suppose we want to create a calculated control, which will show the Total salaries paid to the employees in our company. We could create a calculated control and use the expression builder to enter the expression to calculate the total of all salaries. Follow the steps below to create a calculated control using the expression builder.

1. Click the **Text box** ![ab] tool in the toolbox.

2. Click and drag the text box to the report to create a text box.

3. Select the text box if it is not selected, then click the **Properties** ![icon] button on the toolbar. Microsoft Access displays the **Properties Sheet.**

4. Click the **Data Tab** on the Properties Sheet. You can enter the expression directly into the Control Source property.

   To enter the expression directly into the **ControlSource**, type "=" followed by the expression. For example type "= Sum([Employees]![Salaries])". Click the close button on the property sheet to return to the report in **Design View.**

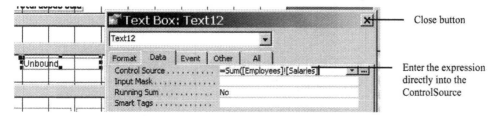

To enter the expression using the Expression builder follow the rest of the steps below.

Click the **ControlSource** property sheet and click on the Builder button.

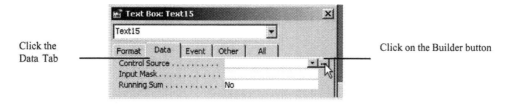

The **Choose Builder** dialog box is displayed.

5. Click on **Expression Builder**, and then choose **Ok.**

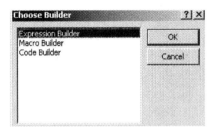

Microsoft Access opens the Expression Builder.

6. Double-click on **Functions** and then click on **Built-in-functions.**

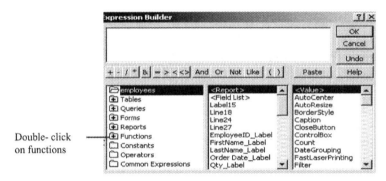

Double- click
on functions

7. Click the category of function you want to use from the middle box and select the function from the box on your right. For example if you want to use **Sum** click on **Sum** in the right box.

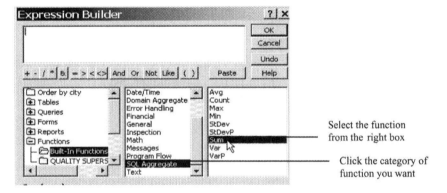

Select the function
from the right box

Click the category of
function you want

8. Click on the **Paste** button. The pasted item appears in the Expression builder window.

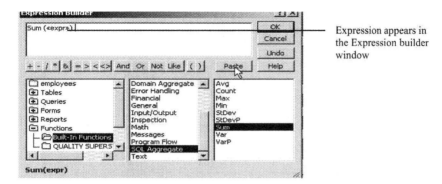

Expression appears in
the Expression builder
window

In this example we want to sum the values in the Salaries field in the Employees table, therefore we need to replace the <<expr>> part of the **Sum** expression with the Salaries field. Follow the rest of the steps to replace the Salaries field with the <<expr>> .

9. Click inside the expression "<<expr>>" to select the expression.

10. In the leftmost box, double-click the **Tables** folder, and then select the table that contains the fields you want to use in your calculation.

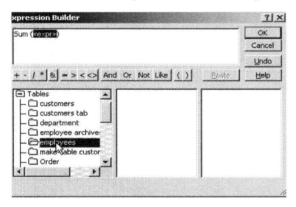

11. Click the field you want to use in the middle box, then click on the **Paste** button. The salaries field replaces the "<<expr>>".

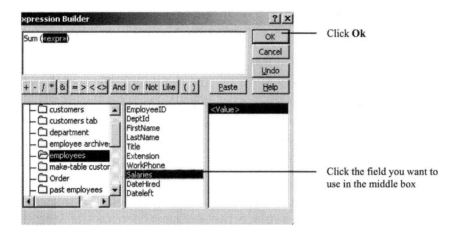

Click **Ok**

Click the field you want to use in the middle box

12. Click on **Ok** to close the **Expression Builder**.

Microsoft Access displays the function in the **ControlSource** property box.

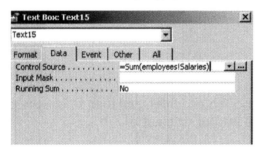

You can double-click the Text box and give it a meaningful name like **Total**

Double-click the text box and change the label

To change an expression in a text box

You can change the expression in a text box in a property sheet. Follow the steps below to change an expression in a text box.

1. Double-click the control to open the property sheet of the control.

2. Click on the **Data** tab.

3. Click the **ControlSource** property box and type the new expression in the **ControlSource** property box or click the **Build** button to display the Expression builder and then change the expression in the expression builder.

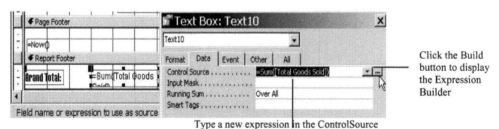

Click the Build button to display the Expression Builder

Type a new expression in the ControlSource

Creating a label

Microsoft Access automatically attaches a label to a control when you create a control. This type of control is known as an attached control. You can add labels on their own which are not attached to any field. An example of a label which is not attached to a field is a labels used as a title in a report or a form.

To create a label that is not attached to any field

1. Click the label button ![Aa] on the toolbox.

2. Click and drag the label to the report to create the label.

3. Type the text you want for your label.

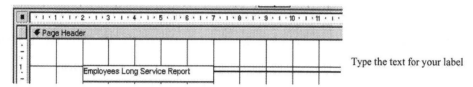

Type the text for your label

Change the Text in a label

1. Click the label.

2. Select the text and then type in the new text.

Select the text   Type in the new text

Deleting Controls

1. Select the **control(s)** you want to delete.

2. Press the **Delete key** to delete the control.

Working with Controls on the Report Design View

Working with controls in the Report Design view is similar to working with a control in the Form Design view. For example you can select, move, resize and format controls.

Selecting a control

Before you can work with a control you must select it. For example before you can change, move or delete a control you must select it.

1. Click the control to select the control. When you select a control, selection handles appear around the control.

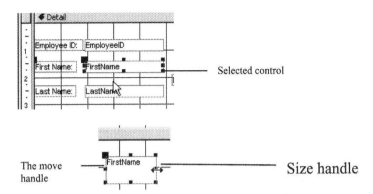

To select more than one control, hold the **Shift key** down and click the controls you want to select. You can also select all the controls in a report by Choosing **Select All** from the **Edit** Menu.

To deselect all selected controls, click in an empty area of the design view screen.

Moving controls

You can move a control and its label together or move a control and its label separately. You can move and position a control anywhere on the design screen.

To move a control and its label together

1. Select the **control** or its **label**.

2. Position the mouse pointer towards the edges of the control or its label. The control changes to a hand.

    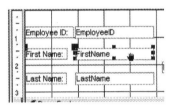

3. Click and drag the control and position it in its new position.

    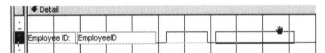

Moving a control and its label separately

1. Click the label or its control.

2. Position the mouse towards the edge of the control or its label towards the top of the move handle. The pointer changes to an upward pointing finger.

3. Move the control or its label to the desired position.

Resizing controls

1. Select the control.

2. Drag the size handle to the size you want.

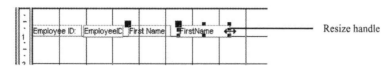

Resize handle

3. The size of the control changes.

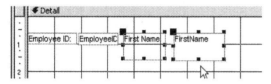

To size selected controls so that their data will fit the contents, click on **Format** then select **Size** and then click on **To Fit**.

To make selected controls the same size, click on Format, then select **Size** and then click on **To Tallest**, **To Shortest**, **To Widest**, or **To Narrowest**. Access will resize all selected controls according to the option you choose.

Formatting a control

You can format a control by using any of the tools on the toolbar or in the property sheet.

To format a control with the toolbar

1. Select the control(s).

2. Click the tool button(s) you want to format the control with.

For example to change all the controls in your report to font size 12, select the controls and select the font size from the **Font size** drop-down list. To apply the bold format, select the control and click on **Bold.**

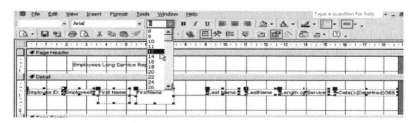

Properties

Every control has properties, which determines its structure, appearance and the data stored in the control.   When you create a bound control, it inherits the same properties as the field in its underlying table or query. With Microsoft Access you can customize some of the properties to meet your needs.   The properties of a control are changed in the properties sheet.

To change the property of a control

1. Double-click the control to open the property sheet of the control. To change the property of more than one control, hold the **Shift key** and then click each of the control you want to change.

2. Choose a property category by clicking any of the following tabs. (Format, Data, Event Other and All).   For example if you want to change the Format of the control, click the **Format tab.**

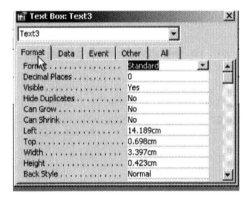

3. Click the property you want to change. Enter a value for the property or select a value from a drop-down list, if a list appears.

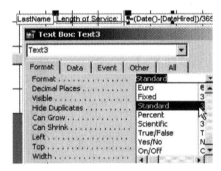

To change the field that a text box or control is bound to

1. Double-click the control to open the property sheet of the control.

2. Click on the **Data** tab.

3. Click the **ControlSource** property box and select the field you want to change the control to from the drop-down list.

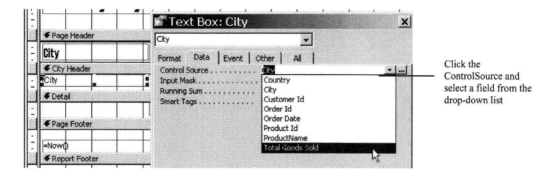

Click the
ControlSource and
select a field from the
drop-down list

The different sections of a report

A report is divided into different sections. Each section has a specific purpose. For example the Detail section of a report is used to display the data in the report. The different sections of a report are well labeled as illustrated in the Report Design view.

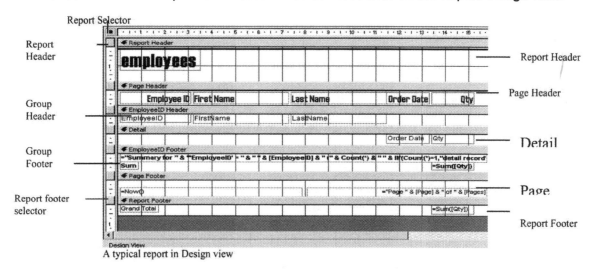

A typical report in Design view

Report Header: Information in the Report Header appears once in a report and is displayed on the first page of a report.

Page Header: The Page Header appears at the beginning of every page.

Group Header: The content of this section appears at the beginning of a new group.

Detail: This section is displayed for every record printed in the report.

Group Footer: The content of this section appears at the end of a group of records.

Page Footer: The Page Footer appears at the bottom of every page.

Report Footer: Information in the **Report Footer** appears once at the end of a report.

Adding Sections to a report

To Add a Report header and footer

1.   In **Design View**, click on the **View Menu**.

2.   Click on **Report Header/Footer**.

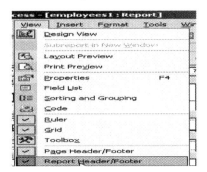

To add a page header and footer

1.   In **Design View**, click on the **View Menu.**

2.   Click on **Page Header/Footer.**

Remove a Report Header

1.   In **Design view**, click on the **View Menu.**

2.   Click the **Report Header/Footer**

3.   Microsoft Access displays a dialog box warning about the consequence of your action.

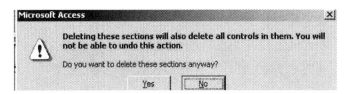

4.   Click **Yes** to delete the **Report Header.**

Remove a Page Header

1.   In Design view, click on the **View Menu.**

2.   Click the **Page Header/Footer**

3.   Microsoft Access displays a dialog box warning about the consequence of your action.

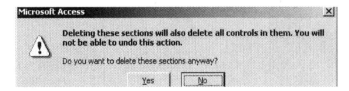

4.   Click **Yes** to delete the **Report Header.**

To show or Hide a section

You can hide sections of your report you don't want to display in your report. For example you could hide the **Detail Section** of a report and display only the Group summary of a report.

To show or Hide a section

1. Open the report in **Design view**.

2. Double-click the section selector you want to hide or show. The property sheet appears.

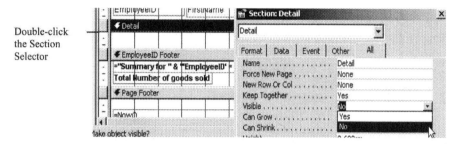

3. Set the visible property to **Yes** or **No.** To hide a section select **No,** to show a section select **Yes.**

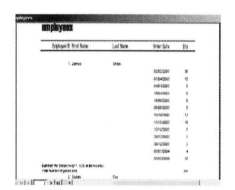
Report before hiding section

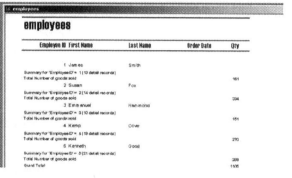
Results of setting the detail section to No

The only exception to this rule is that you cannot hide the Page Header or Footer.

Add Page Breaks

Page Breaks are used to mark the beginning of a new page in a section. For example you may decide to print the Report Header on a separate page and begin the rest of the report on new page. You can use the Page Break to separate the Report Header from the rest of the page.

To Add a Page Break

1. Open the Report in **Design view**, then click the **Page Break** tool on the toolbox.

2. On the Report, click where you want to put the page break. Microsoft Access puts dots on the report where you positioned the **Page Break**

Dots appears on the
report where you
put the Page Break

Tip To avoid splitting data, place the page break above or below other controls.

Adding Page Numbers to your report

There are two ways of adding page numbers to a report. They are using the **Page Property** or using the **Insert Menu.**

To add page numbers to a report using the Page Property

1. Create a text box and position it in the Page Header or Page Footer.

2. With the text box selected, click the properties [icon] button on the toolbar. The Property sheet appears.

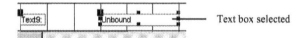

Text box selected

3. Click the **Data** tab and click the **ControlSource** property. Enter the page expression directly into the ControlSource.

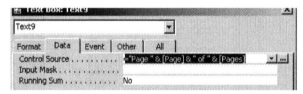

To Add Page Numbers using the Expression Builder

1. Open the report in **Design view.**

2. Create the text box and position it where you want it to be in the report.

3. Select the text box and click the **Properties** button on the toolbar.

4. Click the **ControlSource** property, and then click on the **Build** button and select **Expression Builder** from the **Choose Builder dialog** box.

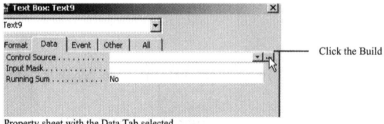

Click the Build

Property sheet with the Data Tab selected

5. Select **Common Expressions** from the leftmost box.

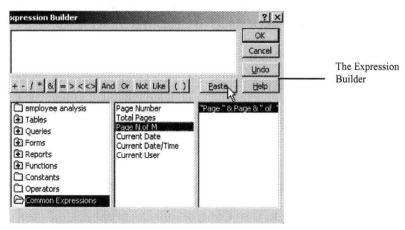

The Expression Builder

6. Select the **Page Number** format you want from the list displayed in the middle box. The right box displays the expression you have selected.

7. Click the **Paste** button to add the expression.

8. Click Ok. The expression is displayed in the **ControlSource** property box.

To add page numbers to a report using the Insert Menu

1. Open the report in **Design View.**

2. Click on the **Insert Menu** and choose **Page Numbers.** The Page Numbers dialog box appears on the screen.

3. Choose a format, position and the alignment you want to use from the Format, Position and Alignment box respectively.

   Accept the Default value for the **Show Number on First Page.** If you don't want a page number to appear on the first page of the report, deselect the box next to **Show Number on First Page**.

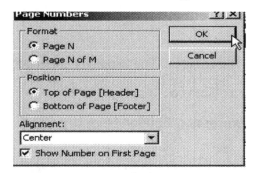

4. Click on **Ok.**

Adding a date to your report

A well-formatted report should not only display the page numbers of the report, it should also display the date the report was printed. There are two ways you can add a date to your report.   These are using the Property sheet or using the Insert Menu.

To add a date to a report using the Property sheet

1.   Open the report in **Design view.**

2.   Create the text box and position it in the page footer.

3.   Select the text box and click the **Properties** button on the toolbar.

4.   Click the properties ⌨ button on the toolbar. The Property sheet appears.

5.   Click the **Data** tab and click the **ControlSource** property.   Enter the date expression directly into the ControlSource. Type =Date() into the **ControlSource** property.

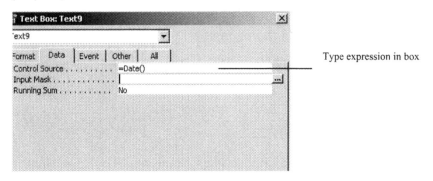

Type expression in box

6.   Click **Ok.**

Enter a date using the expression builder

1.   Open the report in **Design view.**

2.   Create a text box.

3.   Select the text box.

4.   Click the properties ⌨ button on the toolbar. The Property sheet appears.

5.   Click the **Data** tab and click the **ControlSource** property.

6.   Click the **Build** button and choose **Expression Builder** from the **Choose Builder** box.

7.   Select the **Common Expressions** folder from the **Expression builder** and select the **Current Date** function from the middle box.

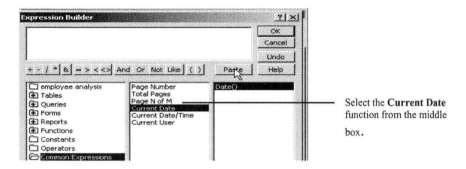

Select the **Current Date** function from the middle box.

8. Click on **Paste** and click **ok.** The expression appears in the **ControlSource** property box.

To add a date to your report using the Insert Menu

1. Open the report in **Design view.**

2. Click the **Insert menu** and select **Date and Time.** The **Date and Time** dialog box appears on the screen.

3. Click the box next to **Date** to add date to your report, then choose the format of the date you want from the options provided below the **Include Date.**

4. Click the box next to **Time** to add the time to your report, then choose the format of the time you want from the options provided below the **Include Time.** Deselect the box next to **Include Time** if you don't want the time to appear in your report.

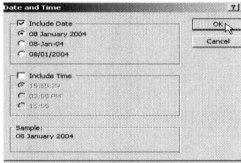

The Date and time dialog box

5. Click on **Ok.** A text box with the date format appears in the upper-left corner of the **Report Header.** If the Report does not have a header, the text box appears in the **Detail Section.** You can move the text box and position it wherever you want.

Changing the size of a section

You can increase or decrease the height and width of a report section. As illustrated in the above report, a report, have many sections but only one width, therefore if you change the width of a report, it affects the whole report.

To change the height of a report

1.   Place the mouse at the bottom edge of the section.

2.   Drag the pointer **up** to decrease the size of the section and **down** to increase the size of the section.

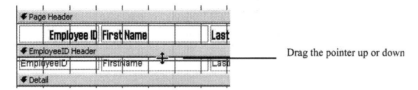

Drag the pointer up or down

To change the width of a section

1.   Place the pointer on the right edge of section.

2.   Drag the pointer to the left or right.

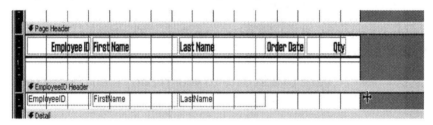

Section Properties

Like controls, the sections of a report also have properties. You can change or set properties of a section in the property sheet.

To set the property of a section

1.   Double-click the section.

    The section property sheet is displayed.

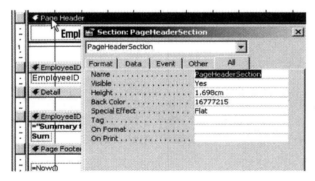

2.   Choose a category tab.

3.   Set the property by entering an appropriate value or selecting the value from a drop-down list.

Setting Report Properties

The Report Properties is used to define properties for an entire report.

Example

You may decide to center the whole report. You can centre the whole report by changing the **Auto Centre** property for the report to **Yes**.

To set property for a Report

1. Double-click on the **Report Selector**. The property sheet is displayed.

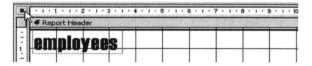

2. Choose a property category. For example choose the **Format Category** by clicking the **Format** tab.

3. Set the property by clicking the drop-down list or by entering a value.

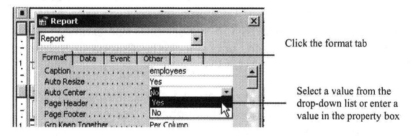

Click the format tab

Select a value from the drop-down list or enter a value in the property box

Chapter

SORTING AND GROUPING DATA

Sorting

Sorting allows you to organise the data in your report in a particular order. For example you can organise the customers list in alphabetical order by their last name and first name, so that it becomes easier to search for a customer. In Microsoft Access you can set or change the sort order in the Sorting and Grouping dialog box. The **Field/Expression** column is used to define the field or expression to sort on. For example if you want to sort your data on the Company name field, you select the **Company Name** field in the **Field/Expression** field.

The Sort Order column is used to define the sort order i.e. Ascending or Descending order. Ascending sort's data from the lowest value to the highest. For example in an ascending order, Text fields are sorted alphabetically and numeric fields are sorted from 0 upwards. (1,2,3,etc.). Descending sort's values from highest to the lowest.

Setting a sort order

1. Open the report in **Design view.**

2. From the view menu, choose **Sorting and Grouping** or click the **Sorting and grouping** button on the toolbar. The sorting and grouping dialog box appears.

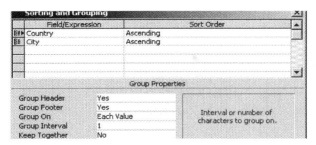

3. In the **Field/Expression** column, select the field you want or if you are using an expression type the expression beginning with an = sign.

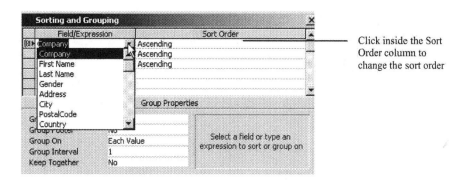

Click inside the Sort Order column to change the sort order

4. By default Microsoft Access sets the Sort Order to **Ascending.** You can change the Sort Order by clicking inside the Sort Order column and selecting the **Sort Order** you want.

5. Repeat step 3&4 until you have selected all the fields you want to sort your data on.

    Enter the fields in the order you want the records to be sorted. Microsoft Access sorts the report in the order the fields are entered in the Sorting and Grouping dialog box. In the example below the report will be sorted first by country and then city.

This symbol shows that records are grouped by the values in this field.

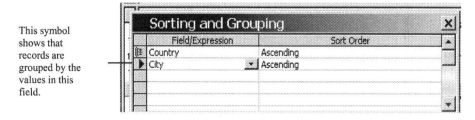

To change sorting and grouping order

You can change the sort order of a report by changing how the data is sorted. For example in a report in which data is sorted by company, last name and first name you can decide to change the sort order and sort the report by last name, first name and last name. Follow the steps below to change the sort order.

1. Open the report in **Design view.**

2. From the view menu, choose **Sorting and Grouping** or click the **Sorting and grouping** button on the toolbar. The sorting and grouping dialog box appears.

3. In the **Sorting and Grouping** box, click the row selector of the field or expression you want to change.

4. Click the selector and move it to the new location.

Click the row selector

The new sort order is displayed in the sorting and grouping dialog box

Deleting a sorting or grouping field or expression

1.   Click the **row selector** of the field or expression you want to delete and press the **Delete key.**

    The Sorting or Grouping Delete box appears prompting you to confirm the deletion.

2.   Click **Ok** to delete the **Sorting or Grouping** or **No** to stop deleting the **Sorting and Grouping.** The header and footer for that group will also be deleted if you click **ok.**

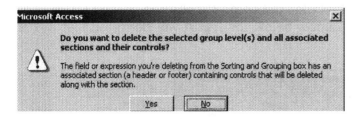

Inserting a sort or grouping field or expression

You can insert an additional field to sort your data on. For example you may decide that you want to sort the data in your report by last name, first name, city and then company name. By default Microsoft Access will sort data by the order in which the fields appear in the Sorting and Grouping dialog box. In order to sort the data by last name, first name, city and company name, you will have to insert the city field before the company name. Follow the steps below to insert a field in the Sorting and Grouping dialog box.

1.   Click the **row selector** of the row where you want to insert the new field or expression.

2.   Press the **Insert key** on your keyboard. Microsoft Access inserts a new blank row.

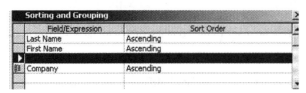

3.   Select a field or enter an expression in the new row.

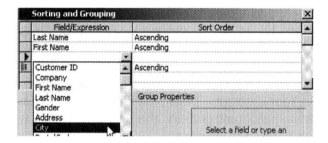

Grouping Data

Sorting only arranges the data in a particular order. Arranging data in a particular order does not help you very much in analyzing your data. You can group your data into different category by fields. For example you could group the customers report by country and city fields. When you organize your report into groups you can calculate total for each group and display the results as summarize data for each group. Because the report is organize in groups you can quickly locate a record you are looking for without much hassle. Also with a summarize report for different groups you could compare the performance of each group. A Group is made up of a group header, detail records and group footer.

The Group Header or Footer property is used to add or remove a group header or footer.

To add a group header or footer

1.   Open the report in **Design View.**

2.   Click the **field** or enter an **expression** you want to group on.

3.   Set the **Group Header** or **footer** or both to yes in the Group property at the bottom of the Sorting and Grouping dialog box.

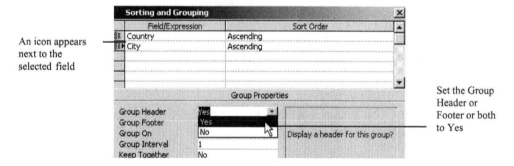

A group header or footer or a header and footer are added to the report depending on the setting you made.

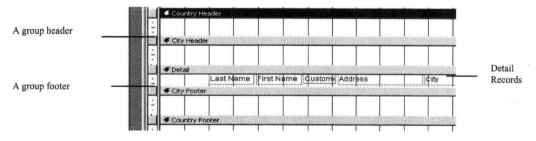

4. Click on the **GroupOn** property and select **"Each value"**. The **GroupOn** property is used to specify how the values are to be grouped. The values displayed for the **GroupOn** property depends on the data type of field you are grouping. For example for a text field the values displayed in the **GroupOn** property sheet are **Each value** and **Prefix**. For date field the values displayed in the **GroupOn** property are **Each Value**, **Year**, **Month**, **Week**, **Day**, **Hour** and **Minute**. For numeric, currency, number or autonumber field, the properties displayed in the **GroupOn** property are **Each Value** and **Interval**.

If you select **Each value** for the **GroupOn** property Microsoft Access will group identical values together.

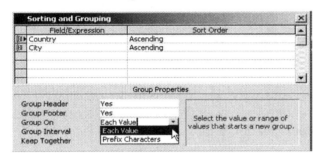

5. Enter a valid value for the **GroupInterval** property. The **GroupInterval** defines the interval between the groups.

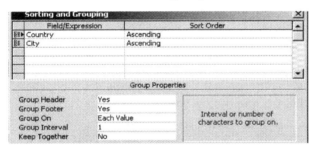

6. Click on the **Keep Together** property. The **Keep Together** property defines how the group is printed. The options displayed in this box are **No, Whole Group or With the First Detail**.

No will print the group without keeping the Group Header, Footer and Detail section together on the same page.

Whole Group will print the whole group on the same page.

With First Detail will print the group header and the first detail record on the same page.

Example

Grouping on a currency data type

Suppose a retailer sells goods with different price range, it will be very handy for the retailer to have a price list with different price ranges. We could create a price list and group the price list by the Unit Price of the product. Because the Unit Price is a currency field you can set the GroupOn field to Interval and the GroupInterval property to the price range you want to group the data. In this example we want the report to group the Unit Price within intervals of 5000.

1. Create a report in **Design view** using the Product table.

2. Include fields such as the ProductId, ProductName, SupplierId and UnitPrice.

3. Click the **Sorting and Grouping** ▐⟮⟬▐ tool on the Report toolbar.

4. Click inside the first row of the **Field/Expression** column and select Unit Price and set the group properties as follows.

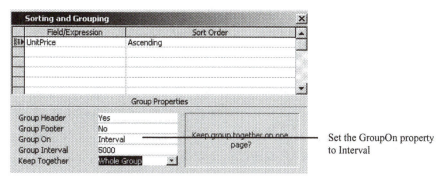

Set the GroupOn property to Interval

5. Move to the next row and select the Unit Price again from the **Field/Expression** column. Set the group's properties as indicated below.

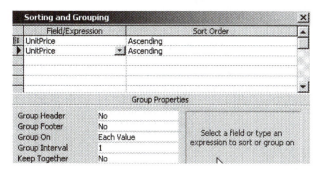

6. Close the Group dialog box when you finish setting the properties. When you close the group dialog box, the UnitPrice header appears in the report.

7. In the Group Header for the **UnitPrice** create a text box. In the label for the text box, enter the text **"Products within the price range of"** and in the control enter the following formula for calculating the price range. This function will display the price range for each group.

=Int((([UnitPrice])/5000)*5000 & " - " & Int(((([UnitPrice])/5000)+1)*5000

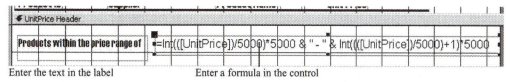

Enter the text in the label   Enter a formula in the control

8. When you finish entering the formula, click the **view** button to view the report.

Price List

Product ID	Supplier	Product Name	Unit Price

Products within the price range of   25000 - 30000

	25	PEWLTERS	BMW	£25,000.00
	32	Schmes	Lincoln	£25,000.00
	30	Sea View	Land Rover	£26,999.00
	29	BRISCOL	Jeep	£27,000.00
	28	Sea View	Jagguar	£28,000.00
	27	Malatan Ltd	Ford	£29,999.00

Products within the price range of   30000 - 35000

| | 26 | Malatan Ltd | Cadilac | £30,000.00 |
| | 20 | Schmes | HONDA | £32,000.00 |

Products within the price range of   40000 - 45000

To remove a group

1.   Open the report in **Design View.**

2.   Click the field or expression you want to delete.

3.   Set the Group Header or footer or both to **No** in the **Group property**.

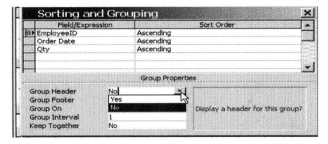

Microsoft Access displays a dialog box warning you about the delete operation. Click **Yes** to delete the header or footer.

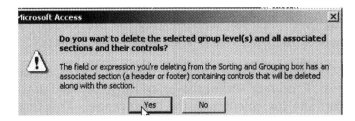

Calculating Totals for a group of records

Sometimes to access the performance of a sector or a group it is necessary to group the data and perform calculation on a group. When you perform a calculation on a group of records it is very important where you place the calculated total. The group total is always placed in the group header or footer.

To calculate a group total

Suppose you decide to analyze your daily sales figures to review your performance daily. You can group your orders by date and calculate the total sales figure daily.

1. Open the report in **Design view.**

2. Create a text box and position it in the **Group Footer.**

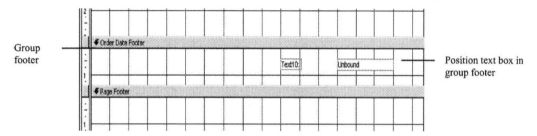

Group footer ← (left label)

Position text box in group footer ← (right label)

3. Select the text box and click on the properties tool.

4. Click the **ControlSource** Property and enter the expression for calculating the subtotal. Type = Sum([Qty]*[Unit Price]). Enter the format for the expression in the format box and enter a name for the expression.

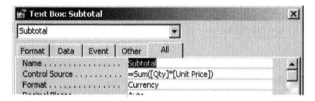

5. Click the close button on the property sheet. The function appears in the text box.

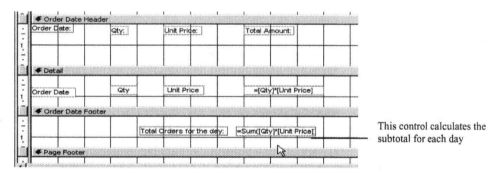

This control calculates the subtotal for each day

Calculating Totals on Several Groups

You can calculate the total on several groups of records. Apart from calculating the total for each group daily, you can also calculate the total sales for the whole company and compare your figures with other company's data if that it available. The overall total for all records is always placed in the Report footer or Header.

To create overall total for all records

1. Open the report in **Design view.**

2. Create a text box and position it in the **Report Footer.**

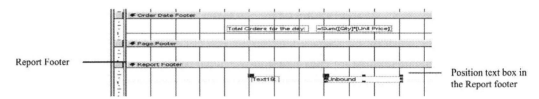

Report Footer ⎯⎯⎯⎯

Position text box in
the Report footer

3. Select the text box and click the properties tool.

4. Click the **ControlSource** Property and enter the expression for calculating the Grand Total. Type = Sum([Qty]*[Unit Price]). Enter the format for the expression in the format box and enter a name for the expression.

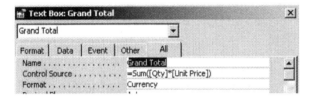

5. Click the close button on the property sheet. The function appears in text box.

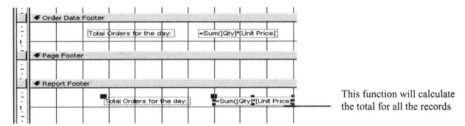

This function will calculate
the total for all the records

Printing One Group of Record Per Page

You can print each group of record on a new page. Printing a group of records on a new page makes it easier to find records or specific items. Follow the steps below.

1. Open the **Report** in **Design View.**

2. Double-click the **Section Selector** to the left of the group. The property sheet opens.

3. Click the drop-down arrow next to **Force New Page** property and select **BeforeSection.**

Double-
click the
Section
Selector

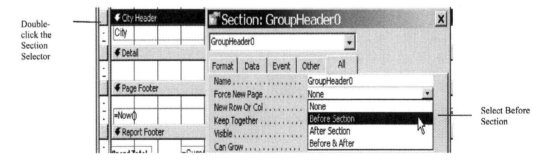

Select Before
Section

SUBFORMS AND SUBREPORTS

Subform

Sometimes you may want to work with related tables in your form. For example you may want to view all the orders placed by a customer. A mainform and a subform may be useful in a situation like this.

A subform is a form within another form. In Microsoft Access, you can add a form to an existing form. When you add a form to an existing form, the existing form becomes the main form and the form you added to the main form becomes the subform. For example if you have an existing form **Order** and you add another form **Order Details** to the form, the **Order** form becomes the main form and the **Order Details** form becomes the subform.

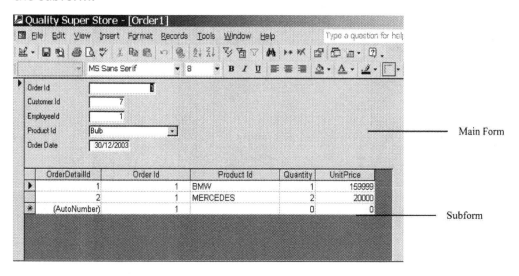

A **subform** is useful for displaying information between tables with a one-to-many relationship. For example in the **Order** and **Order Details** table displayed above, an order may consist of many items. In Database terms, a one-to-many relationship exists between them. Between the Order table and the Order details table, a common field (Order Id) exist which links the Order table to the Order Details table. Microsoft Access uses the common field to display records, which are common to both tables. The Subform will only display records that relate to the current record in the main form. Note that the **Order Id** in the main form is **1** and the **Order Ids'** in the subform are all **1**.

When creating a mainform/subform, use the table for the one-side of the relationship as the main form (i.e. Order) and the tables for the many side of the relationship for the subform (i.e. Order Details).

Before you create the subform, make sure you have created the relationship between the tables.   Refer to the chapter on relationship for further details on creating a relationship.

Creating a form/subform

Creating a form/subform with a wizard

The quickest and easiest way to create a form/subform is with the wizard. Follow the steps below to create a form/subform.

1.   In the **Database window,** click on **Forms** under **Objects.**

2.   Double click **Create form by using wizard,** Microsoft Access displays the **Form Wizard.**

3.   Choose the table you want to use as the main form (One-side of the relationship) from the **Table/Queries** drop-down list. (i.e. Order)

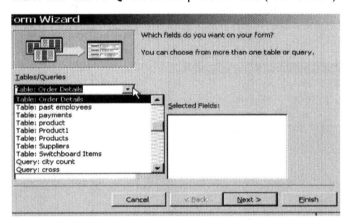

4.   Select the fields you want to use from the table and move the fields to the **Selected Fields** box using > or >> button.

5.   Repeat steps 3&4 to select the table (i.e. Order Details) and fields you want to use for the many-side of the relationship. Click **Next** to continue.

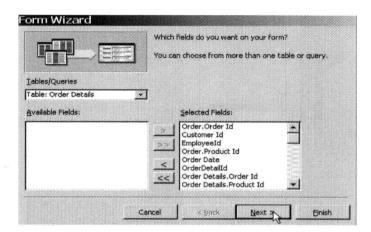

6. The wizards asks you how you want to view your form, click on **By Order** and then click on **Forms with subform(s).** Click **Next** to continue.

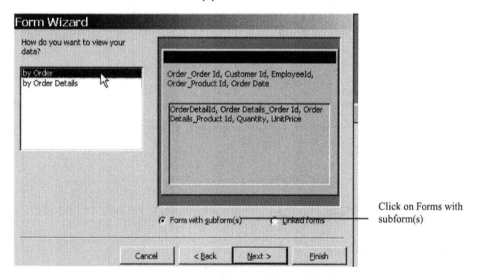

Click on Forms with subform(s)

7. Select the layout for your sub-form. The preview window displays the selection you make. Click **Next** to continue.

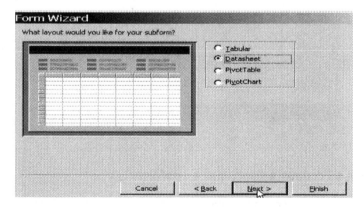

8. Choose a style for your form from the list displayed in the style box. Click **Next.**

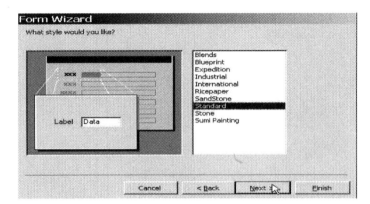

9. The form wizard asks you for a title for your main form and subform. Accept the default name or type a name for your form and subform.

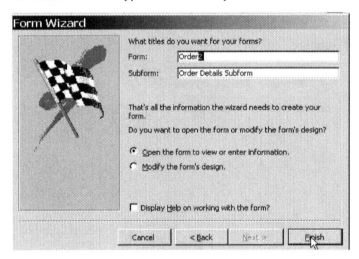

10. Click the **Finish** button.

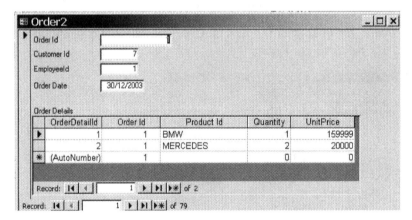

Add a form to another form to create a form and a subform

You can create a mainform/subform by creating the main form and the subform separately and dragging the subform on to the main form. For this example we are going to use the department form and the employees form. A one-to-many relationship exists between the department form and the employees' form.

First step : create the main form

1. Create a main form using any of the methods described in the chapter for creating a form.

Second step: create a subform

The **subform** is quite often created in datasheet view. For this example we will create a form in datasheet view.

1. In the **Database window,** click on the **Forms** object and click **New.**

2. Choose the table or query you want to use for your subform from the drop-down list next to **Choose the table or query where the object's data comes from.**

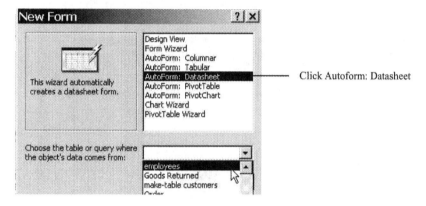

Click Autoform: Datasheet

3. Click on **Autoform: Datasheet.**

The **Autoform wizard** creates a form in datasheet view. The form appears on your screen.

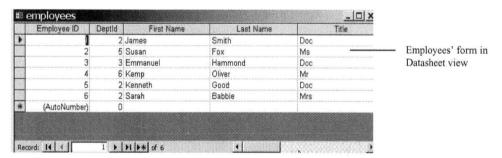

Employees' form in Datasheet view

4. Click the close button. Microsoft Access asks you if you want to save the form, click **Yes** and enter a name for the form.

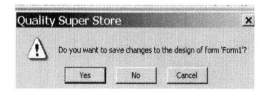

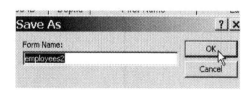

Now that you have created both the main form and the subform separately you can add the subform to the main form.

2. Open the form you want to use as the main form in **Design view**.

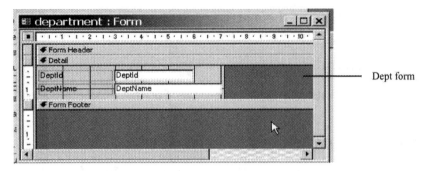

Dept form

3. Switch to the database window by pressing **F11** key. Line up the form and the Database window so that you can see both windows at the same time.

The database window

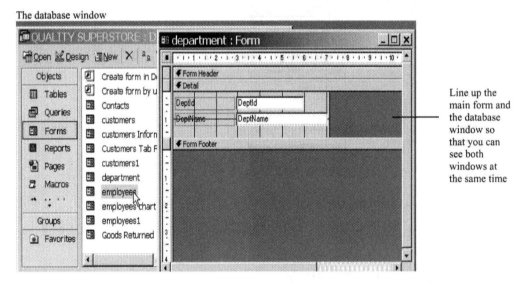

Line up the main form and the database window so that you can see both windows at the same time

5. In the Database window click on the **Forms** tab under **Objects** and select the form you want to use as the subform and drag it to the mainform. The subform appears on the main form.

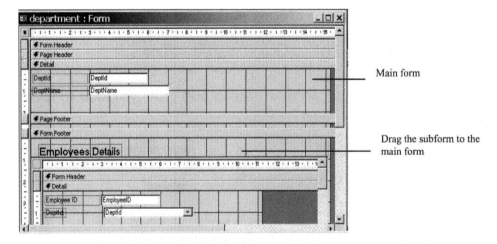

Main form

Drag the subform to the main form

6. Click on the **view** button to view the form.

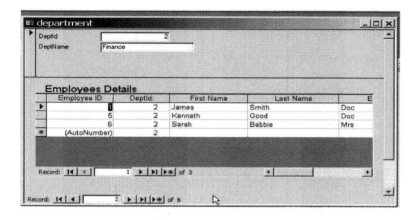

To add a subform to a main form using the Subform/Subreport wizard

Another method is to add a subform to the main form using the **Subform/Subreport wizard.** Create the main form and subform separately. Follow the steps below to add the subfrom to the main form using the subform/subreport wizard.

1. Open the form you want to use as the main form in **Design view**. Make sure the **Control wizard** is selected.

2. Click the **Subform/subreport** tool in the toolbox.

3. Click and draw a rectangle on the form where you want the subform to appear.

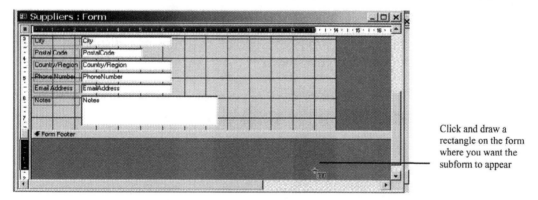

Click and draw a rectangle on the form where you want the subform to appear

When you release the mouse the **subform/subreport** wizard appears.

4. Click on **Use an existing form** and select the **form** you want to use for the **subform** from the drop-down list. Click **Next** to continue.

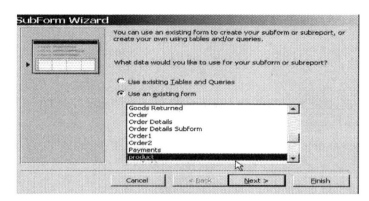

5. Because you have already defined the relationship between the tables, click **Choose from a list**. The wizard displays a list of relationship from which you can choose. If you want to define your own relationship click **Define my own** and define the relationship yourself.

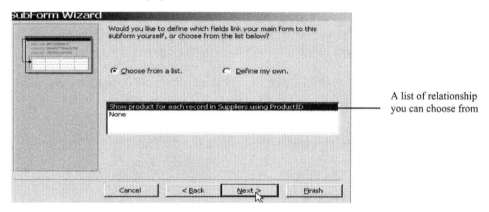

A list of relationship you can choose from

6. Select a relationship from the list of relationships displayed or accepts the default selection and click **Next.**

7. Enter a name for your subform.

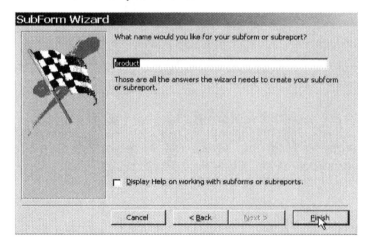

8. Click **Finish.** The subform appears on the main form.

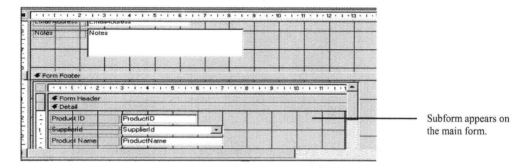

Subform appears on the main form.

You can customize the form in the property sheet. For example you can expand the width of the form, move controls on the form and you can also remove the navigational buttons. You can expand the navigational button by selecting **No** in the Navigation Buttons property of the form property sheet. (Refer to the chapter on customizing a form with the property sheet).

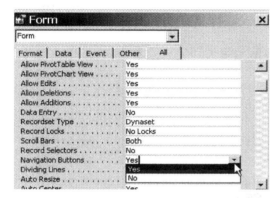

9. Click the view ▦ ▾ button to view the **mainform/subform** you have created.

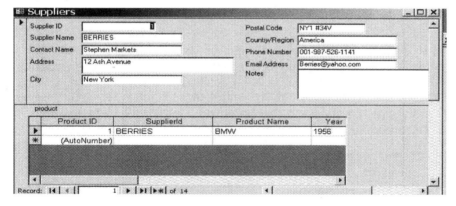

Creating a form with two subforms

Before you create a form with two subforms, make sure all the relationship are define before you start creating the form. For this example we are going to use the **Customers**, **Order** and the **Order Details** table. The Customers table has a one-many relationship with the Order table and the Order table has a one-to-many relationship with the Order Details table.

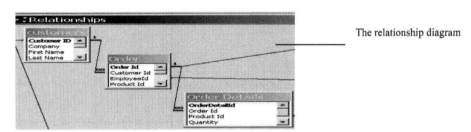

The relationship diagram

1. In the **Database window,** click **Forms** under Objects and then click **New.** The **New form** dialog box appears.

2. Double-click the **form wizard.**

3. Select the table you want to use to create the main form from the **Table/Queries** drop-down list. For example select the customers table.

4. Select the fields you want to use for the table and move the fields to the **Selected Fields**

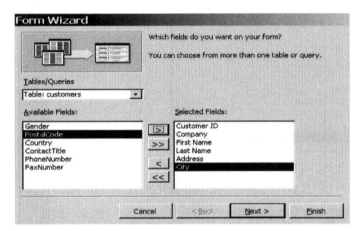

5. In the same dialog box, repeat steps 3&4 to select the first sub-form and move the fields to the **Selected Fields** box. For example select the **Order** table.

6. In the same dialog box, repeat steps 3&4 to select the table for the second sub-form and move the fields to the **Selected Fields** box. For example select the **Order Details** table. Click **Next** to continue.

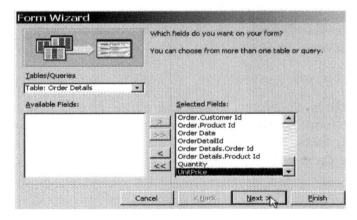

7. The wizard asks you how you want to view your data. Click, **By Customers**. A
    preview is shown on the right window.

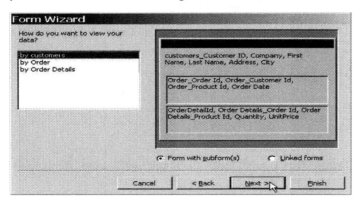

8. Click **Form with subform(s)**. Click **Next**.

9. Select the layout you would like for each subform and click **Next**.

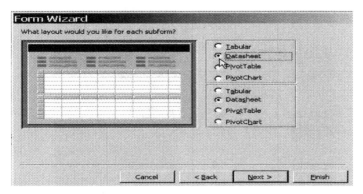

10. Choose the style you want from the list displayed. Click **Next** to continue.

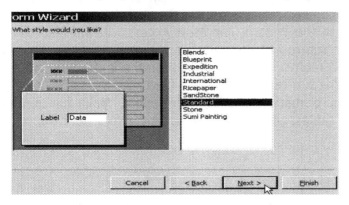

11. Enter Titles for the main form and the two subforms, you can accept the default
    names.

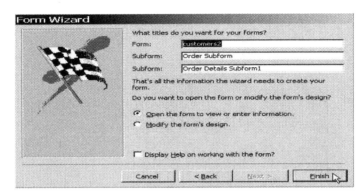

12. Click **Finish**. The main form with the two subforms are displayed on your screen.

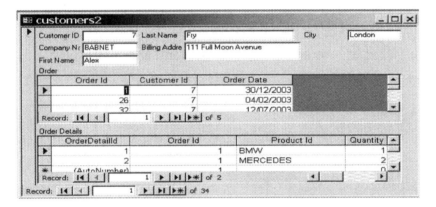

Subreport

A Subreport is a report inserted into another Report. In Microsoft Access you can combine two or more reports together on the same page. When you put two or more report together, one of the reports becomes a main report and the other(s) become a subreport(s). When you create a report with the Wizard, Microsoft Access will automatically display the correct information in the sub-report, if there is a common field that links the main report to the sub-report, i.e. a relationship exists between the underlying table or query that makes the reports. Also the sub-report contains a field with the same name and data type or similar data type as the primary key in the main report. Make sure a relationship exist between the underlying tables/queries you are using for your main-report and sub-report.

Adding a sub-report to a report

There are about two ways you can create a sub-report. They are create:

• Create a sub-report in an existing report.

• Add an existing sub-report to another report as a sub-report.

Create a sub-report in an existing report

1.   Open the report you want to use as a main report in **Design View**.

2. Click on the **sub-form/sub-report** 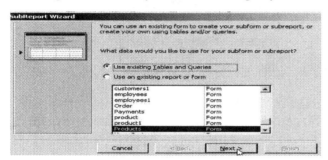 tool on the toolbar.

3. Click and drag the **sub-form/sub-report tool** on the report where you want to position the sub-report. Microsoft Access displays an unbound sub-report on the report. The **Sub-Report** dialog box appears advising you that you can use **existing tables and queries/ existing report or forms**.

4. Select from one of the options displayed above.

5. If you want to use existing tables and queries, click on **Use existing Tables and Queries** and click **Next** to continue. Microsoft Access displays the second dialog box, Select the table and fields you want to use for your sub-report and move the fields you want to use to the selected fields by clicking on the > to move one field at a time or >> to move all the fields to the selected fields box.. Click **Next** to continue.

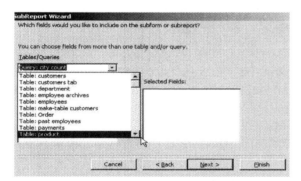

If you want to use existing form or report, click on **use existing form or report**, select the form or report you want to use.   Click **Next** to continue.

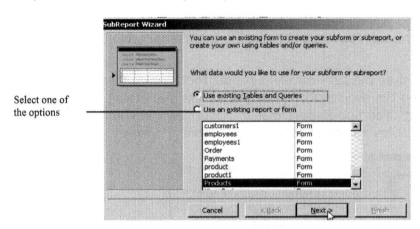

Select one of
the options

6. You can choose from the list in the bottom box how you want the main-report to link the **sub-report** or you can define your own fields to link the main report with the **sub-report**. Click **Choose from a list** and select how the sub-report links the main report from the box below. **Click Next** to continue.

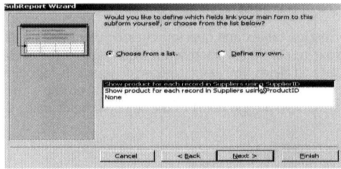

the default choice for this dialog box

    If you choose to define your own links, Microsoft Access presents you with another dialog box from which you can define the fields that **links** your main report to your sub-report. Select the field(s) you want to use in your main report from the drop-down list in the **Form/Report** fields and select the field(s) you want to use for your sub-report in the **Subform/Report** field. When you finish, click on **Next** to continue.

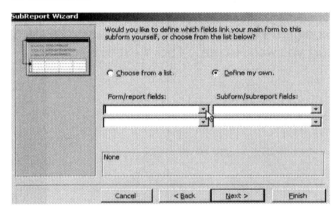

7. Enter a name for your sub-report and click on **Finish**.

    Microsoft Access displays the sub-report in **Design view**.

Adding an existing report to another report as a sub-form

1. Open the report you want to use as the main report in **Design view.**

2. Press **F11 key** to switch to the Database window.

3. In the Database window click on the **Reports** tab under **Objects** and select the report you want to use as a **sub-report** on the Database window and drag the report to the section in the main report where you want to position the sub-report. The sub-form/sub-report control appears in the main report.

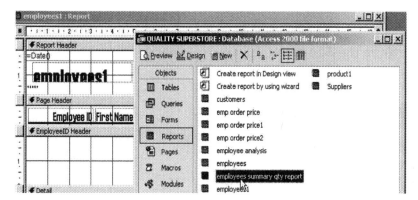

If a relationship exist between the main-report and sub-report, Microsoft Access links the two reports automatically. If the two reports are not related, you will have to link the fields manually. **(see linking fields manually).**

Linking the fields Manually

1. In **Design view,** Select the Sub-report .

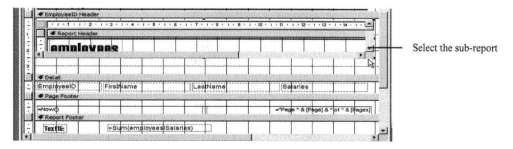

Select the sub-report

2. Click on the **properties tool** button to open the property sheet.

3. Enter the name of the field(s) that links the sub-report to the main report in the **LinkChildFields** property.

    Enter the name of the field(s) that links the main-report to the sub-report in the **LinkMasterFields** property.

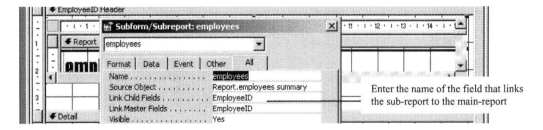

Enter the name of the field that links
the sub-report to the main-report

Printing your report

1. Open the form in **Design view, Layout Preview** or **Print Preview.**

2   Select **Print** from the **File Menu.**

    Microsoft Access displays the Print dialog box.

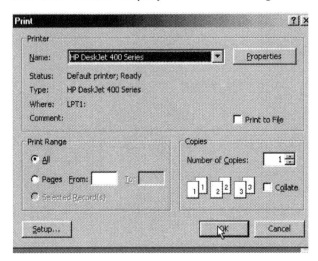

3. Select the **Print Range** you want to print. To print all the report select **All,** to print a selection of the report, select **Selected Record(s),** to print a range of pages, select **Pages.**

4. Enter the Number of copies you want to print.

5. Accept the default setting to print collated copies of your report. If you don't want to collate the report you can clear the box next to **collate**.

6. Click **Ok** to print the report.

    In Access 2003, if the **error-checking** feature is on, Microsoft Access automatically checks common errors like report size. For example if the size of the report is wider than the page, Microsoft displays a warning and gives you the option to fix the error.

    You can enable the **error-checking** feature if it is not enabled. Follow the steps below to enable the error-checking feature.

To set the error checking feature

1. Click on **Options** in the **Tool Menu.**

2. Click the **Error checking** tab.

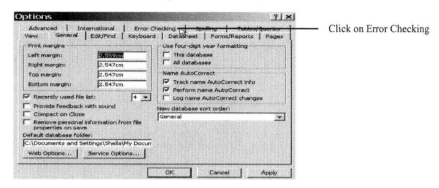

Click on Error Checking

3. Click the check box next to **Enable error checking**.

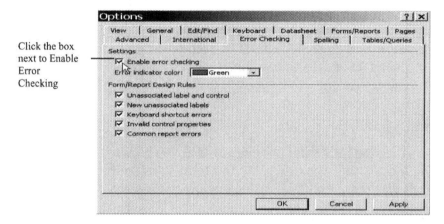

Click the box
next to Enable
Error
Checking

4. Under **Form/Report** Design Rules, select or clear the options you want.

5. Click **Ok.**

Chapter

USING CHARTS TO ANALYZE YOUR DATA

A chart is a graphical presentation of data. People find it easier to read charts than figures. It is very difficult to make sense of large numbers than to look at pictures or a chart. With a chart, users can easily make comparison and spot trends. In Access 2003 you can use the chart wizard to create charts in both forms and reports. you can create different types of charts to anlyse and summarize your data. For example you could create line graphs, pie charts and other types of graphs.

Creating a chart in a form

Suppose you want to see the total sales per employee as you browse through the employees form, you can add a chart that would display the total sales figures of each employee as you browse through the form. Follow the steps below to create a chart.

1. Open the form in **Design view.**

2. Select **Chart** from the **Insert Menu.**

3. Click on the form and draw a box where you want the chart to appear. The Chart Wizard appears.

4. Select the source of data for your chart for example select the query you want to use for your chart from the displayed list and click **Next** to continue.

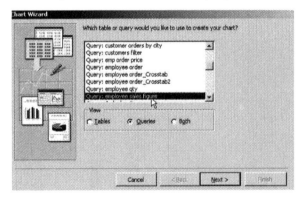

5. Select the fields you want to use in your chart from the **Available fields** and click on > or >> to move the fields over to the box labelled **Fields for Chart.**

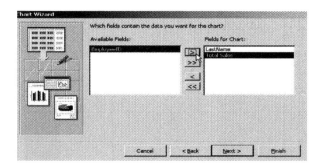

6. Select the **type of chart** you want to create from a variety of charts displayed. Click **Next** to continue.

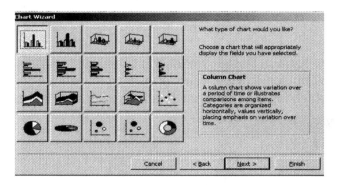

Microsoft Access displays a preview of a sample chart.

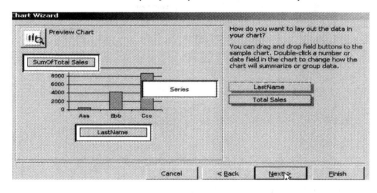

7. You can drag and drop field button to the sample chart the way you want the layout of your report to be. Click **Next** to continue.

8. If you want the chart to change from record to record, select the fields that link the form and the chart. The field that links the employee form with the Employees Sales figures query in this example is **EmployeeId**. Select **EmployeeId** in the box labelled **Forms Fields** and select **EmployeeId** in the **Chart Fields**. Click **Next**.

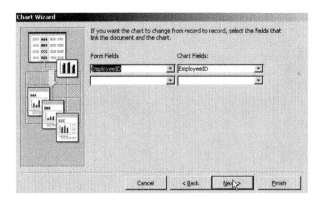

9. Enter a title for your chart and accept the default option to display the chart with a legend.

10. Click on **Finish**.

The chart appears on the form in **Design view**. You can adjust the layout of the form. Click on the **view** button to view your form. As you browse through the employee form the graph changes to show each employees sales figures.

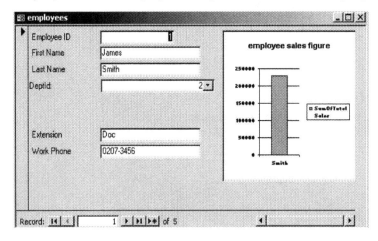

Create a chart report

You can create a chart on its own that retrieves information from many records in a database rather than a particular record in a database. This kind of chart is not link to a particular record as in the previous example; it retrieves its information from many records in the database.

Create a new chart report

1. In the Database window, click **Reports** under **Objects**.

2. Click **New**. The **New Report Dialog** box appears.

3. Select the **Chart Wizard** and select a table or query from the drop-down list at the bottom. Click **Ok.**

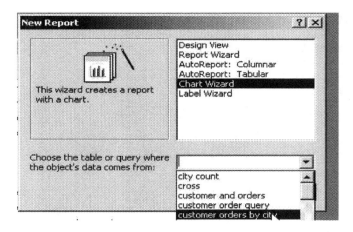

4. Select the **fields** you want to include in your chart from the **Available Fields** box, and click the > or >> button to move the fields to **Fields for Chart** box.

5. Select the chart type from the list displayed.

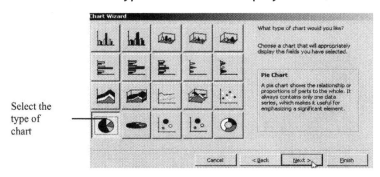

6. Drag and drop the fields in your layout the way you want it or accept the default layout. You can click the **Preview Chart button** to view the changes you have made. Close the Preview window and click **Next.**

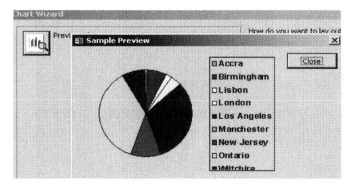

7. Enter a title for your chart and accept the default options to open the report with the chart displayed on it.

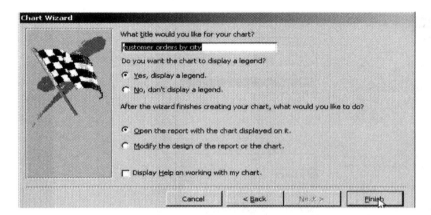

8.   Click on **Finish**. The chart appears.

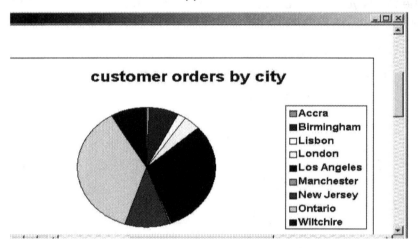

Previewing a chart

1.   Click the 📷 **Print Preview** button to Preview the chart.

Saving a chart

1.   Click the **close** button on the **Print Preview** window.

      Microsoft Access asks you if you want to save changes to your report.

2.   Click **Yes,** and enter a name for the chart.

3.   Click **Ok.**

Printing a chart

1.   Click on the **Print** 🖨 button on the toolbar.

      Alternatively,

      You can click on the **File Menu** and select **Print** from the menu.

Customize a chart

There are many ways you can customize a chart. For example you can resize the chart, format the chart, change the appearance of the chart and change the type of chart.

Change the size of a chart

1. Open the form or report in **Design view**.

2. Click the **chart**.

3. Position the mouse over the sizing handles until it changes to a double-headed arrow. Use the **sizing handles** to resize the chart.

    You can also move the chart to another location by hovering the mouse over the chart, when the mouse changes to a hand shape, you can move the chart to the desired location.

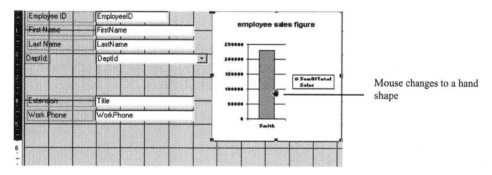

Mouse changes to a hand shape

Change the type of chart

1. Open the Chart in **Design View**.

2. Right click the chart.

3. Select the **Chart Type** from the list displayed.

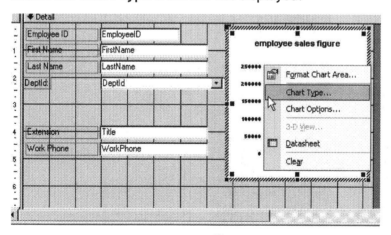

4. Select the chart type from the **Chart Type** box on the left and select the **Sub-type** from the **Chart Sub-type** box on the right.

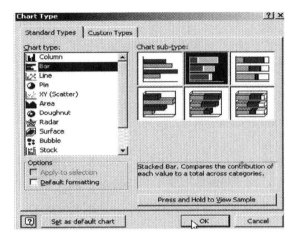

5. Click **Ok.**

To Format the look of a chart

A chart has different parts. For example you have the **Chart Legend**, **Chart Title** and **Axis**. Each part has different characteristic that you can format, For example you can format the **fonts**, **pattern** and **alignment** of a Chart Title.

Follow the steps below to format a chart title.

To Format the Chart Title

1. Right click the Chart Title.

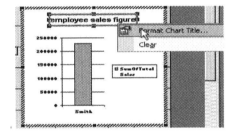

   The format Title dialog box appears

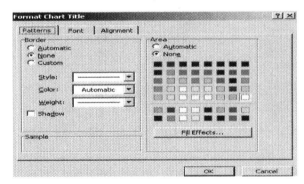

2. Click on the Tab to display a list of options within that format category. For example if you want to apply an Arial font to your **Chart Title,** click the **Font** Tab to display a list of options within the Font category.

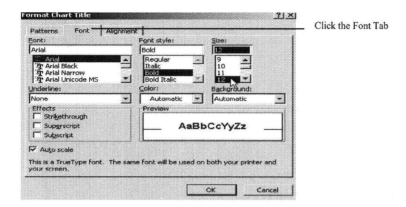

Click the Font Tab

3. Select from the options displayed. For example select the Font, Font style and size you want to apply to the **Chart Title** and

4. Click **Ok.** The fonts you selected is applied to the **Chart Title.**

Chapter

MANAGING DATABASE OBJECTS

You can manage the **objects** in a database in the **Database window**. For example you can open, copy, rename and delete objects and create new objects in the database window.

Objects

A Microsoft Access database is made up of several different objects in the Database window i.e. **Tables**, **Queries**, **Forms**, **Reports**, **Macros** and **Modules**. The different objects in a database appear on the left side of the Database Window under Objects.

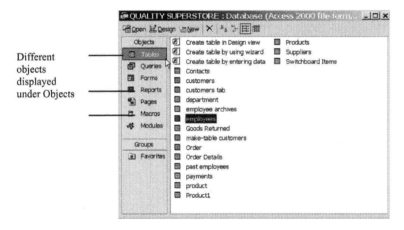

Create a new database object with a wizard

1. In the Database window, click on the type of object you want to create under **Objects**. For example if you want to create a table, click on **Tables** under **Objects.**

2. Click on **New.**

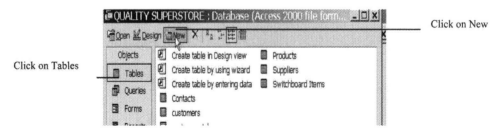

The **New Object** dialog box appears. For example the **New Table** dialog box appears.

3. Click the **Object's wizard,** for example click on the **Table Wizard** to create a table.

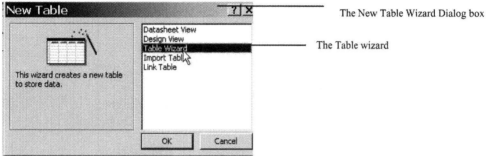

The New Table Wizard Dialog box

The Table wizard

The New Table Dialog box

4. Click **Ok.**

5. Follow the wizard to create the object.

Open a database Object

1. In the Database window, click on the type of object you want to open under **Objects.** For example if you want to open a form, click on **Forms** under **Objects.**

2. Click the object you want to open.

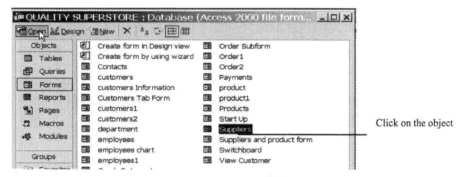

Click on the object

3. Click on the **Open** [icon] button on the toolbar or double-click the object. This will open the object i.e. a form.

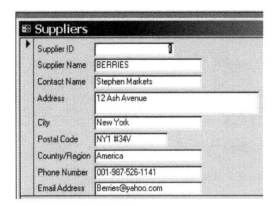

A form in form view

To open the object in Design view, click on 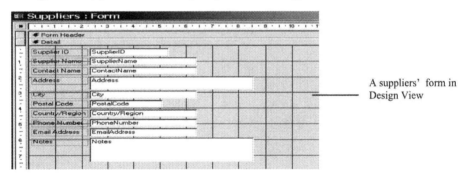 tool. The object opens in **Design view**, you can modify objects in design view.

A suppliers' form in Design View

To copy a database object

You can copy an object to the same database or to another database. Follow the steps below to copy an object.

1. In the Database window, click the **Object type** you want to copy under **Objects.** For example click on **Queries**.

2. Click on the **Object** you want to copy.

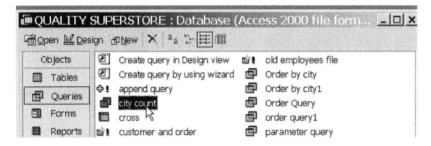

3. Click on the copy button on the toolbar or press the **Ctrl and C** keys at the same time.

    If you are copying the object to another database, close the current database and open the database you want to paste the object.

4. Click on the paste  button on the toolbar or press the **Ctrl and V** keys at the same time.

5. Enter a new name for your object in the **Paste As** dialog box.

6. Click **Ok**.

Renaming a database object

1. In the Database window, click the **Object type** under **Objects.** For example click on **Reports.**

2. Click on the **Object** you want to rename.

3. Click on **Edit Menu** and choose **Rename.**

Alternatively

Right click the object and select **Rename**

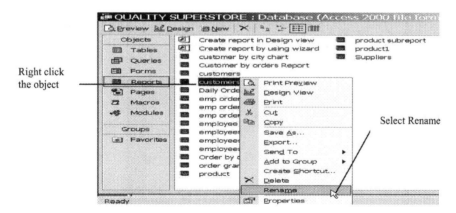

The object is highlighted.

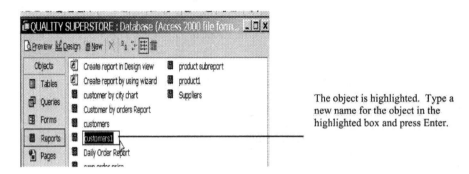

The object is highlighted. Type a new name for the object in the highlighted box and press Enter.

4. Type a new name for the object and press **Enter**.

To delete a database object

1. In the Database window, click the **Object type** under **Objects.** For example click on **Forms**.

2. Click on the **Object** you want to delete.

3. Click on the **Delete** ✕ button on the toolbar or press the **Delete** key.

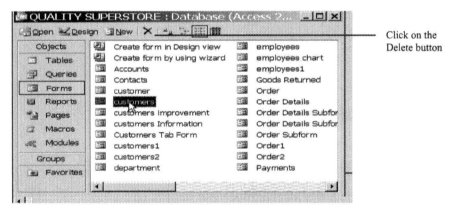

Click on the Delete button

4. Microsoft Access displays a warning about the object you are about to delete.

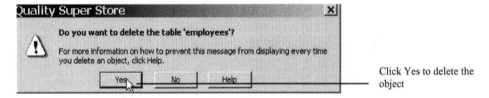

Click Yes to delete the object

5. Click **Yes** to delete the object or **No** if you don't want to delete the object.

Previewing database objects

You can use Print Preview to see how an object will look when printed. For example if you have a report, you can print preview the report to see how the report will look like when printed. Print Preview is used especially for previewing reports and forms.

To Preview Data in a report

You can preview a report from the Design view and from the database window.

To Preview Data in the Design view

1. Open the report you want to preview in **Design view**.

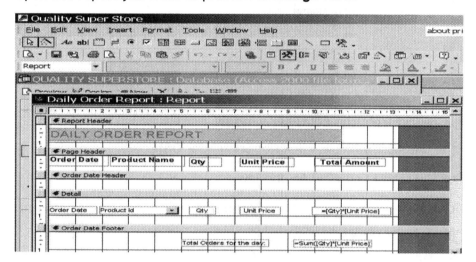

2. Click on the **Print Preview** button on the toolbar.

   Microsoft Access displays the report in Print Preview.

Magnifying the view of the report.

You can magnify the view by clicking on the page or the part of the page you want to view. Click on the page again to reduce the view.

Alternatively

1. Click on the **magnifying** button on the toolbar and select the percentage you want to magnify the object.

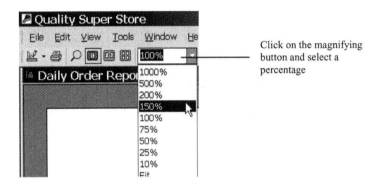

Click on the magnifying button and select a percentage

Previewing a report from the database window

1. In the Database window, click **Reports** under **Objects**.

2. Click the report you want to preview.

3. Click the **Preview** button on the Database window.

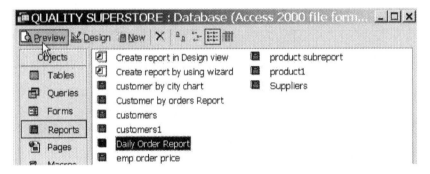

Printing a database object

You can print a database object i.e. a report. Follow the steps below to print a report.

1. Open the **Object** in **Design view, Print Preview or Layout view.**

2. From the **File menu,** choose **Print** (or click on the **Print** button).

   The Print dialog box appears.

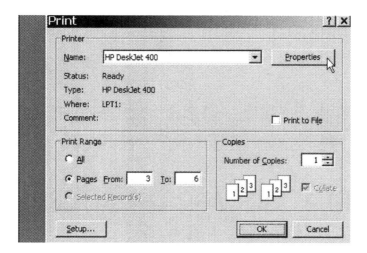

3. Enter the options for printing your document. For example under

    Print Range click **Pages.** You can print selected pages by clicking on the **Pages** options and entering the pages you want to print in the **From** and **To** box. To print all the pages **Click** on **All**.

    To print more than one copy, click inside the **Number of copies** and enter the number of copies you want to print and indicate whether you want to collate the copies by clicking the **Collate** button.

    Click on **Properties** to set the **layout and Paper Quality** properties and click **Ok**.

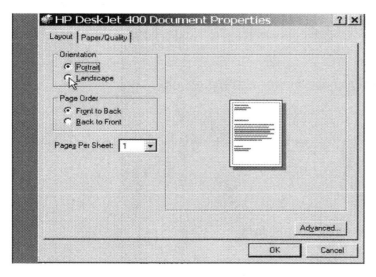

4. Click **Ok** to print.

Chapter

USING MICROSOFT ACCESS AND THE INTERNET

The integration of Microsoft Access with the Internet has extended the capabilities Microsoft Access database. For example it has made it possible to publish information for viewing externally on the Internet or internally on a company's intranet. Users of the Internet can gain access to information in your database by visiting your website or intranet. It has also made it possible to connect to the Internet from a database. For example users of a database can gain access to the Internet by hyperlinks from the database.

Using hyperlinks from your database to gain access to the Internet

A **hyperlink** is a link to another object. A colour or underlined text or picture is often used to show a hyperlink. The text or picture contains the hyperlink address, clicking on the text or picture will connect you to another object for example a web page on the Internet. The hyperlink can also be used to connect users to stored Microsoft document on your local computer and also to send e-mails.

Examples of connections you can make with hyperlinks

http:// Hyper Text Transfer Protocol; opens a web page.

mailto: sends e-mail to a network or Internet address.

File:// opens a local or network file.

ftp:// File Transfer Protocol; links to a FTP server.

Some common terms you may come across

HTML stands for Hyper Text Markup Language. HTML is the format used to store Web Pages. For example all the documents that you create on your computers are stored in a particular format. Word documents are stored in doc format; a web page is stored in HTML format.

The Internet is a vast collection of connected computers. The major component of the Internet is the World Wide World.

Intranet is a network of computers connected to a web site that is available to members of a group or company within a local area network (LAN) or wide area network (WAN). For example a companies website.

URL stands for the words Uniform Resource Locator; In simple terms URL is a web address. Example of a web address is http://www.microsoft.com.

Browser is a program, which enables any computer to read any HTML file. The most common Browsers are Microsoft Internet Explorer, Netscape and Oracle PowerBrowser.

Creating a hyperlink

There are two ways to add a hyperlink to an Access database. They are as follows

• Creating a field in a table and setting its data type as a hyperlink.

• Adding a hyperlink to a form or report.

Adding a hyperlink field to a table

With this method, you create a field in a table and set its data type as a hyperlink. Any valid text entered into this field becomes a hyperlink that you can use to connect to a web page. The hyperlink is associated to the selected record. For example in our product table we can add a field with a hyperlink data type that will link users to the websites of our suppliers.

1. Open the table in **design view**.

2. In the **Field Name** column enter a name for the field you want to add.

3. In the **Data type** column select a hyperlink data type.

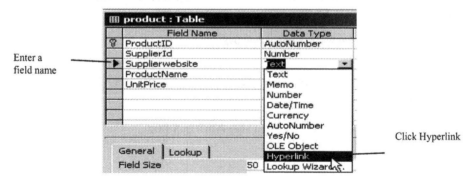

4. Click on the save button to save the table.

Entering data into the hyperlink field

When you enter data into a hyperlink field the hyperlink field automatically formats itself. You can enter the web address of the suppliers into the **supplierwebsite** field in your table.

1. Click on the **view** ▦ button on the toolbar to switch to database base view.

2. Enter a web address in the Supplierwebsite. The data you enter into the hyperlink field becomes a hyperlink. Microsoft Access automatically formats the data you enter into the hyperlink field.

▦ Product1 : Table				
Product ID	Supplier ID	Supplierwebsite	Product Name	Unit Price
2	1	www.Berries.com	Honda Accord	£20,000.00
▶ (AutoNumber)				

Enter a supplier website address in the supplierwebsite field

Using the hyperlink

1. Connect to the Internet or your network.

2. Open the database that contains the table you want to use.

3. Open the table that contains the hyperlink.

4. Click the hyperlink address. The **Internet Explorer** opens and the website of the supplier appears on the screen.

▦ Product1 : Table				
Product ID	Supplier ID	Supplierwebsite	Product Name	Unit Price
2	1	www.Berries.com	Honda Accord	£20,000.00
▶ (AutoNumber)				

http://www.Berries.com

Adding a hyperlink to a form or report.

With this method, a hyperlink is added to a form or report. The hyperlink is not associated to any particular record, but to the entire form or report.

1. Open the form or report in **Design view**.

2. Click the **Insert hyperlink** 🖼 button on the toolbar. The Insert Hyperlink dialog box appears

3. Enter the file or URL to link to in the **Address** box.

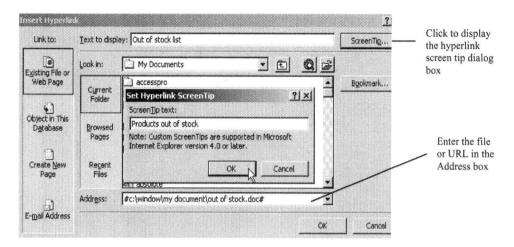

Click to display the hyperlink screen tip dialog box

Enter the file or URL in the Address box

4. Click the **screen tip** button to enter a screen tip text. (optional). Click **ok** to close the screentip dialog box.

5. Click **Ok.** Microsoft Access inserts the hyperlink in the active section. You can move the hyperlink to the position you want it to be.

6. Open the form in form view.

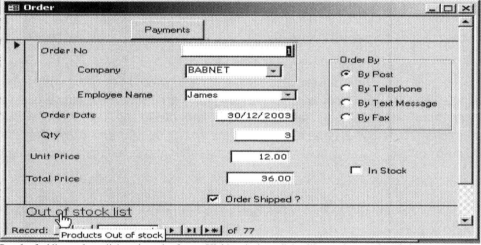

Result of adding an hyperlink to the order form. Clicking the hyperlink will open the out of stock document.

Using the property sheet to specify a hyperlink address

1. Open the form or report in **Design view**.

2. Make sure the Control Wizard is not highlighted. When the Control Wizard is not highlighted it has no box around it.

3. Click on the command button on the toolbar and click on the form or report to insert a command button.

4. Select the command button and click the property button to display the property sheet.

5. Click on the **Format tab.**

6. Type an address in the **Hyperlink Address** text box.

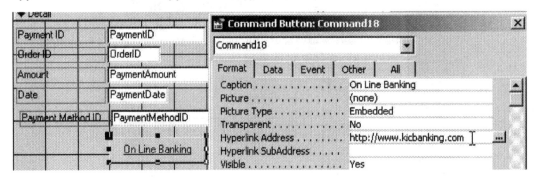

7. Close the **property sheet.** Microsoft Access inserts a hyperlink on the command button. When users click on the command button it will open the website of kicbanking.

Publishing your data on the web

There are two ways you can publish your data on the web. They are using **Static** and **Dynamic** pages.

Using Static pages to publish your data

This is simplest form of publishing your data on the Internet. The way this method works is by converting your objects (forms, tables, queries) into HTML, users will then download and display the data. Data remains static, and users are unable to change or edit records. If you add more records to your table, and want to include the data on the web page, you will have to create the web page again. This method is useful for information that doesn't change quite often. For example we can use this method to publish our product list.

Creating a Static web page

1. In the **Database window,** click on the name of the table, form or query you want to export.

2. Click on **Export** from the **File Menu.** Microsoft Access displays the **Export dialog box.**

3. In the **Save as type** box, select **HTML Documents**

4. In the **Save In** box select the drive or folder you want to export your object to.

5. Select **AutoStart** if you want to display the results in your **default browser**.

6. Click **Export.** The HTML Output dialog box is displayed.

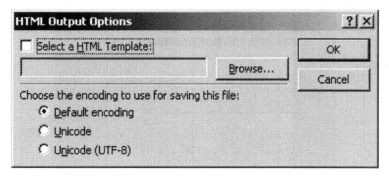

7. Click **Ok**. Microsoft Access exports the object and because you selected **AutoStart** in step 5, when Microsoft finishes exporting the form it will display the **HTML** page in your default browser.

8. Close the **HTML** report.

Using Dynamic pages to publish your data

If you want users to be able to view your data, edit or delete data, you can use Data Access Pages to create your web page. A Data Access Page is a type of web page designed purposely for viewing, editing, adding or deleting data on the Internet or intranet. A Data Access Page is similar to a form in presentation and function. For example it looks like a form and you can use it to view, enter, edit data. It also has the navigational tools for working with forms. Unlike a form the Data Access Page is not stored in the Database. It is stored in an external file, which can be opened in a database as well as a web browser. You will need to transfer both the web page and the data folder to the web server for visitors to view your data as well as your web page.

Creating a Data Access Page

There are about four different ways of creating a Data Access Page.

They are as follows:

*   Create a data access page using Auto Page.

*   Create a data access page with the Page wizard.

*   Use an existing Web Page.

*   Create a data access page in Design view.

Creating a Data Access Page using Auto Page

This method uses all the available fields to create the page.

1. In the Database window, click **Pages** under **Objects.**

2. Click **New.** The **New Data Access Pages** dialog box is displayed.

3. Click **AutoPage: Columnar**

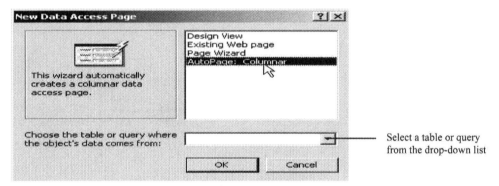
Select a table or query from the drop-down list

4. Select a file or query from the **table or query** drop down list.

5. Click on **Ok.** Microsoft Access displays the Data Access Page

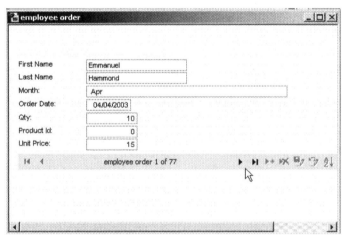
A data Access Page based on Employee Order query

6. Close the **Data Access Page** window. Microsoft Access displays the **Save** dialog box.

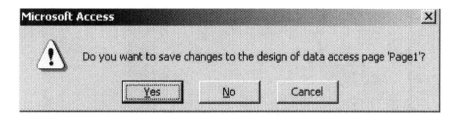

7. Click **Yes.** The **Save As Access Page** dialog box appears. Select the folder you want to save the file and **enter a name** for the Data Access Page.

8. Click **Save.**

    Microsoft Access displays this message. Click **ok** to ignore the message if you are not working on a network.

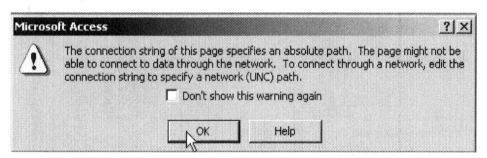

The **UNC Path** is a path that connects the HTML file to the data source. It defines the computer, the drive and folders on which the data source is stored. This is useful if you are working in a network environment.

Microsoft Access saves this page as a Data Access Page and saves an external file containing the data.

Creating a Data Access Page with the Page Wizard

Using the Page Wizard gives you more flexibility than using the AutoPage. For example you can choose the fields you want to include in your page and also the layout of our page.

1. In the Database window, click **Pages** under **Objects.**

2. Click the **New** button on the Database toolbar. The **New Data Access Page** dialog box is displayed.

3. Click **Page Wizard.**

4. Select the table, query and view that contains the data you want to use for your page form the **Choose a tables/Queries** drop-down list.

5. Select the fields you want to include in your **Data Access Page**, from the **Available fields** to the **Selected fields** using > or >> button. Click **Next** to continue.

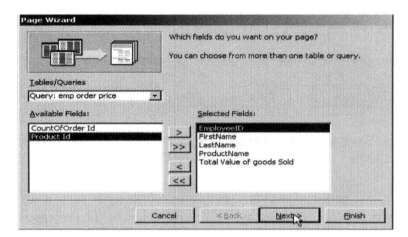

7. If you want to include a group, select the group and click **>** to move the group to the box on your right. Click **Next** to continue.

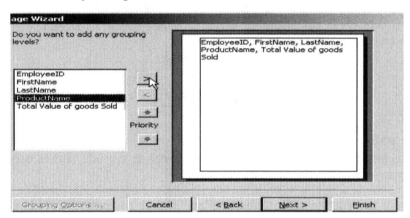

8. Select a sort field and a sort order for your records.

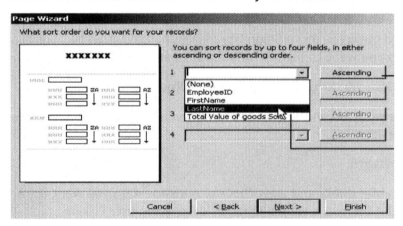

9. Enter a title for your page.

10. If you want to apply a **theme to your page,** Click the box next to **Do you want to apply a theme to your page.** Click **Finish.** Microsoft Access creates the page and displays it in design view.

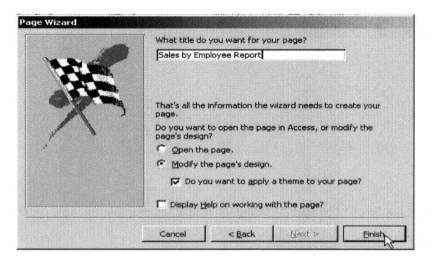

11. If you selected the **Theme** box, Microsoft Access displays the **Theme** dialog box. Click the **Theme** you want to apply and preview in the Preview window.

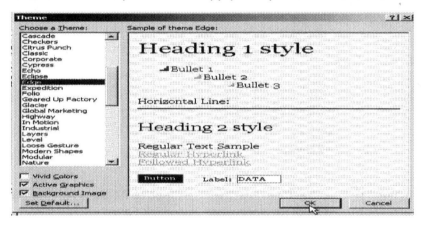

12. Click **Ok.** The new page appears in design view.

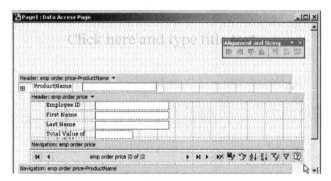

Data Access Page in Design view

13. Click the view ![view icon] button to change to **Page view.**

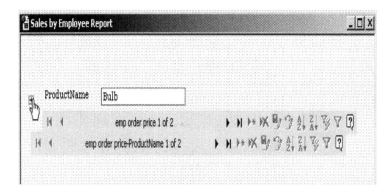

14. click the + button to the left of **Product Name** to display the full record.

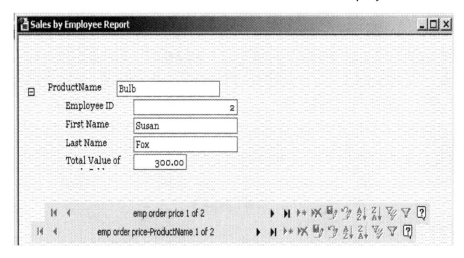

15. Click the **Save** **Button** to save the file. The **Save As Data Access Page** dialog box appears. Enter a name for your page and click **Save.**

16. Click **Ok.**

Creating a Data Access Page in Design view

1.   In the Database window click **Pages** under **Object.**

2.   Click the **New** button on the **Database window toolbar**.

Microsoft Access opens **the New Data Access Page** dialog box.

3.   Click **Design view.**

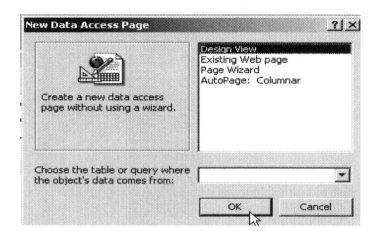

4. Select a table/query or view from the **table or query** drop-down list.

   If you want to create a blank form, don't choose any table/query or view.

5. Click **Ok**. Microsoft Access displays the following warning about creating a Data Access Page using this version. Click **Ok** to continue.

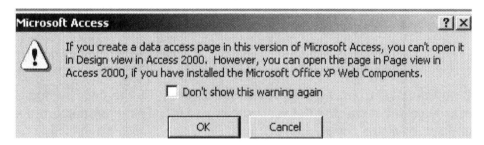

6. Microsoft Access displays the **Data Access Page** in Design view. You can customize the page to suit your purpose.

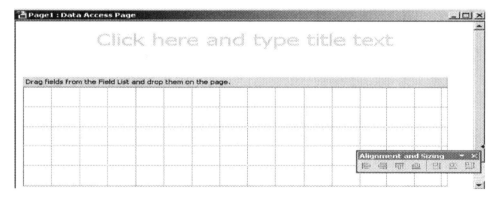

Modifying a Data Access Page

1. Click on the field list button on the toolbar. Microsoft Access displays all the tables in your tables and queries in the database.

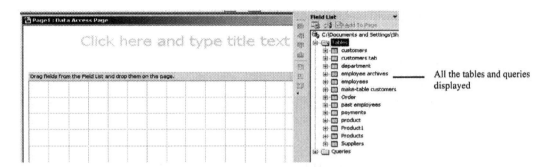

All the tables and queries displayed

2. Click on the + sign next to the table/query you want to include on your page. All the fields in the table are displayed.

3. Select the field(s) you want to include on your page.

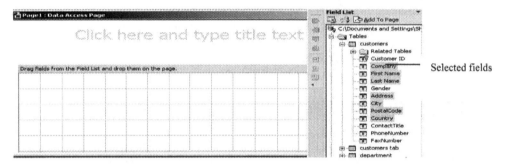

Selected fields

4. Drag the fields from the field list and drop them on the page. You can move, rearrange and resize the fields. You can also modify the properties of any of the controls or of the page itself.

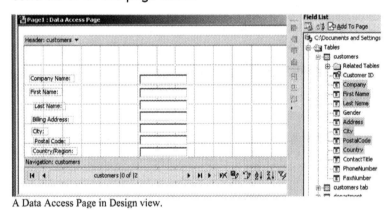

A Data Access Page in Design view.

5. Click the **view** button to view the page.

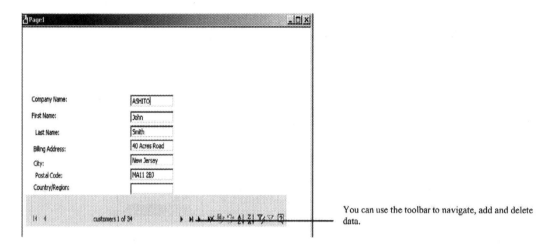

You can use the toolbar to navigate, add and delete data.

Viewing or modifying records

You can use the same techniques for viewing and modifying forms, to view and modify records in a data access page. For example you can add records to the Data Access Page. Follow the steps below to add records to the **Data Access Page**.

Add New Records

1. Click the **New Record** button on the **toolbar.** Microsoft Access displays a blank record.

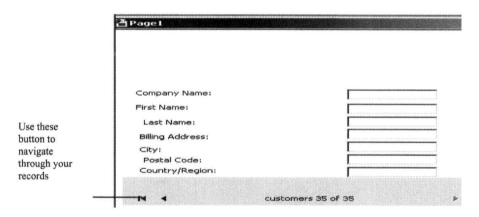

Use these button to navigate through your records

2. Click inside the field you want to enter the data.

3. Enter the Data and press the **Tab key** to move to the next field. When you come to the end of the record, Press the **Tab** key to move to the next record.

Using properties to format controls

1. Double-click the control. The property sheet is displayed.

2. Click on **Format** tab.

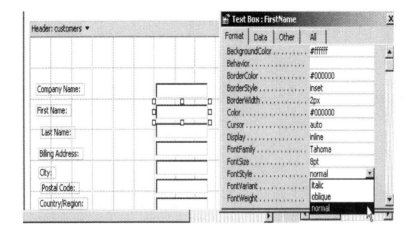

3.   Click the box next to the property you want to change.

4.   Enter a value or select a value from the drop-down list.

Example

You can customize the toolbar using the property sheet.

To show or hide the toolbar using the property sheet

You can show or hide the toolbar depending on how you want to present information to users. Some people hide the toolbar so they can have more room to display the page.

To show or Hide the toolbar

1.   Double click the toolbar. The property sheet is displayed.

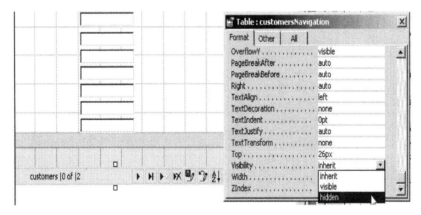

2.   Click on the **Visibility** property.   Click **Visible** to display the toolbar; **Hidden** to hide the toolbar.

If you choose **Hidden** the toolbar will disappear.

Show or Hide a tool on the toolbar

By default users should be able to view, add, delete data on the page, but you can hide some of the tool buttons on the toolbar to restrict the activities of users on your page.

For example you can hide the **Delete** and **Add** button on the toolbar so that users can only view records on your page. .

To show/hide a tool on the toolbar

1. Double-click the tool you want to hide.

Double-click the tool you want to hide.

2. Click the **Visibility** property.

3. Select **Hidden** to hide the property.

4. Click the view button to view the page. The tool disappears from the toolbar. Users will not be able to add data to the page. Follow the same steps to hide the **Delete** tool.

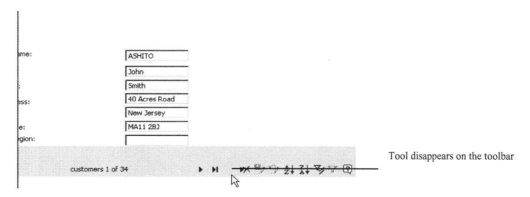
Tool disappears on the toolbar

Saving a page

1. Click the Save 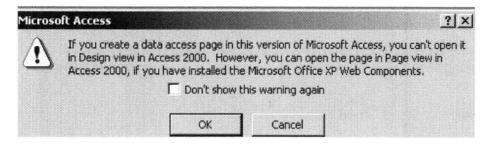 button on the Design Toolbar.

2. The Save As Data Access Page dialog box appears.

3. Enter a name for your page and click the **Save button.**

    Microsoft Access displays the following dialog box.

> **Microsoft Access**
>
> ⚠ If you create a data access page in this version of Microsoft Access, you can't open it in Design view in Access 2000. However, you can open the page in Page view in Access 2000, if you have installed the Microsoft Office XP Web Components.
>
> ☐ Don't show this warning again
>
> [OK]   [Cancel]

4. Click **Ok.**

Show/Hide a records in Page View

When a page is organized in a group, the group appears with a positive sign before it. All the detail records are not displayed. You can **Show/hide** the records in a group by following the steps below. For example the Customer Order Query Page displayed below.

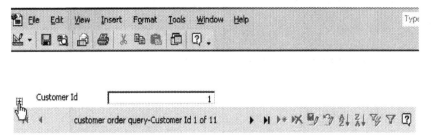

To show or hide records in a group in Page View

1. Click the + sign to show records in the group

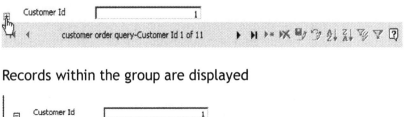

Records within the group are displayed

Customer Id	1
Order Id:	24
Order Date:	02/01/2004
First Name	Samuel
Last Name	Payne
Billing Address	12 Tollgate Road
Qty:	4
Unit Price:	£11.00

customer order query 1 of 7

customer order query-Customer Id 1 of 11

or

Click the – sign to hide records in the group.

Customize a Group

You can use **ExpandedByDefault** property in the property sheet to set the default view of a grouping Page View. This means that you don't have to expand the group when you view the page.

1. Right click the **Group Header.**

2. Select the **Group Level Properties** as indicated below.

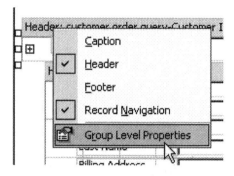

3. Select **True** for the **ExpandedByDefault** property in the property sheet.

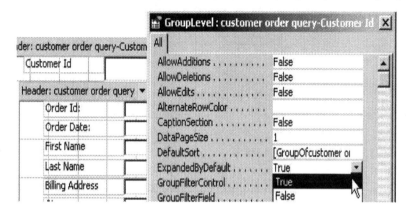

4. Click the **view** button to view the page. The group is displayed with all the records when you click the view.

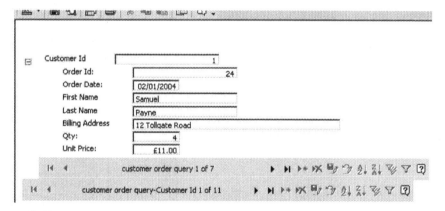

Customizing a section

You can customize a section in many ways for example you could change the section height. Follow the steps below to change the section's height.

1. Right click the section you want to customize.

2. Select **Section Properties** form the list displayed.

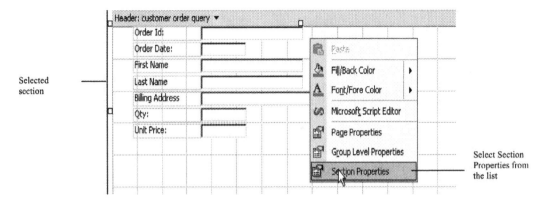

3.   Enter a value for the height and Press the **Enter** key.

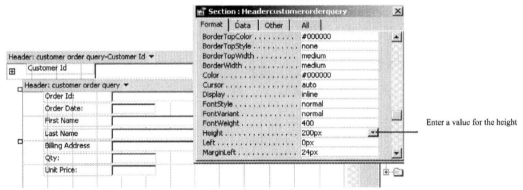

The height of the section is changed to reflect the changes.

Customize a page

You can customize a page in many ways. For example you could change the **title** of a page.   You could also change the **DataEntry** property to True to use a page only for data entry. Follow the steps below to change the page title of a page.

1.   Right click on the page.

2.   Select **Page Properties** from the list displayed.

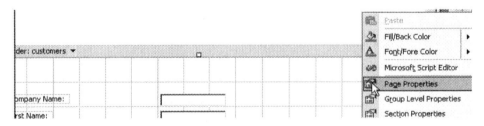

3. Click the **Other** Tab and click inside the **Title** property and enter a new title for the page.

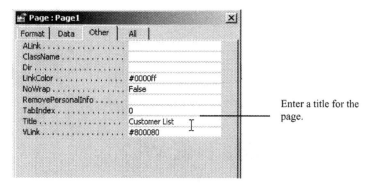

Enter a title for the page.

Chapter

ANALYSING YOUR DATA ON THE WEB

On the Internet you can analyse data on your web pages by using the Pivot Table and Pivot Chart.

A **Pivot Table** is a data analysis tool used to analyse data on the web. Data in a Pivot table are presented in rows and columns like a table. The table is interactive in that users can pick and choose different view to analyse the data in the database. A Pivot Table is connected to database, therefore any changes you make to your database is immediately reflected in the pivot table.

To create a pivot table on a Data Access Page

1. In the **Database window**, click **Pages** under **Objects**.

2. Double-click the **Create data access page in Design view.**

    Microsoft Access displays the following warning.

    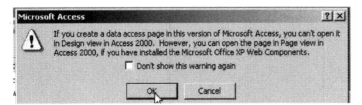

3. Click **Ok.**

    A blank data access page is open in Design view.

4. Click the **PivotTable** button on the toolbar. If the **PivotTable** button is not displayed click the toolbox to display all the tools.

5. Click the upper-left corner of the data access page where you want to position the pivot table. Microsoft Access displays a pivot table frame on your page.

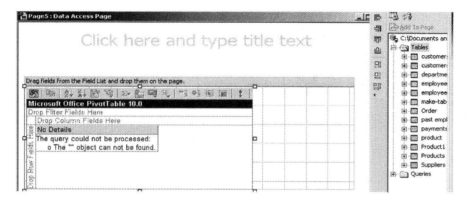

6. Choose a data source for your pivot table. For this example the data source is from a query, so click the + sign next to the **Queries** folder to display all the queries in your database. Select the query you want to use from the list of queries displayed.

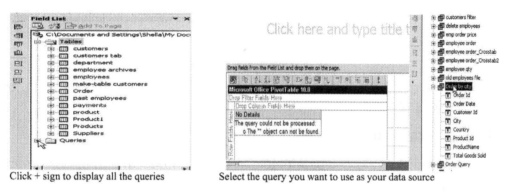

Click + sign to display all the queries   Select the query you want to use as your data source

7. Drag the field you want to use as the filter field in this example drag the (City field) from the **Field list** to the horizontal box labelled **Drop Filter Fields here.**

8. Drag the field you want to display as row in this example (Product Name) from the field list to the vertical box labelled **Drop Row Fields** here.

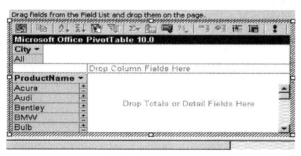

9. Drag the field you want to display as columns from the field list to the horizontal box labelled **Drop column Fields here.**

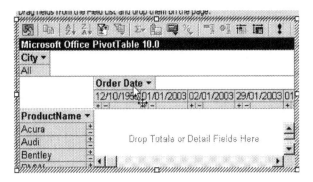

10. Drag the field whose value you want to display as **Totals** or **Details** to the **Drop totals or Details Fields Here.** Drag **Total Goods Sold** to the box labelled **Drop Totals or Details Fields Here.**

11. Click on view to view your page.

Formatting the Order Date column

You can format the Order Date column so that it displays the date by month, instead of displaying a long list of dates.

To display the Order Date in month format

1. Right click the Order Date field and select **Command and options** from the list.

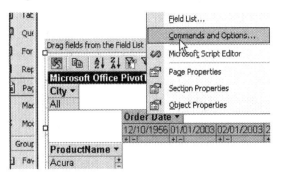

2. Click on the **Filter and Group** tab. The **Command and options** dialog box is displayed. Select **Months** from the **Group items by** box.

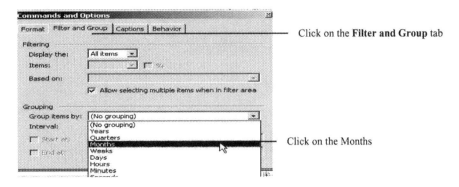

3. Click on **View** to see the pivot table displayed in **Page view**

City ▾									
All									
		Order Date ▾							
			Mar		Apr		May		Jun
			+ −		+ −		+ −		+ −
ProductName ▾	d: ▾	Total Good: ▾		Total Good: ▾		Total Good: ▾		Total Good:	
Audi	±							15	
Bentley	±					100000			
BMW	±					183330			
Bulb	±		200		225				
Cadilac	±								

4. Click the **Save** button to save the page. Name it **Order by city**.

Using a chart to analyse your data

As the saying goes a picture is better than thousands of words and figures. With a chart you can present data visually and people can easily understand the trend and changes in your data without much difficulty. In Access 2003 you can use the Pivot Chart to create charts on your Data Access Page.

The Pivot Chart

The Pivot Chart is a data analysis tool used to present data visually in charts. Like a pivot table a Pivot Chart is interactive and is connected to a database. Because the chart is connected to your database any changes you make to your database is updated immediately on your chart.

To create a pivot chart on your Data Access Page

1. Open a **Data Access Page** in **Design View.**

2. Click the **Office Chart** tool [📊] on the toolbar.

3. Click and drag the office chart tool onto the **Data Access Page.** The mouse pointer changes to a rectangle. Draw a rectangle box the size you want on the Data Access Page. You can position it below the Pivot Table.

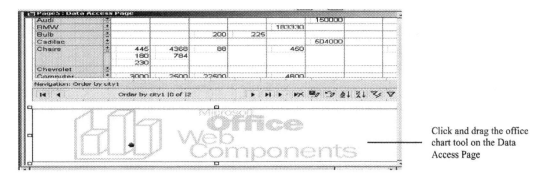

Click and drag the office chart tool on the Data Access Page

4. Click the frame to display the **Command and Options** dialog box.

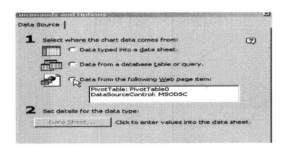

5. Select **Data from the following Web page item**.

6. Select **DataSourceControl:MSODSC.**

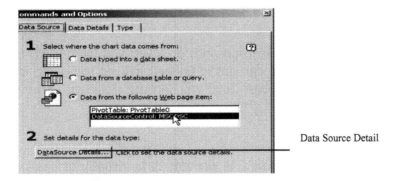

Data Source Detail

7. Click the **DataSource Detail** tab and click on **Data member, table, view or cube name.**

8. Select a table or query from the drop-down list.

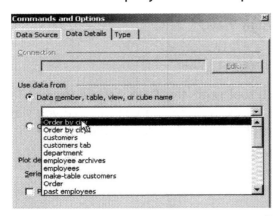

9. Click on the **Type** tab and select the type of chart you want to create from the category box on the left and select from the available options on the right box.

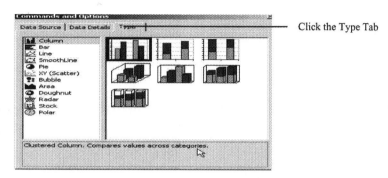

Click the Type Tab

10. Close the **Command and Option** dialog box.

11. Drag the **City** field from the **field list** to the box labelled **Drop Filter Fields Here**.

12. Drag the **ProductName** field from the **field list** to the box labelled **Drop Category Fields Here**.

13. Drag **OrderDate** field to the box labelled **Drop Series Here**. To format the Order date field to months i.e. Jan, Feb, etc., right click the **OrderDate** field and select **Command and Options** from the list. Click the **Group and Filter** tab and select Months from the drop-down list under Months. Close the **Command and Options** box.

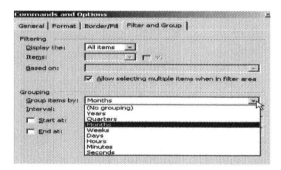

14. Drag **Total Goods Sold** to the box labelled **Drop Data Fields Here**.

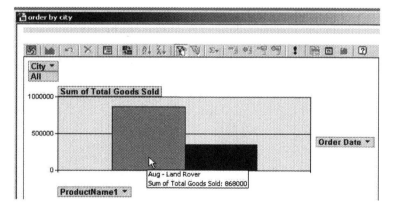

15. Resize the chart the way you want it.

16. Click **Save** to save the **Page.**

17. Close the page.

You can experiment by selecting different products and different months and different cities.

Chapter

TURNING YOUR DATABASE INTO AN APPLICATION

In most cases the people who would use the database do not have much experience with databases. You can make it easier for them to use your database by turning it into an application. When you turn your database into an application, the different tasks in your database are organised into Menus and users will just click a menu and perform a task.

For example in our Order Database System, we could organise our database into the following menu.

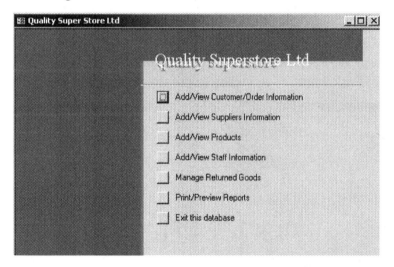

Users will just have to click the menu and perform a task. For example if a user wants to enter data into the Order table, they don't have to worry themselves about how to open the table, they will just click from the available menu to carry out the operation. Microsoft Access will open the table and they can enter information into the order table.

Apart from making it easier for users and colleagues to use your database, the information in your database will be safer and secured. Users can mess around with the objects in your database, for example they can delete your table deliberately or accidentally when working in the Database window. You can prevent this from happening if you automate all the tasks.

To make it easier for users to use your database and to prevent users from messing about with your database, you can create a **Switchboard** and **Startup** form, which will open each time you open your database. For this example we want to create a switchboard that will enable users to enter and view orders, retrieve information about orders and print reports. Also users should be able to enter other information like product information etc. Our Switchboard should look like the above menu when finish.

Create a Switchboard

In Microsoft Access you can create a switchboard by using the **Switchboard Manager** in the **Tool Menu**.

Creating a Switchboard by using the Switchboard Manager

1. Open the database.

2. From the **Tools Menu** select **Database Utilities** and click on **Switchboard Manager.**

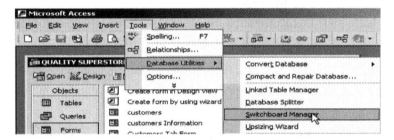

If this is the first time you are creating a switchboard Microsoft Access displays the following message and ask whether you want to create one. Click **Yes**.

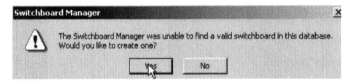

The switchboard Manager dialog box appears

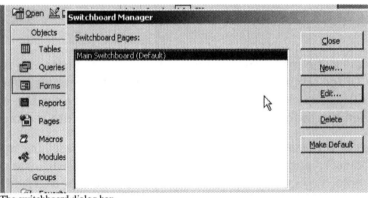

The switchboard dialog box

3. Click **Edit**. Type a name in the **Switchboard Name box**. The next step is to add switchboard items to the switchboard that you have created.

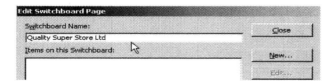

4. Click **New.** The **Edit Switchboard Item** dialog appears. This dialog box is used to enter the items that will appear on the switchboard. For example one of the items we want to appear on the main switchboard is **Add/View Orders**.

5. Enter **Add/View Orders** in the **Text Box.**

6. Click the drop-down list next to **Command** and select a command from the **Command box.**

   Select **Open Form in Edit Mode.** The command you select depends on the **Object** you want to open and how want to use it. For example to open a form you can edit, select Open Form in Edit Mode.

   Press the **Tab key** to move to the next box.

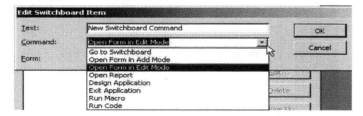

7. Select the form you want to open when this item is clicked on the Switchboard.

   Click **Ok.** For example if you want to open the Order form, select Order from the list of forms displayed.

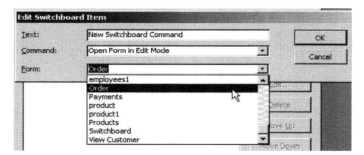

8. Repeat steps 4-7 until you have added all the items to the switchboard.

   To create a switchboard item that will return you to a switchboard, select **Go to Switch board** from the **Command** list, and select the name of the switchboard to go to from the **Switchboard** box. This command is useful for switchboard item like **Return to Switchboard**.

To create a **Switchboard** item that will close the database and exit the application, select **Exit application** from the **Command** drop-down list.

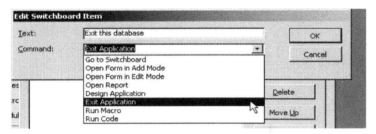

9.   When you finish creating the switchboard items click the **Close** button.

To view the switchboard

1.   In the Database window, double-click **Switchboard**. The **Switchboards** opens.

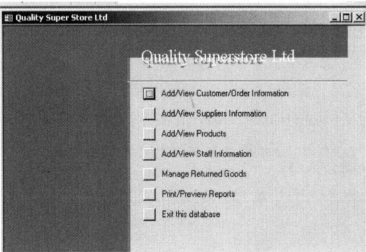

The Quality Superstore Switchboard

You can create the switchboard above with the following **Commands** and **Text**

Main Switchboard

Switchboard Item	Text Box	Command Box	Name of Object to select

Add/View Customer/Order Information	Add/View Customer/Order Information	Open Form In Edit Mode	Customer Tab Form
Add/View Supplier Information	Add/View Supplier Information	Open Form In Edit Mode	Suppliers
Add/View Products	Add/View Products	Open form In Edit Mode	Product
Add/View Staff Information	Add/View Staff Information	Open Form In Edit Mode	Employees
Manage Returned	Manage Returned	Open Form In Edit Mode	Goods Returned
Goods Preview/ Print Reports	Goods Preview/ Print Reports	Go To Switchboard	Report Menu The report menu is another switchboard

The Report Menu is another switchboard with various items on it.

The Report Menu

Switchboard Item	Text Box	Command Box	Name of Object to Select
Print/Preview Customers Orders	Print/Preview Customers Orders	Open Report	Customer by Orders Report
Preview/Print Daily Order Report	Preview/Print Daily Order Report	Open Report	Daily Order Report
Preview Employees Sales Report	Preview Employees Sales Report	Open Report	Sales by City Report
Preview Products List	Preview Products List	Open Report	Product List
Print/Preview Returned Goods	Print/Preview Returned Goods List	Open Report	Returned Goods List
Return To Main Menu	Return To Main Menu	Go To Switchboard	Quality Super Store Ltd

Example

To create the Report Menu switchboard and add the following items to the switchboard follow the steps below.

1.   Open the database.

2. From the **Tools Menu** select **Database Utilities** and click on **Switchboard Manager.** The Switchboard manager appears on screen.

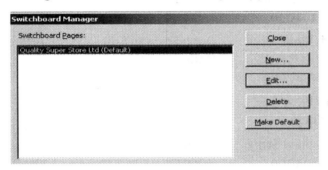

3. Click on **New.**

4. Enter a name for the **Switchboard Page** and click **Ok.**

5. Click on Report Menu in the **Switchboard Manager** dialog box.

Adding Items to the Report Menu.

6. Click on **Edit.**

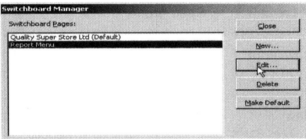

The Switchboard Manager dialog box

The **Edit Switchboard** appears.

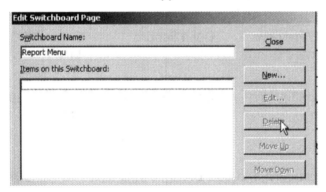

6. Click on **New.** The **Edit Switchboard Item** is displayed on your screen.

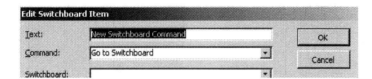

7. Enter the text you want to appear on the Switchboard Item Page in the **Text** box.

8. Click the drop-down list in the **Command** box and select a command i.e. **Open Report**. Depending on the option you select from the **Command** box another box or a **Third box** is displayed.

   If for example you want to open another switchboard, select **Go to Switchboard** and select the switchboard you want to open from the **Switchbaord** drop-down list.

9. If you select **Open Report** in step 8, then select the name of the report from the Third Box i.e. from the **Report Box**.

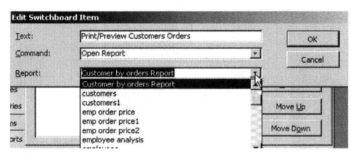

10. Click **Ok**.

11. Repeat steps 6-9 until you finish entering all the items you want to appear in the Report Switchboard.

12. When you finish, click **Close**.

Working with your switchboard

From the switchboard you can select any of options displayed to perform the action you require.

Example

Suppose you want to enter information about a customer, you can click on "**Add/View Customer Information**" on the Switchboard, Microsoft Access will open the **Customer Tab** form.

The customer Tab form in Edit Mode.

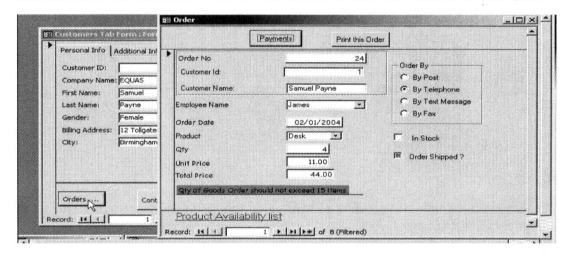

When you click on the Order button on the customer tab form, Microsoft Access opens the Orders relating the customer displayed. If no orders exist for this customer, a blank order form appears on screen, you can enter orders for this customer on the blank form. You can also click the **Add button** on the toolbar to add new records to the form.

The Report Menu

On the switchboard, clicking on Preview/Print Reports will open the report menu. The **Report Menu** is a sub-switchboard within the Preview/Print Reports Menu.

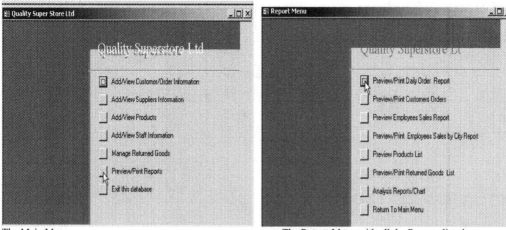

The Main Menu   The Report Menu with all the Reports listed

When you click on **Preview/Print Daily Report** on the **Report menu**, the **Daily Order Report** will open in Preview form. You can click on the **Print** button to print the **Daily Order Report.**

Click on the Print button to print the report

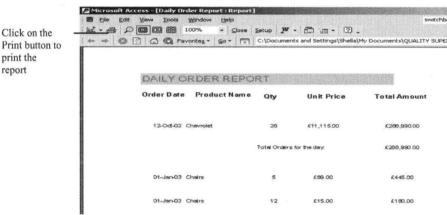

The Daily Order Report in preview

Customize a Switchboard

You can customize a switchboard by creating a new switchboard, deleting and editing the switchboard. You can also customise the items in a switchboard by adding a new item, deleting an item, editing an item or moving items in a switchboard.

To create a new switchboard Page

1. In the Database window, click on **Tools,** select **Database Utilities** and click on **Switchboard Manager**. The **Switchboard Manager** dialog box appears.

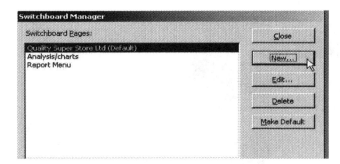

2. Click on the **New** button.

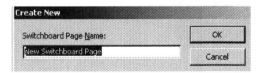

3. Enter a name in the **Switchboard Page Name**.

To edit a switchboard

1. In the Database window, click on **Tools,** select **Database Utilities** and click on **Switchboard Manager**. The **Switchboard Manager** dialog box appears.

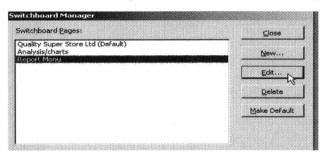

2. Click on the **Switchboard Page** you want to edit, and click on the **Edit** button. Edit the text in the **Switchboard Name** box.

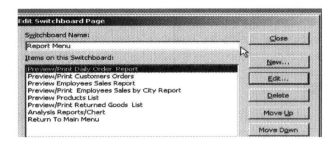

3. Click on **Close** button.

To Delete a Switchboard

1. In the Database window, click on **Tools,** select **Database Utilities** and click on **Switchboard Manager**. The **Switchboard Manager** dialog box appears.

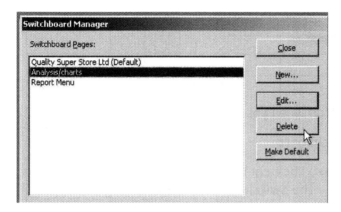

2. Click on the **Switchboard Page** you want to delete, and click on the **Delete** button.

3. Click on **Close** button when you finish.

To edit items on the Switchboard

1. In the Database window, click on **Tools,** select **Database Utilities** and click on **Switchboard Manager**. The **Switchboard Manager** dialog box appears.

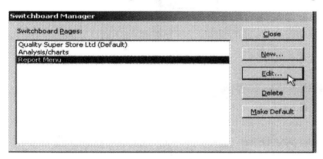

2. Click on the **Switchboard Page, which** contains the items you want to edit, then click on the **Edit** button.

3. Select the **Switchboard item** you want to edit from the box labelled **Items on this Switchboard.**

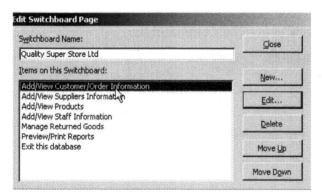

4. Click on **Edit**. Make the changes you want. You can edit text in the **Text** Box; select another command from the **Command** box or the **Report** box. When you finish making the changes, click on **Ok** to close the box.

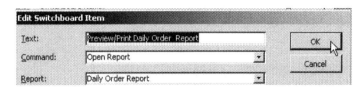

5.   Click on the **Close** button when you finish.

To add a new item to the switchboard

1.   In the Database window, click on **Tools,** select **Database Utilities** and click on **Switchboard Manager.** The **Switchboard Manager** dialog box appears.

2.   Click on the **Switchboard Page** you want to add an item on, and then click on the **Edit** button.

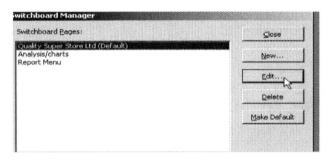

3.   Click on **New.**

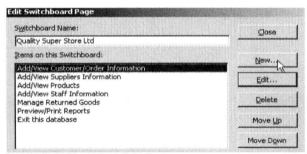

The Edit Switchboard Page dialog box

4.   Enter a text in the **Text box,** Select a command from the **Command** box and select an item from the box below the **Command** box.

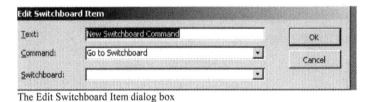

The Edit Switchboard Item dialog box

5.   Click on **Ok.**

To delete a switchboard item

1.   In the Database window, click on **Tools,** select **Database Utilities** and click on **Switchboard Manager.** The **Switchboard Manager** dialog box appears.

2. Click on the **Switchboard Page** that contains the item you want to delete, click on the **Edit** button.

3. Select the item you want to delete from the box labelled **Items on this Switchboard:**

4. Click on the **Delete** button.

   The **Switchboard Manager** displays the delete dialog box; click **Yes** to delete the item.

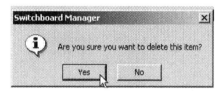

Move an item

1. In the Database window, click on **Tools,** select **Database Utilities** and click on **Switchboard Manager.** The **Switchboard Manager** dialog box appears.

2. Click on the **Switchboard Page** that contains the item you want to move, click on the **Edit** button.

3. Select the item you want to move from the box labelled **Items on this Switchboard:**

4. To move the item up, click on **Move Up,** to move the item down, click on **Move Down.**

Startup Form

Another way of making your database easier for users who are less proficient with Access database is to create a **Startup form.** A **Startup form** is a simple form with settings, which automatically opens your database. It is the first form that opens when users open the application.

You can use the **startup** form to open your database by adding command buttons to the Startup form, when users click on the command button it opens your database. You can also use a **Startup form** to display useful information to the user, display copyright agreement or instructions about how to use the program.

To display the **Startup** Form Automatically, you need to first create the **Startup** form and set up the options that display the Startup form automatically. Follow the steps below to create the StartUp form and set the options for displaying the form automatically.

Example

In this example the **startup** form that we will create, will display the company logo with two command buttons, **Continue** and **Quit.** Clicking on the continue button will open the switchboard, clicking on the Quit button will quit the application.

To create a Startup Form

1. In the **Database window**, click on **Forms** under **Objects**.

2. Click **New**.

3. Click on **Design view,** and then click on **Ok.**

   A blank form appears on your screen.

4. Add text and any images or logo you want to display on the **startup form**.

Add images and
logo to your form

Add text

(Optional) Customise the form by double-clicking on the **Form Selector** and making changes to the settings in the property sheet. For example you can decide to remove the scrollbar, and the Navigation bar from the form since you are not showing any record on this form, To remove the scroll bar and the Navigation bar, Click inside the **Navigation Buttons** box and select **No** from the form property box, click inside the **Scroll Bars** box select **Neither** from the form property sheet.

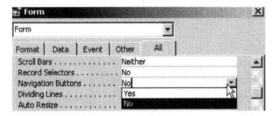

Click the **Save** button to save the form as **Start Up.**

Creating the Continue command button

5. Make sure the control wizardis [icon] highlighted, and click on the **Command button** [icon] tool on the toolbar.

6. Click on the form where you want to display the command button. Microsoft Access opens the **Command Button Wizard.**

7. In the box labelled **Categories**, select **form Operations**. In the box labelled **Actions** select **Open Forms** and click **Next** to continue.

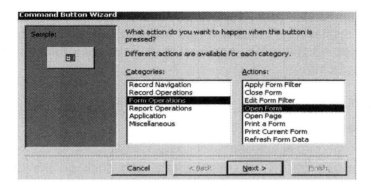

Microsoft Access displays a box with a list of all the forms in your database.

8. Select **Switchboard** from the list of forms and click **Next**.

9. Accept the default settings to open the form and show all the records. Click **Next**.

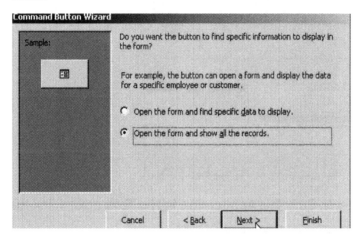

10. Click on **Text** and enter **Continue** in the **Text** box. Click **Next**.

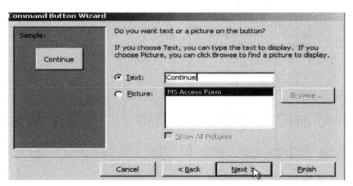

11. When Microsoft Access requests a name for the button enter **Continue** and click **Finish**. Microsoft Access adds a button with the caption **Continue** on your form. This button will be used to open the **switchboard** form, which gives users access to your database.

Creating the Quit button

You must create another command button, for users who want to quit the program as soon as the **startup** form is displayed. Probably, these users think they can't follow the instructions displayed or selected the wrong application or have something else to do. This button will close the application.

To create Quit command button

1. Open the form in **Design view**.

2. Make sure the control wizardis ![wizard icon] highlighted, and click on the **Command button** ![button icon] tool on the toolbar.

3. Click on the form where you want to display the command button. Microsoft Access opens the **Command Button Wizard**.

4. In the box labelled **Categories**, select **Application**. In the box labelled **Actions** select **Quit** and click **Next** to continue.

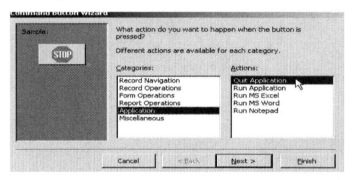

5. Click on **Text** and enter **Quit this Application** in the **Text** box. Click **Next**.

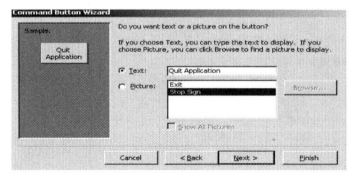

6. When Microsoft Access requests a name for the button enter **Quit** and click **Finish**.

   Use the label button on the toolbar to enter the text "**To continue click Continue and to quit this application click on Quit this Application**".

   Your startup form may look like this.

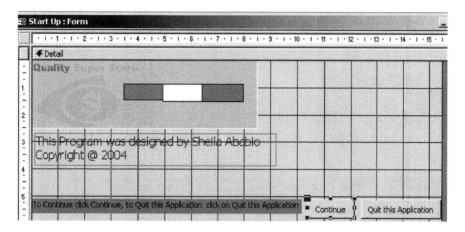

To set up options that will display the Start Up form automatically

Now that you have created your startup form, you need to set up options to display the startup form automatically.

1. Click on **Startup** on the **Tool Menu**. Microsoft Access displays the **Startup** dialog box.

2. Enter a title for your application in the box labelled **Application Title**.

3. Select the **Start Up** form, in the box labelled **Display Form/Page:**

4. **(Optional)** if you want to display an icon for your application, specify the path. If you don't know where the icon is stored on your computer, click on the **icon browser** and locate your icon.

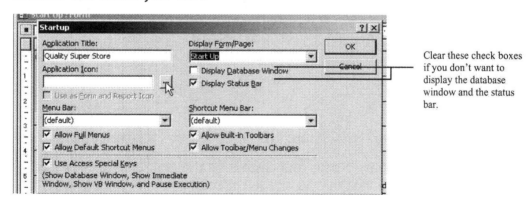

5. Accept the other default settings and click on **Ok**.

Use any of the methods described in this book to open your database. For example click on **File** and click on **Quality Super Store**.

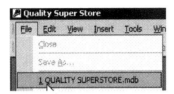

The startup form is displayed. Clicking on the **Continue** button will display the switchboard; clicking on the **Quit this Application** button will close the application.

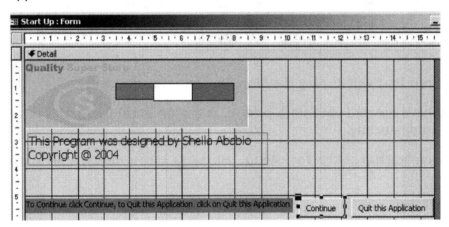

Displaying your database on the desktop

Another way of making your database application easier to use by users who are less proficient with Access Database is to put the database on your Desktop. Users will just double-click the application icon and the database will be open.

To put your database on the desktop

1. Open **Windows explorer.**

2. Click the file you want to move to the **Desktop** i.e. click on **Quality Superstore.**

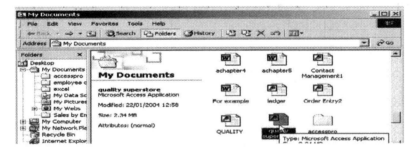

3. Drag the file to the **Desktop.** The file appears on the **Desktop.**

    You can also copy the file and paste it on the desktop. To copy the file onto the desktop, right-click the file and select copy.

4. Minimize all the programs and right click the **Desktop,** select **Paste** from the list displayed.

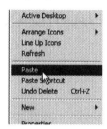

The file appears on your desktop. Users who do not have any experience with Access could just double-click quality superstore and the database will be open.

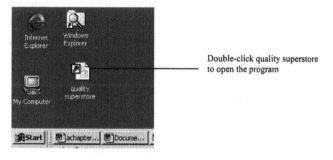

Double-click quality superstore to open the program

SHARING DATA AND SECURING YOUR DATABASE

Sharing Data in a network environment

A database may contain information useful to different departments or operations in the company. Thus, different departments may need to access the database. For example the sales department may need information about sales, the human resources team may need information about employees and their salaries. As different departments and users access the database, it may so happen that different users may want to access the database at the same time. Users can access the same database at the same time if working in a network environment. In a network environment many users can work with one database at the same time.

Sharing Data

There are many ways of sharing data with other users, for example you can share the entire database on the network server or share only the tables in a database. The most common way of sharing data is to put the entire database on a network server. When you put the entire database on a network server, more than one person can open the database at the same time. Also more than one person can work with the database in different ways for example one person can be viewing data and another person may be changing or adding data in the same database. Like anything you share there are often conflicts and there must be a way of resolving or avoiding these conflicts. This chapter will explain how data can be shared in a multi-user environment.

Ways of sharing data

There are many ways of sharing a database with other users in a network environment. Some of ways are:

- **Share the entire database**

The easiest way is to put the entire database in a network server or shared folder. With this method there is consistency; everyone shares the same data and objects in the database.

- **Share only tables in the database**

You can put the tables in a network server and the rest of the other objects i.e. forms and reports etc. on the users computer. This method increases performance.

Opening an Access Database in a shared or exclusive mode

You can open your database in a shared or exclusive mode. To allow users to share the database on a network environment the database must be open in a shared mode.

Opening your database in shared mode allows other users to share your database. Opening the database in exclusive mode gives access only to only one person at a time.

Setting up options to open a database in shared or exclusive mode

1. Click **Options** in the Toolbar. The **Options dialog** box is displayed.

2. Click the **Advanced Tab.**

3. In the **Default Open mode** box, select the option you want. For example if you want others to be able to open the database whilst you have opened it click **Shared,** if you want one person to be given access to a database at a time click **Exclusive.**

4. Click **Ok.**

Editing Data in a multi-user environment

Sharing data in a multi-user environment is excellent and economical, however, there are often problems with editing and updating records in a multi-user environment. For example, there may be situations where more than one person may try to edit the same record. This can cause a lot of problems. To avoid this conflicting situation, you can customize your environment to resolve this problem. For example you can set the multi-user option to **Edited Record** so that a record is lock while a user edits the record. Microsoft Access also informs you about the status of a record when editing by displaying the following current record symbols.

Current Records Status

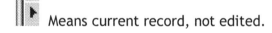 Means current record, not edited.

Means current record is being edited or record has been edited but not saved.

Record is locked by another user, therefore cannot be edited.

Example of a record displaying a locked record status

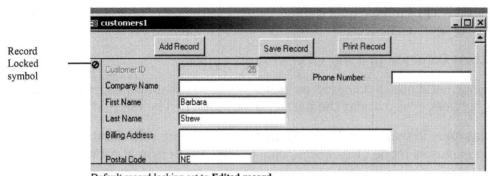

Record
Locked
symbol

Default record locking set to **Edited record**

Setting up options for editing in a multi-user environment

You can set up editing options to prevent another user from gaining access to the record that you are editing. Follow the steps below to set options for editing in a multi-user environment.

1. From the Tools Menu, click on **Options**. The **Options dialog box** is displayed.

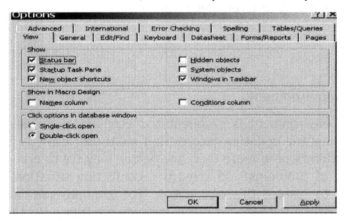

2. Click the **Advanced Tab**.

3. In the **Default record locking** box, select the option you want.

    No locks: is the default setting, it allows others to edit and overwrite the same record you are editing.

    Edited record locks the record you are editing so that no other user can change the record.

    All records: lock all the records in a form or datasheet for the period you have open the record. No one else can open or lock the record.

    Select **Edited record** to lock the record you are editing so that no one can change the record whilst you are editing it.

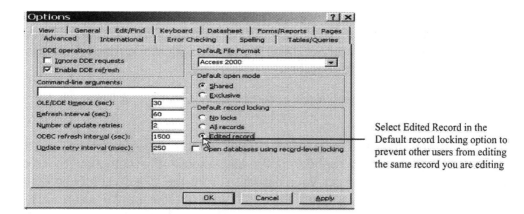

Select Edited Record in the Default record locking option to prevent other users from editing the same record you are editing

4.   Click **Ok.**

Examples of setting default record locking to No locks

When you set the **Default record locking** to **No locks,** Microsoft will allow you to edit the record and give you the chance to overwrite the changes made to the record.

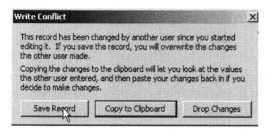

Example of setting default record locking to edited record

When you set the default record locking to **Edited record**, Microsoft will not allow another person to edit the same record. It displays the stop record symbol. Only that record is lock.

Record Locked symbol

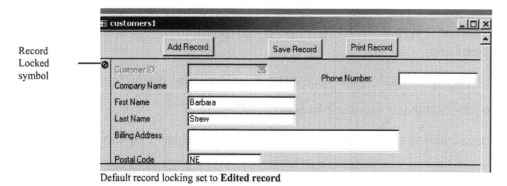

Default record locking set to **Edited record**

Examples of setting default record locking to All Records

When you set default record locking to **All Records,** all the records in a form are locked for as long as long as the form is open. Use this sparingly.

Securing your database

Caution: This section is for advance users; if you are a novice please skip this section. This is because if you don't set your password for your database correctly, you may not be able to gain access to your database. Also if you lose your Workgroup information file you may not be able to access your database.

This topic involves setting passwords and user level security. A Database Administrator usually does this job.

Security is a very important issue in any organization using a database. Unauthorized access to data can breach confidentiality and expose the company to competitors. Securing a database can protect your database from malicious users who may want to make changes to your codes and design to ruin your database application. Also securing your database can protect sensitive data in your database. There are many ways of protecting your database from unauthorized access. For example you can use a password or user level security measures to secure your database.

Protecting your database with a Password

The easiest way to prevent unauthorized access and changes to your database is to assign a password to it. Anyone who tries to open the database will be asked for a password, if they enter the right password they will have access to the database, if not they will not be allowed access. When setting and removing a password you must open the database in **Exclusive mode**. After you set the password for the database, you can open the database in shared mode.

Setting a password

If you are working in a multi-user environment, make sure all users have closed their database. Also make a backup copy of your database, should you forget your password or lose your password. The first step is to open the database in Exclusive mode and then setting up the password.

1. Click on the **Open** tool on the Access toolbar. The Open dialog box appears.

2. Click on the database you want to open.

3. Click on the down-arrow next to **Open,** and click on **Open Exclusive.**

4. On the **Tools Menu,** Click on **Security** and then click on **Set Database Password.** The **Set Database Password** dialog box appears.

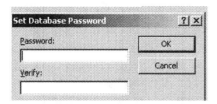

5. Type a password into the box labelled **Password.** Press the **Tab key**.

6. In the box labelled **Verify,** type the same password you typed in the box labelled **Password** again.

7. Click **Ok**.

Any time you open the database, Microsoft Access displays the Password Required dialog box, which ask you for a password, if you type in the right password, the database is open, if not Microsoft Access warns you that the password is not valid.

Removing a password

1. Open the database in **Exclusive mode.**

2. Type a valid password in the **Password** box and click **ok.**

3. Click on **Tools,** click **Security** then click on **Unset Database Password.** The **Unset Database Password** dialog box appears.

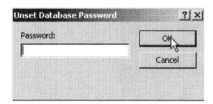

4. Type your current password in the **Password** box and click **ok.**

   Note: Passwords are case sensitive, so bear this in mind when you enter your password.

User-Level Security

Another way of securing your database is to use User level Security. User level security is used in a network environment to secure a database. With User-level security, passwords and permissions are used to secure a database. Permissions are granted to groups and individuals to control how they can work with objects in the Database. Different workgroups and users are created and assign passwords. After establishing the workgroup and the level of access you want for an individual or group, you grant specific permission to control how an individual or group works with objects such as forms, tables, reports etc. in a database. For example you may decide that the data entry group can have access to the Order table but not to the employee table. You may also decide the Data Entry group may insert and update rows in a Order table but not delete data in that table. Again you may also decide that the Data Entry Manager group may be able to insert, delete, update and delete data in the Order table.

The major steps involved in creating user-level security are as follows

- Establish and create the group.

- Give permissions to the group.

- Assign users to the group. Users inherit the permissions of the group they are assigned to.

The easiest way to create a user-level security is by using the wizard.

Using the User-level Wizard to secure your database

1.   Select **Security** from the **Tools** menu, and then click **User-Level Security Wizard.** Click **Next.**

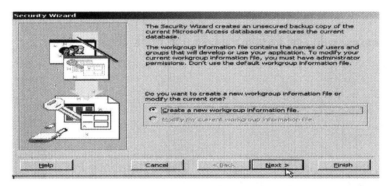

2.   Enter an id in the box labelled WID:

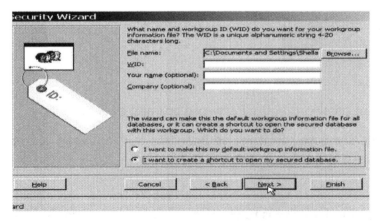

Write down your exact name, organisation and working group ID whether lowercase or uppercase and keep it in a secured place. You may need to use it to recreate the workgroup information file. If you lose this information, you can't recover them and you might not be able to access your database.

3. Click on **I want to make this my default Workgroup Information File** to make this your default workgroup information file. The Workgroup Information File contains information about the workgroup, the users and permissions. Microsoft Access uses this information at start up to define the members of the group. Click **Next** to continue.

4. Accept the default selections or click on the **Deselect** or **Select All** or **Deselect All** button to select or deselect objects. You can also select or deselect individual objects by clicking the left box next to object. Click **Next**.

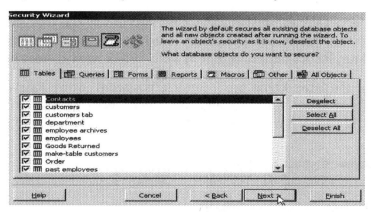

5. Select the group you want to include in your work group information file and click **Next**.

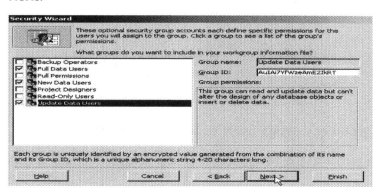

6. Click **Next**.

7. Click **Yes I would like to grant some permission to the Users group**.

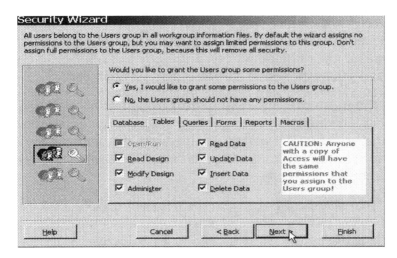

8   Click on the objects tabs and assign various permissions to the User group. For example click on the Tables tab and assign **Read Design, Modify Design, Read Data, Update Data, Insert Data and Delete Data**. Click **Next** to continue.

9.   Enter a name in the **User Name** box. Enter a password in the **Password** box. **Enter** a personal id in the **PID:** box and then click **Add This User to the list**. Repeat this step until you have added all the users to list. When you finish click **Next**.

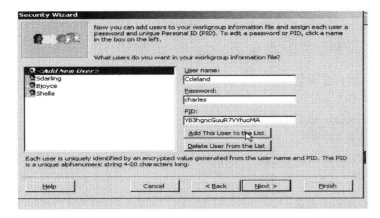

10.   Click **Select a group and assign users to the group** option.

11.   Click the down arrow to the box labelled **Group or User name** and click a group from the list.

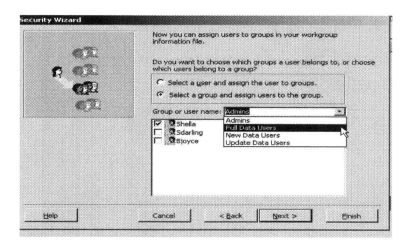

12. Select the users you want to assign to this group by clicking the check boxes next to the users.

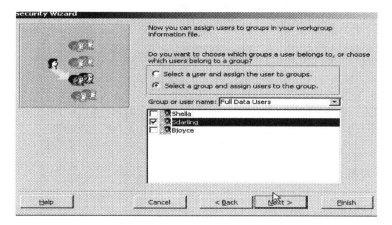

13. Repeat steps 11&12 to select different groups and assign users to the group. When you finish adding different users to different groups Click **Next** to continue.

14. Write down the default name and path for the backup copy of your unsecured Database. You may need this information if you have to recreate the **Workgroup Information File**.

    Click on the **Finish** button to accept the default name for the unsecured database.

    Microsoft Access displays a report, which you will need to re-create your workgroup file information.

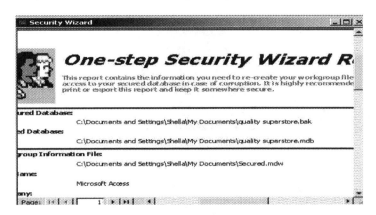

15. Close the report. Microsoft warns you that you may need this information to recreate a workgroup file if you lose or corrupt your file and advises you to save the file. Click yes to save the file.

The security wizard displays a message informing you that it has encrypted your database and advises you to close and re-open Access.

16. Quit Microsoft Access.

The Workgroup Information File

The wizard created a new workgroup and a Workgroup Information File. The Workgroup Information File (WIF) stores information about members of a group, users in a group and the permissions granted to the group and different objects in the database. By default when you install Microsoft Access, a default workgroup with two groups **Admins** and **Users** were created. A default Workgroup Information file was also created to hold the security information for the default workgroup. Before you created the new workgroup, Microsoft Access uses the default Workgroup Information File at startup to define the members of the group. If you click **I want to make this my default Workgroup Information File** in step 3 when creating a new workgroup, Microsoft Access will use the information in your new workgroup information to define members of your group at startup.

Workgroups

A workgroup is a group of users in a multi-users environment with the same information needs. For example the Data Entry group, admin Group and Management Group.

Each group will need access to different tables and will need to work with different tables in the database in different ways. For example the Data Entry Group will need access to the Order, Customers and payment tables but not the Employees table. The Data Entry Group will need to Enter/View, Update the Order, Customers table and Payment table, but not delete/change information in the payment table. The Management Group will need to Enter, View, Update, change and Delete information from the Order, Customers and

Payment table. The Human Resources team will need to have access to the Employees table but not the Orders, customers and payment table.

To control how each of these groups access these objects and work with these objects you can implement **User-level security**. User-level security is the process of organizing users with the same information needs into groups and assigning permissions to the group. Groups are created and permissions are assigned to the groups. Users are created and assigned usernames and password; they are then added to the groups. The users inherit the permissions assigned to the Group they are added to. The permissions, which the user inherits, determine which database objects (i.e. forms, reports etc.) they can access and how they can work with the objects in the database.

Managing and maintaining Workgroups

You can use the security wizard or the workgroup command to maintain the Workgroup Information File, which contains information about your workgroup, users, password and permissions. For example you use the wizard to add new users to the workgroup and assign them to a group. You can make any changes to your workgroup Information file by using the wizard. The only thing you cannot change is the user name and the password of an existing user.

Using the security wizard to modify a workgroup

1. Open the Database whose Workgroup Information File you want to modify.

2. From the **Tools Menu**, click on **Security**, and then click on **User Level Security Wizard**. The **Security Wizard** dialog box appears.

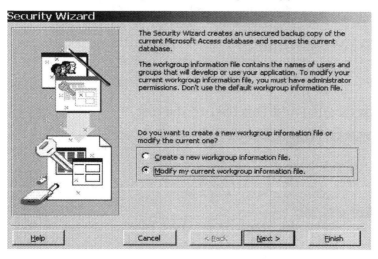

3. Click on **Modify my current workgroup information file**. Click on the **Next** button until you come to the **Add User** Page as illustrated below.

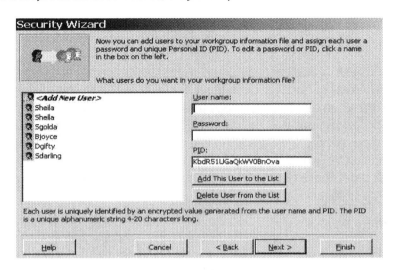

4. Enter a user name in the box labelled **User Name**. Enter a Password in the box labelled **Password.** Enter a unique PID in the box labelled **PID**.

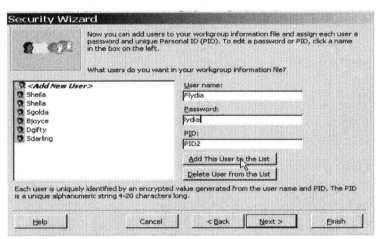

5. Click on the box labelled **Add This User to the List**.

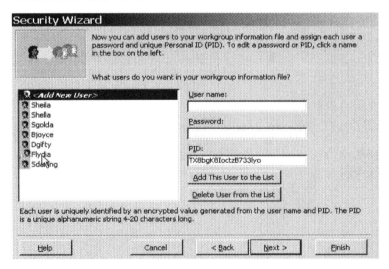

6. Repeat steps 4&5 to continue to add more users to the Workgroup Information File. After adding users to the **Workgroup Information File** you can assign users to a group. Click on **Next** to continue.

7. Click on **Select a user and assign the user to groups**.

8. In the box labelled **Group or user name,** select the user from the drop-down list.

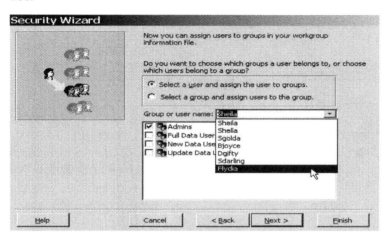

9. Select the group you want to assign this user to in the list of groups under the box labelled **Group or user name**.

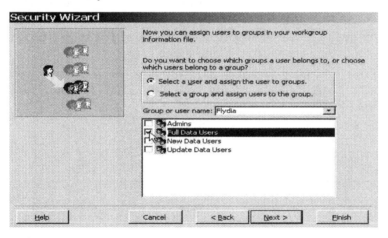

10. Click **Next** to continue.

11. Accept the default name and path for the backup copy of your unsecured database and click on **Finish**. Microsoft Access displays a report. You can use this report to re-create the Workgroup File. Save this file and click the close button to exit from this report.

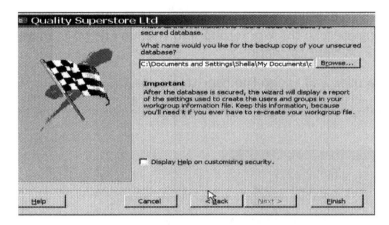

Using the workgroup command to manage the Workgroup

Microsoft Access provides different commands, which you can use to maintain the workgroup that you have created. For example you can use the **User and Group Accounts** to add and delete users and groups. You can also use the **User and Group Permissions** command to change permissions of users and groups in your database; you can use the Workgroup administrator to change workgroups. All these commands are accessible through the Security command on the Tools Menu.

Joining a Workgroup by using the Workgroup Administrator

By default Microsoft Access uses the default workgroup and workgroup information file at startup. If you have secured your database using another workgroup, you will need to make this information available to Microsoft Access so that it can use the settings at startup to open database and give access to the objects in your database. If you don't use the workgroup you secured your database with to open your database, Microsoft Access displays a message informing you that you do not have permission to open the database. You will need to join a workgroup or change the WIF. Follow the steps below to join a workgroup or change the workgroup information file.

1. Start Microsoft Access.

2. Click on **Tools,** click on **Security** and then click on **Workgroup Administrator**. The current **Workgroup Information file** is displayed in the Workgroup Administrator dialog box. Write down the exact name and path of the current workgroup, you may need this information later.

4. Click **Join**.

5. Enter the path and name of the workgroup information folder that defines the workgroup you want to join, alternatively, Click on **Browse** and locate the workgroup information file from the **Select Workgroup Information File** dialog box and click **Open**.

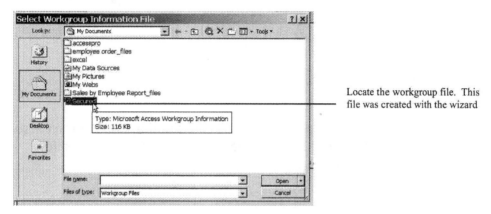

Locate the workgroup file. This file was created with the wizard

6. Click **Ok**.

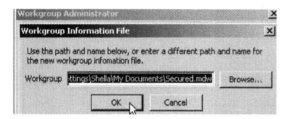

Microsoft Access displays an alert box, informing you that you have successfully joined the selected workgroup. The information in the WIF will now be used to open your database. Quit the database and log on as a member of the new workgroup.

Using the workgroup command to create a group account

1. Start **Microsoft Access Database** and Open the database using the workgroup in which you want to use to create your group account. If the current workgroup is not the workgroup you want to use to create the group account you can change the current workgroup by clicking the **Tools, Security, Workgroup Administrator, join..** and then selecting the **workgroup information file** you want to use or **(Refer to the section on joining a workgroup for more details about joining a workgroup)**.

2. Choose **Security** from the **Tools Menu**, then click on **User and Group Accounts**.

3. Click on the **Groups Tab** and click on **New**.

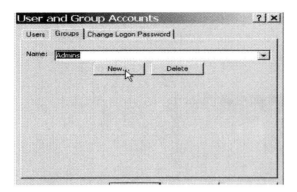

4. Enter a name for the group in the box labelled **Name,** and enter a **Personal Id** for the group. Write down the **Name** and **Personal Id** and keep it safe.

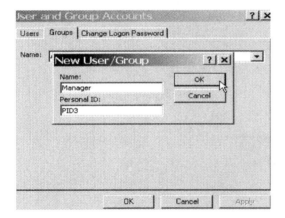

5. Click **Ok** to create the new user group.

Using the workgroup command to Add users to a group

To add a users to the workgroup you must log on as a member of the **Admins Group**.

1. Open the database using the workgroup, which contains the user and group accounts you want to use. If the current workgroup is not the workgroup you want to use follow the steps in the previous section for joining a workgroup to change to the desired workgroup.

2. Choose **Security** from the **Tools Menu,** then click on **User and Group Accounts.**

3. Click on the **Users Tab.**

4. Select the User from the **Name** drop-down list box.

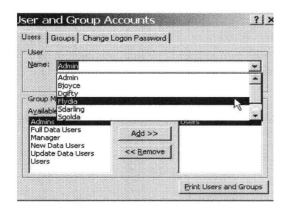

5. Click the Group you want to add the user to from the list of groups in the **Available Groups** box. Click on **Add >>**

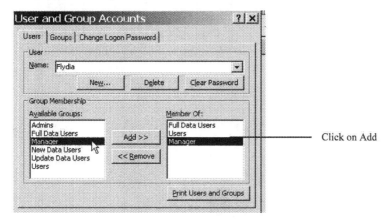

Click on Add

6. The group you added is added to the box labelled **Member of**.

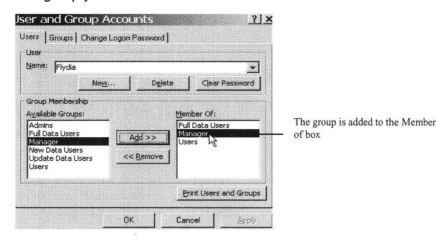

The group is added to the Member of box

7. Repeat step 5 to add this user to another group. Repeat steps 4&5 to add other users to the groups.

8. When you finish click **Ok**.

Delete a group account

You need to be a member of the **Admins Group** before you can delete a group.

1. Start Microsoft Access and Open the database using the workgroup, which contains the workgroup you want to delete. If the current workgroup does not contain the group you want to delete you can change the current workgroup by clicking the **Tools, Security, Workgroup Administrator, join..** And then selecting the workgroup information file you want to use.

2. Choose **Security** from the **Tools Menu,** then click on **User and Group Accounts.**

3. Click on the **Groups Tab.**

4. Select the group from the **Name** drop-down list and then click on **Delete**

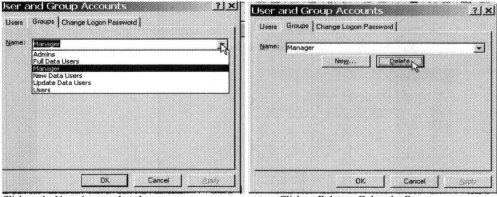

Click on the Name box to select the group   Click on Delete to Delete the Group

5. Click on **Yes** to the delete the group.

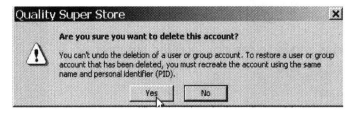

6. Repeat steps 4&5 to delete other groups.

    Important: The default groups **Admins** and **Users** group cannot be deleted.

Delete a user account

You need to be a member of the **Admins Group** before you can delete a user.

1. Start Microsoft Access and open the database by using the workgroup, which contains the workgroup you, want to delete. If the current workgroup does not contain the group you want to delete you can change the current workgroup by clicking the **Tools, Security, Workgroup Administrator, join..** and then selecting the workgroup information file you want to use.

2. Choose **Security** from the **Tools Menu,** then click on **User and Group Accounts.**

3. Click on the **Users Tab.**

4. Select the user from the **Name** drop-down list and then click on **Delete.**

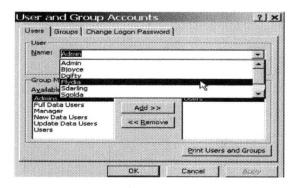

5.   Click **Yes** to delete the user account.

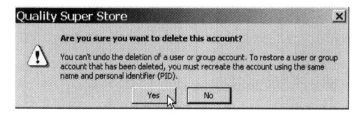

6.   Repeat steps 4& 5 until you have finish deleting all the users.

Remove a user from a group account

Removing a user from a group account is not the same as deleting the user. All you are doing is just removing the user from that particular group. The user may however, be assign to another group. You cannot remove users from the default **Users Group**.

1.   Start Microsoft Access using the workgroup that contains the group you want to remove the user from.

2.   Open the database.

3.   Choose **Security** from the **Tools Menu** and then click on **User and Group Accounts**.

4.   Click on the **Users** Tab.

5.   Select the User you want to remove from the **Name** drop-down list.

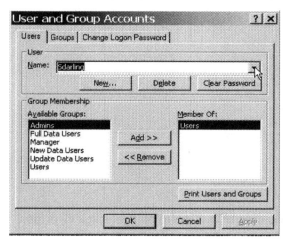

6. In the box labelled **Member of** click the group you want to remove the user from and then click on **Remove.**

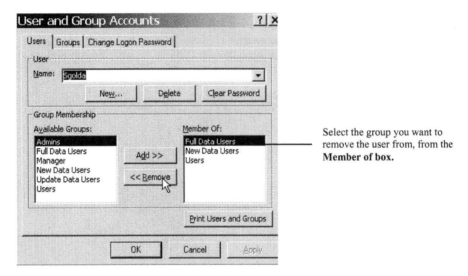

Select the group you want to remove the user from, from the **Member of box.**

7. Repeat step 6 to remove the user from any other groups.

8. Repeat steps 5 & 6 to remove other users from a group.

Permissions

Permissions are granted to control how an individual or group of individual can work with data and objects in the database. A user can be granted direct permission or a user can inherit permission from the group it is added to when it was created.

Setting/changing Permission for a group

Permissions are set for each user and each object type they can access. Permission can be set or changed for a database object by a **member of the Admins group**, the **owner** of the object or a user with the Administer permission on the object. There are different permissions you can assign to a group or user. For example you can assign **Open/Run, Insert or Delete data** permission to a user or a group. Follow the steps below to set or change permission for a User Group.

1. Click on **Security** on the **tools menu,** and then click on **User and Group Permissions.**

2. Click on the **Permission** tab.

3. In the **lists Options** displayed under **User/Group Name:** click **Groups.**

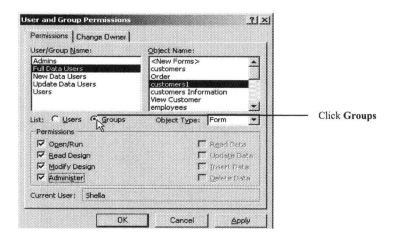

Click **Groups**

4. Select a group from the box labelled **Users/Group Name**.

5. Select the **Object type** you want to assign permission to from the **Object Type** drop-down list. Click the object from the **Object Name** box.

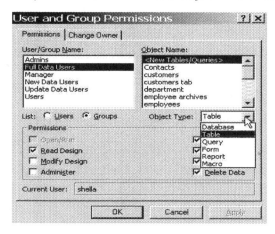

6. Set or change the Permissions by selecting or deselecting the options under the **Permissions** box. Click **ok.**

7. Repeat step 4 - 6 until you have finish setting or changing the permissions for the groups. Members of the group will automatically inherit the permission you have assigned to the group.

Setting/changing Permission for a user

1. Click on **Security** on the **tools menu,** and then click on **User and Group Permissions.**

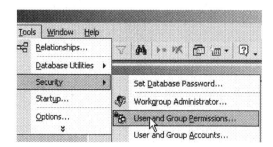

2. Click on the **Permission** tab.

3. In the **list Options** displayed under **User/Groups Name:** click **Users.**

4. Select a user from the box labelled **User/Group Name.**

5. Select **the object type** from the **Object Type** drop-down list and select the **object** you want to give permission to from the box labelled **Object Name.**

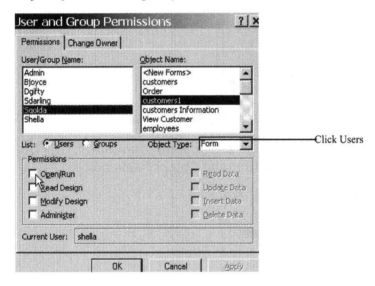

6. Assign the permission you want to assign to the user and click on **Ok.**

7. Repeat steps 5& 6 until you have finish, assigning permissions to all the objects you want to give permissions to. Repeat steps 4-6 to give permissions to different users in your database.

Clearing a user password

No one except a user can change his or her password. If a user loses a password, any member of the Admins group can clear the password. A user will then logon without a password as the password has been cleared and then use the **Tools, Security, User** and **Group Accounts** to set his or her password again.

1. Logon as a member of the **Admins** group.

2. On the **Tools Menu**, click on **Security,** and then click on **User and Group Accounts.**

3. Click on the **Users** tab and select a user from the drop-down list.

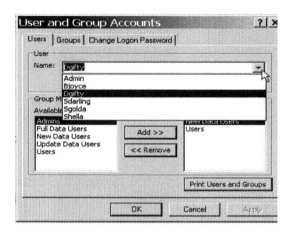

4. Click on **Clear Password** to clear the password.

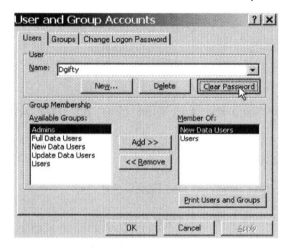

A user whose password has been cleared can now log on without a password and then assign himself/herself a password.

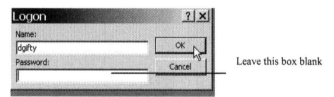

Leave this box blank

When the user logs on he/she will be able to assign a password to himself or herself, by click on **Tools, Security, User and Group Accounts** then click on the **Change Logon Password** tab. On the Logon Password tab the user can leave the old password box blank and enter a new password in the **New Password** box. In the **verify** box enter the same password again.

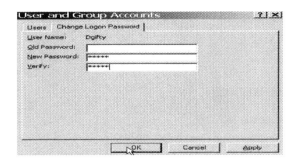

Click on **Ok**. The user can now use the new password to open the database.

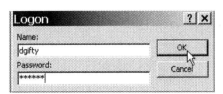

Changing your logon password

1. Logon to the database.

2. On the **Tools Menu**, click on **Security,** and then click on **User and Group Accounts.**

3. Click on the **Change Logon Password** tab.

4. Enter your old password in the box labelled **Old Password**.

5. Enter your new password in the box labelled **New Password**.

6. Enter the same password you entered in the box labelled **New Password** in the **Verify** box.

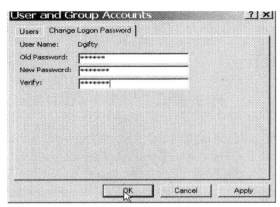

7. Click **Ok**.

Creating an MDE file

Another way of protecting and improving performance of a database with codes is to save the database file as an MDE file. For example if your database contains codes and you don't want users to change the codes and objects in your database you can save the database as an MDE file. Saving a database as an MDE file removes all the editable codes and denies access to the Design view. Users can however, view forms, reports and update, change or delete data, but they cannot change the design of your objects.

It also secures your forms and other objects in your database. Because the forms and other objects are secured, users can work with the database without any need for user-level security. One of the limitations of this method of protecting a database is that users cannot import or export forms, reports and modules. They can however import and export tables, queries and data access pages.

Before you save your database as an MDE file, make sure you have finish with the design because if you need to modify the design of the database you have to modify the database in the original database and save it again as an MDE file. If the database is in Access 2003 format you may need to convert it to Access 2002 before you can save the file as an MDE file.

Converting a database into an Access 2002 format

1.   Close all databases.

2.   Click on **Database Utilities** on the **Tools Menu** and then select **Convert To,** and then click on **To Access 2002-2003 File Format...**

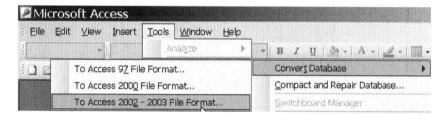

The Database to convert from dialog box appears.

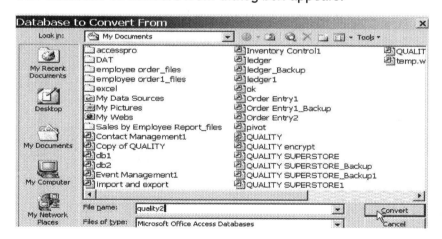

3.   Select the file you want to convert and click on **Convert.**

The **Convert Database Into** dialog box appears. Enter the file name and click on Save.

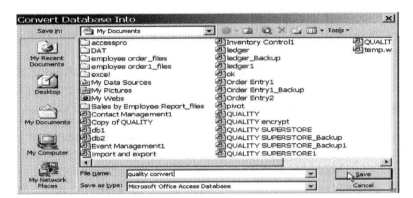

Microsoft displays the following information.

4.   Click on **Ok**.

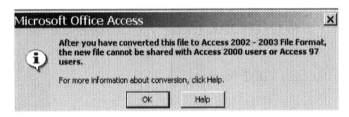

You can now save this database file as an MDE file.

Saving a Database as an MDE File

1.   Open the Database you want to save as an MDE file.

2.   Choose **Database Utilities** on the **Tools Menu** and then click on **Make MDE file**.

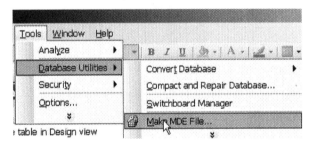

The **Database To Save As MDE** dialog box appears.

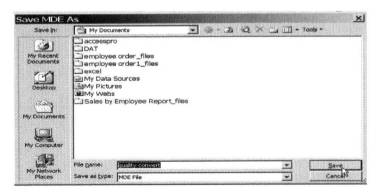

3. Click on **Save**.

Opening an MDE Database

1. In the Database window, click on the **open** button. The **Open** dialog box appears.

2. Select **MDE Files** from the **Files of Type** drop-down list.

3. Double-click the **MDE** file you want to open.

Encrypting your database

Encrypting a database prevents users from reading your program with other programs like Microsoft Word, Excel or other utility program. For example users with other programs like Word, Excel or other packages will be able to open your database file but will not be able to decipher the information. Encrypting the database also compacts the database. The contents of the database will be completely unreadable. This method of securing a database can be an additional measure of securing a database, which is already secured with a password. You need to be a member of the **Admins Group** or the owner of the database in order to secure a database.

To Encrypt a database

Close all databases.

1. Choose **Security** from the **Tools Menu** and then click on **Encode/Decode Database**.

   The **Encode/Decode** dialog box appears.

2. Double-click on the database you want to encrypt.

3. Enter a new name for the encrypted file.

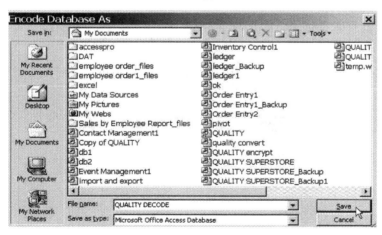

4. Click on **Save**.

   The database file is encrypted; the original version remains the same.

To open an Encrypted database

1. Close the database.

2. Start another program for example, Microsoft Word.

3. Click on **open.**

3. Select **All Files** in the **File Type** box.

4. Double-click on the encrypted file you want to open. The encrypted file opens it is very difficult to decipher anything.

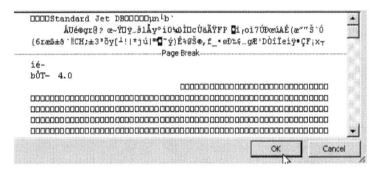

Decrypting a database

1. Close all database files.

2. Choose **Security** from the **Tools Menu** and click on **Encode/Decode Database**.

3. Select the database you want to **Decrypt** and click **ok**. The **Encode/Decode** database dialog box appears.

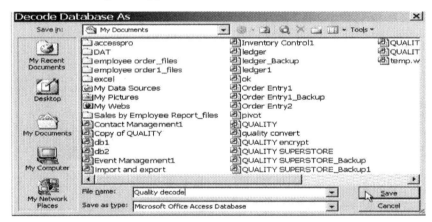

4. Enter a name in the **File Name** box.

5. Click on **Save.**

Chapter

30

MAINTAINING AND IMPROVING THE PERFORMANCE OF YOUR DATABASE

Maintaining your database
Backing up your data

To backup a database is to make a copy of the database. Backup protects your database against accidental loss, damage, hard disk malfunction and corruption. If any of these happens you can fall on the backup copy to restore your lost or damaged data. Lots of time, efforts and money have been wasted in designing and building the database, sudden lost or damage to the database will be a disaster to the company. Accidental damage or any form of damage will mean redesigning and building the database again. It will cost money and effort. To avoid these problems it is advisable to always backup your database. Also creating a backup copy of your database will ensure flexibility in your database design as you know that you can always fall on the most recent version of the program in the event of overwritten file or unwanted changes to your database design.

Ways you can backup your database

There are many ways you can create a backup copy of your database. They are as follows:

- Use the Backup command on the File Menu.

- You can copy the file to another folder on the network.

- Copy the file to another floppy disk using the Windows Explorer. This method is useful for small databases.

- You can also use the backup program that comes with the operating system i.e. Windows 98, Windows 2000 and Windows XP.

Using the Backup command on the File Menu to backup a database

Close all objects in the database.

1. On the **File Menu** choose **Backup Database**. The **Save Backup As** dialog box appears.

2. Accept the default name or enter a new name for your backup copy.

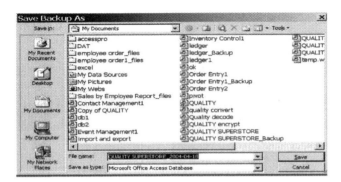

3. Click on **Save**. Microsoft Access creates a backup copy of your database.

    Note : If you are using a user level security to protect your database, you need to also copy the Workgroup Information File, i.e. System.mdw.

Using the Backup program that comes with Microsoft Windows.

1. Click on **Start Program** ➔**Accessories** ➔**System Tools** ➔**Backup** as indicated below. The **Backup Wizard** appears.

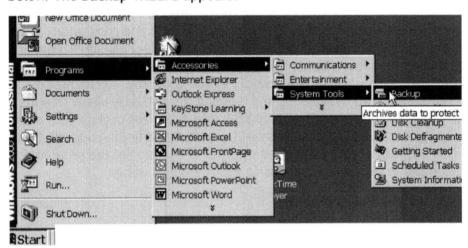

2. Click on the **Backup Wizard.**

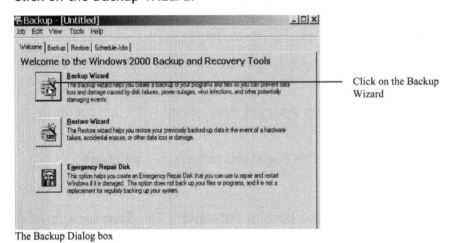

The Backup Dialog box

3. The Backup Welcome Page appears, click **Next** to continue.

4. Click **Back up selected files, drives or network data.** This will give you the opportunity to select the files you want to backup. Click **Next** to continue.

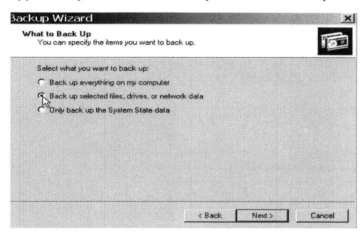

5. Locate the drive and folder that contains the file you want to backup.

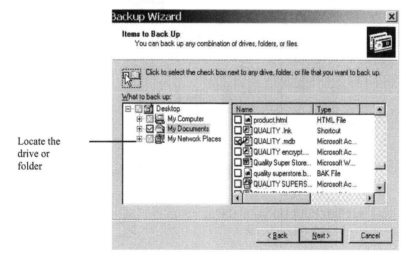

6. Click to select the check box next to the file. Click **Next** to continue.

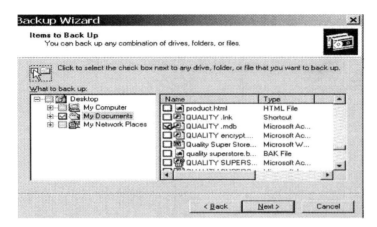

7.   Choose a media to store the Backup copy. Accept the default to **Backup your file on a floppy disk**. Click the **Browse** button to locate a media to store the backup copy. The **Open** dialog box appears.

8.   Enter a name in the **File name** box and click **Open**.

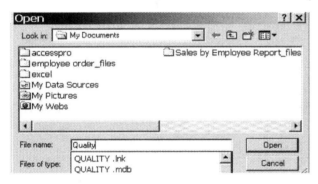

9.   Click **Next**.

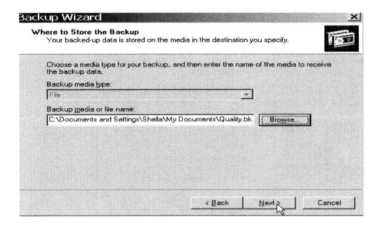

10. Click **Finish** to start backing up your data.

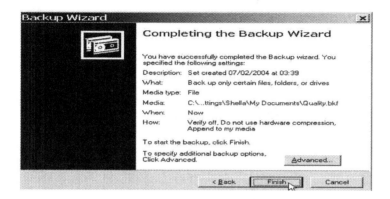

The Backup process starts. It takes a few minutes. When it finishes, the Backup progress report is displayed.

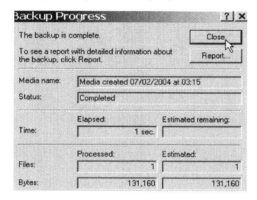

11. Click **Close**.

Restoring your Backup copy

1. Click on **Start Program →Accessories, →System Tools →Backup** as indicated below. The **Backup Wizard** appears.

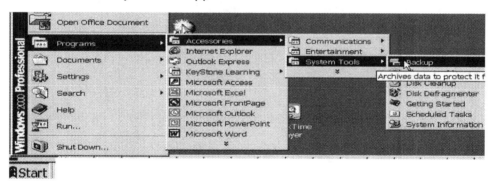

2. Click on the **Restore Wizard**. The Restore Wizard appears.

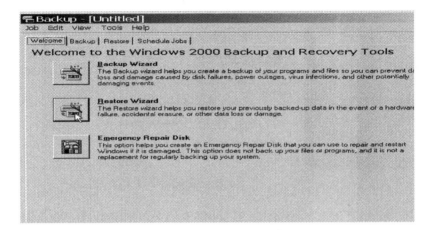

3. Click **Next** to continue.

4. Locate the drive and folder that contains the backup file. Click on the **C: drive**. The Backup File Name dialog box appears. **Enter** the path and file name or click on Browse.

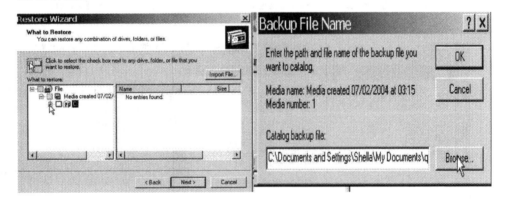

If you click on browse, select the file you want to restore and click **Open**.

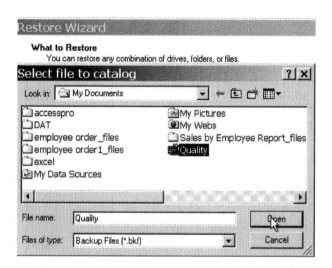

4. Click to select the check box next to the file you want to restore. Click **Next** to continue.

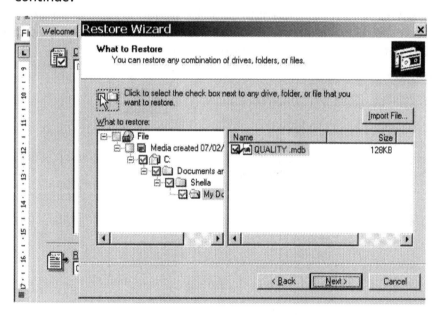

5. Click **Finish** to close the wizard and to proceed with the restoration..

    The file is restored in the original folder.

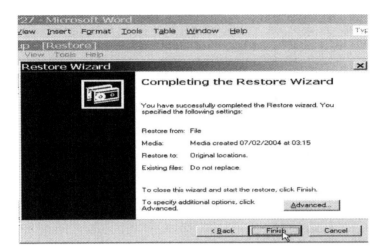

Continue with the rest of the steps if you want to restore your backup file in another folder.

If you want to restore the file into another folder, click the **advanced** button and specify the location for the restored file. Click the **Restore files To** box and select the option you want from the drop-down list.

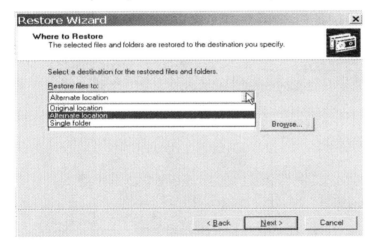

Click on **Browse** to select the alternate location. When you finish, click **Next** to continue.

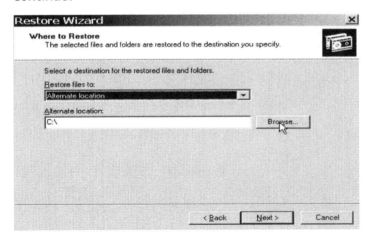

Select how you want to restore your file from the options listed below and click **Next** to continue.

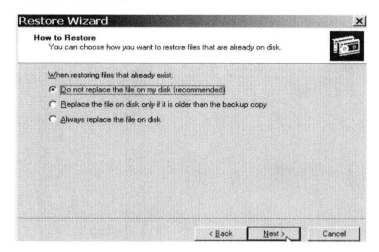

If you want to restore security or special systems files click the check box next to **Restore Removable Storage Database**. Click **Next** to continue.

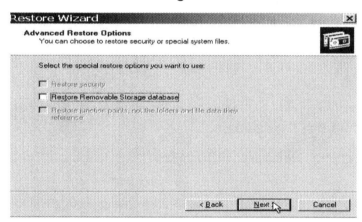

Click **Finish** to close the wizard and to proceed with the restoration.

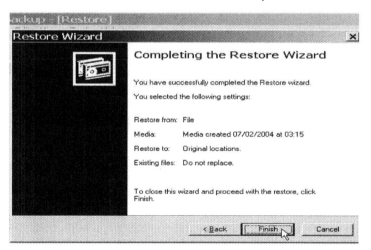

When Microsoft Access finishes the restoration, it displays a summary report. You can click the **Report** button to display detailed report about the restoration.

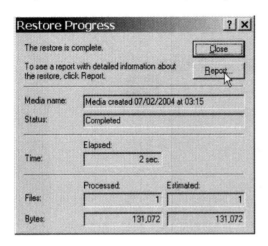

Compacting and repairing your database

The database file like a car needs periodic maintenance to work smoothly and efficiently. Day in and day out you add data and delete data to your database, this can cause your database file to become fragmented and use disk space inefficiently. Also disk error can damage your database. To avoid these problems you should often compact your database. Compacting your database file de-fragmentize your database by re-arranging your data so that it can make optimum use of the disk space. Microsoft Access resets your **Autonumber fields**.

Compacting a database

Make sure that no one else is using the database.

1. On the **Tools Menu,** choose **Database Utilities** and then click on **Compact and repair Database.**

    Microsoft Access displays **Compacting** at the bottom of your screen.

    Note: You can set options to automatically compact your database each time you close your database.

To automatically compact your database

1. On the **Tools Menu** choose **Options.** The **Options** dialog appears.

2. Click on the **General tab.**

3. Click the box next to **Compact on Close** as indicated by the mouse pointer below.

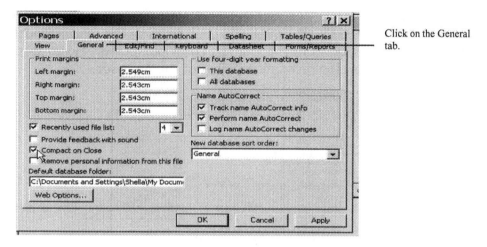

Click on the General tab.

4. Click **Ok.**

Improving the performance of your database

There are several ways you can improve the performance of your database. One of the ways in which you can improve the performance of your database is to use the **Performance Analyser.** The Performance Analyser is a utility provided by Microsoft Access, which helps you to analyse the entire database or selected objects in the database. When you run the Performance Analyser, the Analyser makes recommendations and suggestions, which you may if you want, incorporate in your database design. Follow the steps below to analyse your database.

1. Open the database you want to analyse.

2. From the **Tools Menu,** Choose **Analyse,** and then click on **Performance.** The Performance Analyser dialog box appears.

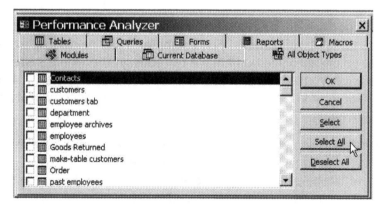

3. Click the tab of the object you want to analyse. You can click the **All Object Types** tab to display all objects in your database.

4. Click the names of object you want to analyse or click **Select All** to select all the objects in your database.

5. Repeat steps 3&4 to select other objects you want to analyse. When you finish selecting the objects click **Ok.** Microsoft Access displays the results on your

screen. The Performance Analyser, categories the results into **Recommendation, Suggestion, Idea and Fixed**. When you click an item, the recommendations and suggestions are displayed in the Analysis notes box below. Go to step 7 if you don't want to follow the recommendations of the **Analyser**.

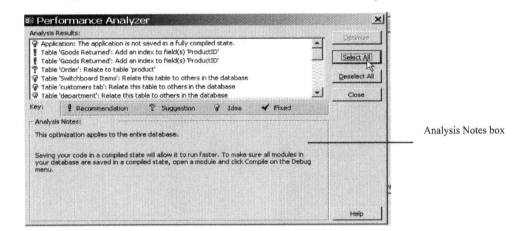

Analysis Notes box

6. To follow the recommendations of the **Performance Analyser,** select the recommendations or suggestions you want to perform and click on **Optimise**. You can make the **Analyser** perform the recommendations for you or you can do it manually yourself. You must consider the suggestions and recommendations carefully before clicking on the **Optimiser** because not all the recommendations may be suitable for your database. You can click **Select All** to perform all the recommendations.

7. When you finish, click the **Close** button to close the **Performance Analyser** dialog box.

Documentation

Documentation is very important in any system you build. Documentation ensures continuity and can be a source of reference. For example if you decide to expand the scope of your system (i.e. go on-line) you don't have to redesign the whole system again, you have a source of reference from which you can move your systems forward. Also when you keep a documentation of your system you can always fall on the documentation if you have to rebuild your system again.

You can document your system as you go through the different stages of database design or you can have Microsoft Access automatically generate documentation for you. Microsoft Access provides a utility, which helps you to generate detail results of your system. For example you can use the documenter to generate code, properties and permissions of different objects in your database. Follow the steps below to automatically generate a detail report of your database.

Using the Documenter to generate detail results of your database

1. Open the database you want to document.

2. Choose **Analyse** from the **Tools Menu,** and then click on **Documenter**. The Documenter dialog box appears.

3. Click the tab of the object you want to document or click on **All Objects Types** to display a list of all the objects in your database.

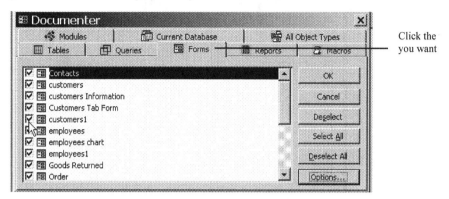

4. Select the objects you want to document by clicking the check box next to the object name. You can click on **Options** to specify which feature you want to document. For example you may decide to print the **Permissions** by user and group or just the code for the object.

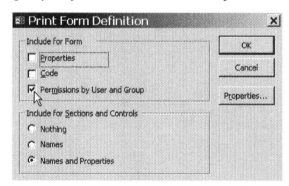

5. Click **Ok**.

6. Click **Ok** again to generate the report. You can print the report or export the report to a variety of formats, for example **HTML** or **Text** file. I will recommend **Rich Text Format**. Click on the **Print** button to print the report. Before you print the report, check the length of the report before printing, sometimes the report can be very long and may take a very long time to print

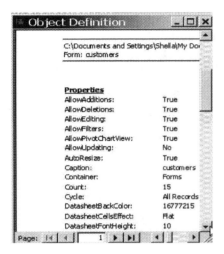

To export the report, click on **File**, **Export** and select the format you want for your report in the **Export Report As** dialog box. Accept the default **File Name** and click **Export**.

Microsoft Access displays the following message informing you that it is now outputting the results of your report to the **Rich Text File** (.RTF).

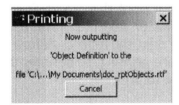

7.   Close the **Report**.

Chapter

IMPORTING AND EXPORTING DATA

Microsoft Access allows sharing of data between different programs. Some of the ways in which data can be shared in Microsoft Access is through Import, Export or Linking to the data.

Importing Data

Data can be shared between different programs or external sources by importing the data into Microsoft Access. You may choose to import data to your database because you want to keep all the data you are working with in one database. Also Microsoft Access works faster with its own table. When you import data, a copy of the data is copied into a new table in your database or appended to an existing table with the same data structure. Access supports the following formats. Always backup your data before importing or exporting your data.

Data Source	Version
Microsoft Access	2.0,7.0/95,8.0/97,9.0/2000,10.0/Access 2002
Dbase	III, IV, 5.0 and 7
Paradox, Paradox For Microsoft Windows	3.x, 4.x, 5.0 and 8.0.
Microsoft Excel	3.0,4.0,5.0,7.0/95,8.0/97
Microsoft Excel Spreadsheets	3.0,4.0,5.0,7.0/95,8.0/97,9.0/2000 and 10.0/Excel 2002
Lotus 1-2-3 Spreadsheets	.wks, .wk1, .wk3, .wk4
Microsoft Exchange	All versions
Delimited Text Files	All character set
Fixed-Width Text Files	All character set
HTML	1.0 (if a list) 2.0,3.x (if a table or list)
XML Documents	All versions
SQL (table, Microsoft Visual FoxPro and data from other programs and database that support the ODBC protocol	Visual FoxPro 2.x, 3.0, 5.0 and 6.x (import only)

Importing Information from Excel

You can import a named range of cells or an entire Excel spreadsheet into Microsoft Access. Follow the steps below to import data from another program.

1. Open the database into which you want to import the data.

2. On the **File Menu,** choose **Get External Data,** and then click on **Import.** The Import dialog box opens.

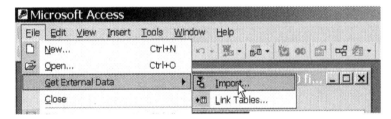

3. Click the **File Type** drop-down list and select **Microsoft Excel.**

4. Locate the drive or folder that contains your spreadsheet by clicking in the **Look in** box and navigating to folder that contains your file.

5. Click on the file you want to import. The **Import Spread Sheet Wizard** appears.

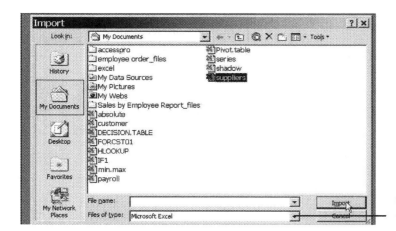

Click the File Type drop-down list and select Microsoft Access

6. Click on **Show worksheet** and then on the worksheet you want to import. Click **Next** to continue.

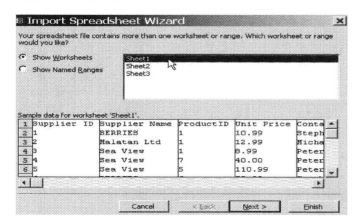

7. Click the box next to **First Row Contains Column Headings** and click **Next** to continue.

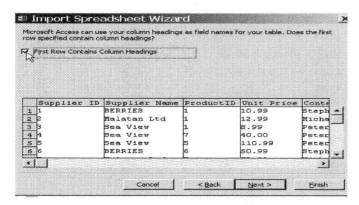

8. Choose where you want to store your data. Click **In a New Table** or **In an Existing Table**. If you chose **In an Existing Table** select the table from the drop-down list next to the box with **In an Existing Table**. Microsoft Access can only import data into an existing table, if the field names and data types match exactly.

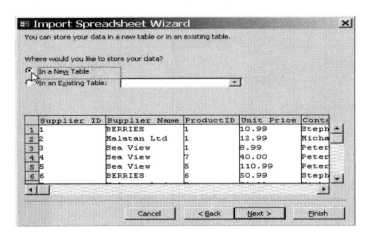

9.   Accept the default field names or change the field information in the **fields Options** area. Click **Next** to continue.

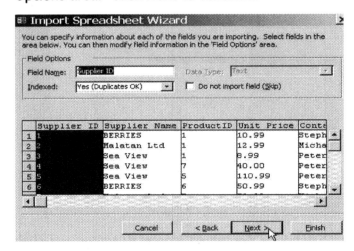

10. Define a primary key for your new table by choosing from the list of three options provided. Click **Choose my own primary key** and select the primary key from the drop-down list. You can also let Microsoft Access create a primary key for you by clicking **Let Access add primary key** or click **No primary key** if you don't want any primary key. Click **Next** to continue.

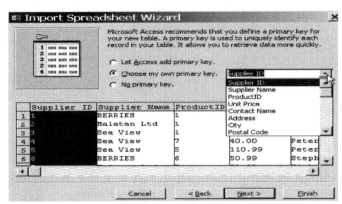

11. Enter a name for your table and click **Finish**.

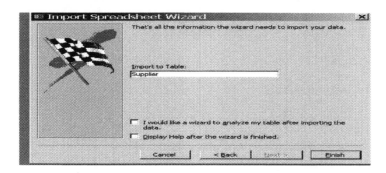

12. Microsoft Access displays a message informing you that the file has been imported. Click **Ok.** The imported table appears in the Database window.

Importing from a Delimited or Fixed-width Text File

Microsoft Access can import data from a text file. There are two types of text files that Microsoft Access can import data from. They are the Delimited or Fixed width text files. A delimited text file is a text file, which is separated by comma, tab or semi-colon. A Fixed Width Text file is a text file, which is arranged in columns. A Fixed-Width file does not have separators. Before you import a delimited file make sure the text file has the same type of data in each field and the same fields in every row. Follow the steps below to import a Text file into your database.

1. Open the database into which you want to import the data.

2. On the **File Menu**, choose **Get External Data,** and then click on **Import.** The Import dialog box opens.

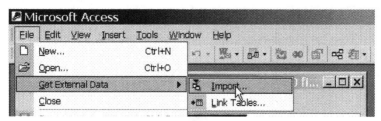

3. Click the **File Of Type** drop-down list and select **Text Files**.

4. Locate the drive or folder that contains your Text File by clicking in the **Look in** box and navigating to folder that contains your Text File. Click on the file and click on **Import.** The **Import Text Wizard** appears.

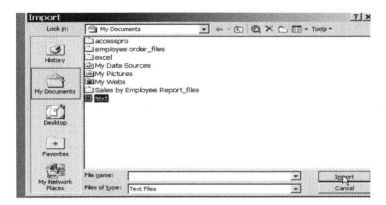

5.   Click **Delimited** if your text file is separated by comma, tab or semi-colon. If not choose **Fixed-width**. Click **Next** to continue.

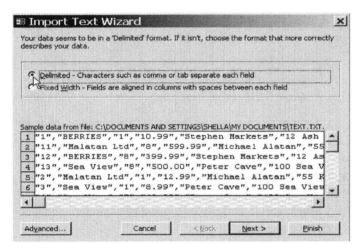

6.   Choose the **Delimiter** that separates your data. If the first row contains your field names click the box next to **First Row contains Field Names**. Click **Next** to continue.

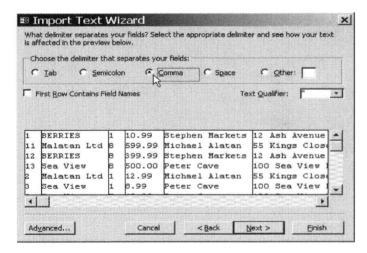

7.   Indicate where you want to store your data. Click **In a New Table** if you want to store your data in a new table. Click **In an Existing table** and select the table from the drop-down table. Click **Next** to continue.

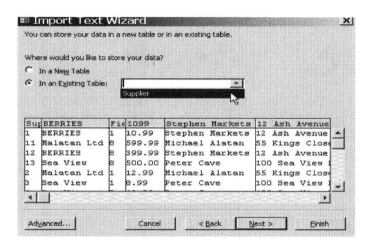

8. Click **Finish** to import the text file into the existing suppliers table. Microsoft Access displays a message informing you that the file has been imported.

9. Click **Ok** to close the message box.

Importing Data from another Database file into Access Database

1. Open the database into which you want to import the data.

2. On the **File Menu**, choose **Get External Data,** and then click on **Import.** The Import dialog box opens.

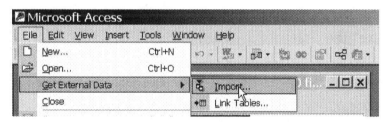

3. Click the **File Of Type** drop-down list and select **Microsoft Access Database**.

4. Locate the drive or folder that contains your access file by clicking in the **Look in** box and navigating to folder that contains your file.

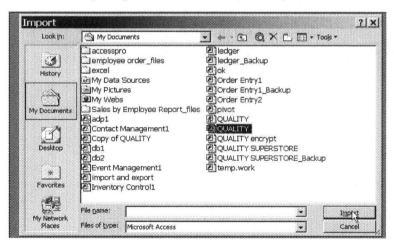

5. Select the file you want to import and click on **Import**.

6. Click the tab of the object you want to import, for example if you want to import **Tables,** clicks on the **Tables** tab.

7. Select the tables you want to import. If you want to import all the tables **Click** on **Select All**. Click on **Options** to display the other options available. If you want to import only the definition (the structure of the table without any data), click on **Definition Only** under the box **Import Tables**. If you want to import the structure and the data in the table, click on **Definition and Data**, if you want to import only the structure of the table, click on **Definition Only.**

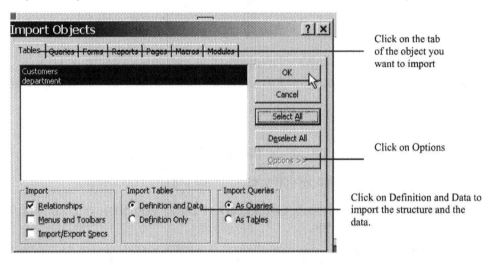

Click on the tab of the object you want to import

Click on Options

Click on Definition and Data to import the structure and the data.

8. Click **Ok** to import the tables.

Importing a Data Access Page from a Microsoft Access file into Microsoft Access

1. Open the database into which you want to import the data.

2. On the **File Menu**, choose **Get External Data,** and then click on **Import**. The Import dialog box opens.

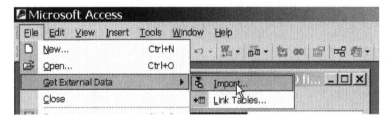

3. Click the **File of Type** drop-down list and select **Microsoft Access**.

4. Locate the drive or folder that contains your access file by clicking in the **Look in** box and navigating to the folder that contains your file.

5. Select the file you want to import and click on **Import**.

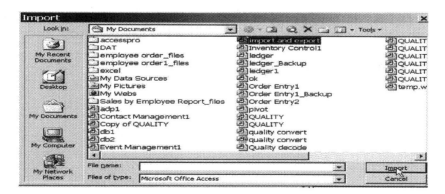

6. Click on the **Pages tab** and select the Page(s) you want to import.

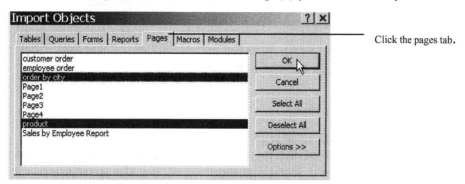

Click the pages tab.

Click **Select All** to select all the pages that you want to import.

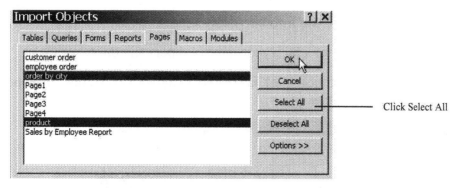

Click Select All

7. Click **Ok**. The Import Objects dialog box appears informing you about the import.

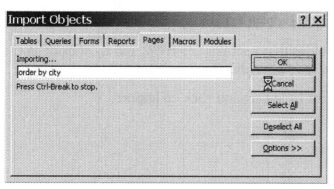

The Save As Data Access Page then follows this. Accept the default name in the **File name** box or enter a new file name. Click the **Save** button.

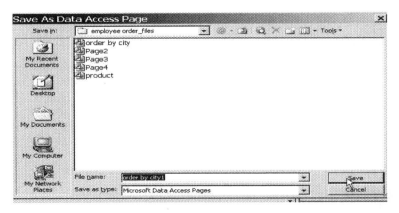

The Data Access Page(s) you imported appears in your database. Click the **Pages** tab of your database to see the imported page(s).

Importing data from an HTML FILE

HTML means Hypertext Markup Language. It is a computer language used to create web pages. HTML uses tags to format the layout i.e. appearance and alignment of text on a web page. HTML describes how a Web page should look, but the structure of the table. It can also be used to display a table on a web page. In HTML format, a table and its other elements are enclosed in HTML tags.

Importing Data from an HTML file into Microsoft Access

1. Open the database into which you want to import the data.

2. On the **File Menu,** choose **Get External Data,** and then click on **Import.** The Import dialog box opens.

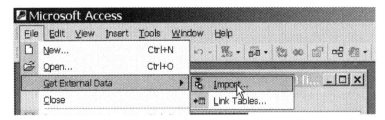

3. Click the **File of Type** drop-down list and select **HTML Documents**.

4. Locate the drive or folder that contains the **HTML** file by clicking in the **Look in** box and navigating to the folder that contains your file.

5. Select the file you want to import and click on **Import.**

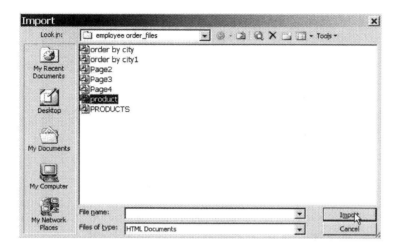

The wizard displays the contents of the table in rows and columns. If the file contains more than one table the wizard displays the tables, select the table you want to import from the list displayed.

6. Click **Next.**

7. Click **In an Existing Table** from the options displayed and select the table you want to import the table into from the drop-down list.

   Click **Next** to continue.

8. Click **Finish** to import the file. Microsoft Access starts importing the file when it finishes a message appears in a message box.

9. Click **Ok** to close the message box.

Importing data from an XML file

XML means Extensible Markup Language. XML is a standard language used by developers in organizing, presenting and delivering data on the web. Prior to the development of XML, exchanging data on the web and between different programs was difficult, because different programs store data in different formats and structure. XML makes it easier for exchanging data between dissimilar systems and applications.

It is similar to HTML files. Like HTML files, XML is suitable for displaying text and images for web browsers and uses tags to format its content. However, unlike HTML, XML defines the data and its structure. Whereas HTML files uses tags and attributes to describe the data and how it will look in the browser, XML defines the data and how it should be structured. Using the **Transform** feature, you can transform the data into a format that Microsoft Access supports before importing the data.

Follow the steps below to import data from an XML file.

1. Open a **database**, or if you have already opened a database, press **F11** to switch to the **database window** for the open database.

2. Click on the **File** menu, click on **Get External Data**, and then select **Import**. The **Import dialog** box appears.

3. In the **Import** dialog box, click the **Files Of Type** box and select **XML Documents.**

4. Locate the drive or folder that contains the **XML** file by clicking in the **Look in** box and navigating to the folder that contains your file.

5. Select the file you want to import and click on **Import**.

6. A list of tables is displayed in the **Import XML** dialog box. **Note** all the tables will be imported.

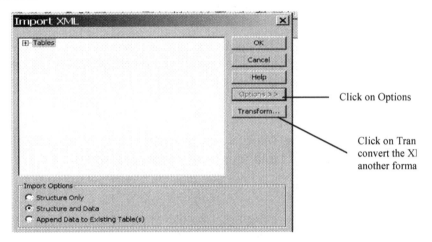

Click on Options

Click on Tran
convert the XI
another forma

You can set options for importing the data. Click on **Options** to display the options available. If you want to import only the **definition** (the structure of the table without any data), click on **Structure Only** under the box **Import Tables Options**. If you want to import the structure and the data in the table, click on **Structure and Data**, to append the data to an existing table, click **Append Data To Existing Table(s).**

A new feature in Microsoft Access is the **Transform** feature. Transform is a template, which is used to convert XML data to the other formats. When you apply **Transform** during import, the data is transform before a new table is created or the data is appended to an existing table.

7. Click on **OK** to start importing the file.

Exporting Data

Exporting data is a way of making data and other objects in your database available to other database or program. You can export data to a variety of databases, program and file format. You can export data to the same format listed for importing data.

Exporting a Microsoft Access table to a text format

1. Open the database containing the table you want to export.

2. In the Database window, click the table you want to export and click on **Export**. Microsoft Access displays the Export dialog box.

3. In the **Save as type** box, click **Text Files**.

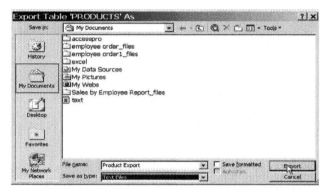

4. Select the drive and folder you want to export to, by clicking the arrow next to **Save in** and then select the drive and folder.

5. Enter a name in the **File Name** box or accept the suggested name.

6. Click **Export**. The Export Text Wizard appears.

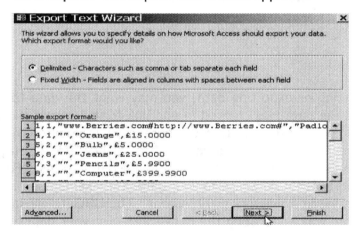

7   Click **Delimited** if you want characters such as comma, tab or semi-colon to separate the fields, choose **Fixed-width** if you want your fields to be aligned in columns with spaces. Click **Next** to continue.

8. If you selected Delimiter in the previous step, Microsoft Access presents you with the option to select the character you want to use to separate the field. Choose the Delimiter that separates your fields from the options displayed. Click the box next to **Include Field names on First Row** to include filed names.

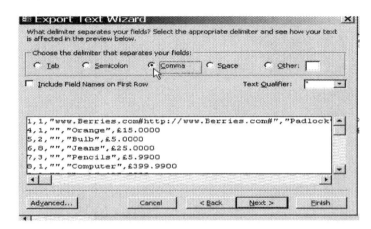

9. Click **Finish** to export your table. When Microsoft Access finishes exporting the table it displays a message box indicating the path where your export file is stored.

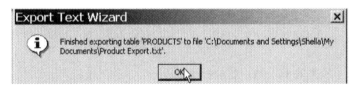

10. Click **Ok.**

Linking a Database

Sometimes instead of importing or exporting data, you may want the data to be kept in the original program that the data was created in and link to it. One of the reasons for linking data instead of importing may be that the data is being updated by another program other than Microsoft Access or because you don't own the data. When you link data you can edit the data in the original program as well as the database file. Follow the steps below to link a table in another database to your database. Remember to use the UNC path when you are working in a network environment. The **UNC** (Universal Naming Conversion) is a more reliable way of locating the data source for your data because it includes the name of the computer as well as the drive and folder.

1. Open the database into which you want to link the data.

2. On the **File Menu**, choose **Get External Data,** and then click on **Link Tables.** The **Link Table** dialog box opens.

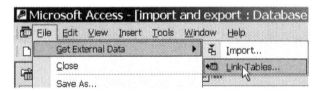

3. Click the **File Type** drop-down list and select **Microsoft Access.**

4. Locate the drive or folder that contains the access file by clicking in the **Look in** box and navigating to folder that contains the file you want to link to.

5. Select the file you want to link to and click on **Link**. The **Link** table dialog box appears.

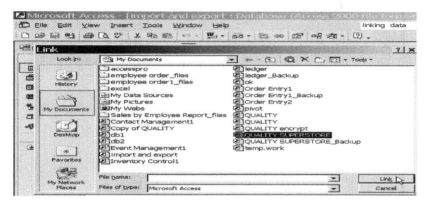

6. Select the table(s) from a list of tables available and click **Ok**. You can select all the tables by clicking on **Select All**.

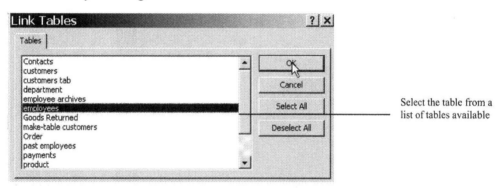

Select the table from a list of tables available

The table you selected is added to your database window. The link table has an arrow to its left. You can view, and update data as you would view and update other tables you have created.

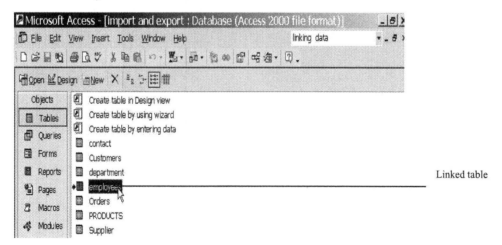

Linked table

A

Action query is a type of query, which makes changes to many records in just one operation. There are different types of Action queries they are **Delete Query, Append Query, Append Query, Make-table.**

Append query is a type of query which add records from one or more tables to the end of one or more tables.

AutoForm creates a form without any questions and displays all the fields in the underlying table or query.

AutoReport creates a preformatted report displaying all the fields and records in the underlying table or query.

B

Browser is a program, which enables any computer to read any HTML file.

Bound control : A control, whose source of data is from a field in a table or query.

C

Calculated control A calculated control is a control, whose source of data is from an expression.

A **chart** is a graphical presentation of data

Check boxes, **Option** buttons and toggle buttons are used to set Yes/No values. When selected they indicate a **Yes** or **True** value. When deselected or cleared they indicate a **No** or **False** value.

A **Combo box** is similar to the list box except that users can type in new values.

Command buttons are buttons used to perform actions.

Controls are the elements of a form that enables you to display fields from your table.

Crosstab query is a type of query that summarises the information in your database in rows and columns for easier analysis. The information in a crosstab query are grouped on the left side of the datasheet and across the top of the datasheet.

D

Database A Database is an organized collection of related information about a particular subject or purpose. A Microsoft Access database is made up of several different objects in the Database window i.e. **Tables, Queries, Forms, Reports, Macros** and **Modules.**

Delete query delete records from one or more tables.

Datasheet view The **datasheet view** is where you view the data in your table. The datasheet view displays the data in your table in rows and columns.

A **Data Access Page** is a type of web page designed purposely for viewing, editing, adding or deleting data on the Internet or Intranet.

Data Type is the type of data that can be entered in a field, for example, Number, Text and Memo.

Datasheet View is a view in which data is arranged in columns and rows similar to a table.

DefaultValue is a value that is automatically entered into a field when a new record is created.

A **delimited text file** is a text file, which is separated by comma, tab or semi-colon. A

E

Encrypting a database prevents users from reading your program with other programs like Microsoft Word, Excel or other utility program.

F

A **Filter** provides a subset of the data in your table or form.

Fixed Width Text file is a text file, which is arranged in columns.

A **form** is a database object, which provides an easy way to enter, edit and view data in your database.

G

Group level is the level by which reports are group in a report.

H

A **hyperlink** is a link to another object.

HTML stands for Hyper Text Markup Language.

I

Indexed Property

An **Indexed field** is a field Microsoft Access uses to search a table or sort records with.

Intranet is a network of computers connected to a web site that is available to members of a group or company within a local area network (LAN) or wide area network (WAN)

An **Internet** is a vast collection of inter-connected computers.

L

Layout Preview: In this view Microsoft Access uses a few sample data to display the layout of the report.

LAN local Area Network

A **list box** is a fixed list of values you can choose from.

Linking is the method of connecting to data in other databases.

M

Make-table is a type of query, which creates a new table from all or part of the data in one or more tables.

Many-to-Many Relationship

This type of relationship is complex and very difficult to implement. In this type of relationship a record in Table A can have many matching records in Table B, and a record in Table B can have many matching records in Table A.

MDE Microsoft Database Executable (MDE) Another way of protecting and improving performance of a database with codes is to save the database file as an MDE file. For example if your database contains codes and you don't want users to change the codes and objects in your database you can save the database as an MDE file. Saving a database as an MDE file removes all the editable codes and denies access to the Design view.

N

Normalization

Is the process of breaking down a table so that each table contains information about only one subject.

O

One-to-one Relationship In a one-to-one relationship, each record in table A can have one matching record in Table B and each record in Table B can have only one matching record in table A..

One-to-many Relationship : each record in a table (A) can have many records in a relating table (B), a record in a relating table (B) can only have one record in table (A).

An **Option Group** is a group of options for a field enclosed in a frame. It provides users with a set of options or alternatives from which users can choose.

P

Parameter query is a type of query that prompts you for information such as the criteria to use to retrieve the information you want.

Permissions are granted to control how an individual or group of individual can work with data and objects in the database.

Pivot Chart is a type of interactive chart that is link to a database.

Pivot Table is a type of table interactive table that is linked to a database.

Primary Key A primary key is a field or set of fields in the table, which uniquely identify an individual record or row.

Property Sheet you can change the properties of a control by using the Property Sheet.

Q

A **Query** is a database object, which enables you to ask questions about the data stored in your database

QBE Query By Example is the process of designing queries based on entering examples of the data you require in the results of the query.

R

Record is a group of fields in a table. The fields in a table make up a record, which describes an individual item in a table.

Reports

In Microsoft Access a report is used to present data in an organised and formatted way.

S

Select Query is the most commonly used query. You can use a select query to retrieve data from more than one table, group the data and perform calculations on the data.

Sorting allows you to organise your data in a particular order i.e. ascending and descending order.

Subform A subform is a form within another form.

A **Subreport** is a report inserted into another Report.

The **System Development approach** is a top-down systematic approach to designing a database.

Smart tags appear as short cut menus with a list actions to choose from. They are time saving tags attach to fields or control in Microsoft Office to perform specific actions.

T

A **Tab Control** is used to display the different pages on separate tabs. The content of each page is displayed on a tab.

A **Table** is the basic storage unit of a Relational Database Management System and it consists of columns and rows.

Transform feature, you can transform the data into a format that Microsoft Access supports before importing the data.

U

Unbound control: A Control, whose source of data is not from a table or a query. Unbounded controls are used to display lines and pictures on your form.

The **UNC Path** is a path that connects the HTML file to the data source.

Update query is a type of query, which makes changes to one or more tables.

URL stands for the words Uniform Resource Locator; in simple terms URL is a web address.

User level security is used in a network environment to secure a database. With **User-level security**, passwords and permissions are used to secure a database.

User is an authorized person who has access to a database.

V

The **ValidationRule** property is a field property that checks the data entered in a field to ensure accuracy.

Validation Text property is a field property that provides immediate feedback on data validation. The text or feedback when inaccurate data is entered is entered in the Validation Text property box.

W

Wizard is a Microsoft tool, which guides users to complete a task.

The **Workgroup Information File** (WIF) stores information about members of a group, users in a group and the permissions granted to the group and different objects in the database.

A **workgroup** is a group of users in a multi-users environment with the same information needs.

Wizard is a tool that which provides step by step guidance on how to perform a task.

XML means Extensible Markup Language. XML is standard language used by developers in organizing, presenting and delivering data on the web.

INDEX

A

Action Query
  Append query 155
  Creating Action Query 155
  Delete query 155
  Make-table query 155
  See also Queries 155
  Update query 155
Adding Controls 208
Adding Records 74
Advanced Filter
  Creating Advanced Query 152
Align 116, 117
And Operator 172
Append Query
  Creating an append query 197

B

Builder
  expression builder 211
Build button 53, 104, 134, 214, 222, 224

C

Calculated controls 208
Caption 54, 55
Check boxes 127, 375
Columns
  Freeze a column 88
  Hide a column 87
  See also fields 88
  Unhide Columns 87
Combo boxes
  See also controls 125
Command buttons
  Creating Command Buttons 131
Controls
  aligning 116
  Calculated control 208
  Moving 86, 114, 216
  selecting 35, 68, 123, 156, 158, 165,
    185, 190, 194, 208, 209, 226, 229,
    245, 296, 331, 334, 337, 355
  sizing 115, 259
Control property
  Setting Control Properties 102
Control sources
  Bound control 208
  Check boxes 127
  combo boxes 126
  Disabling a control* 106
  Locking a control 106
  Option Buttons 127
  Unbound control 208
Creating
  creating a database 21
  Creating a Data Access Page 275
  Creating a form 89
  Creating a query
    Action query 155
    Append query 155
    Delete query 155
    Make-table 155
    Update Query 155
  Creating a report
    Creating subreports 248
    Without a Report Wizard 200
    With a Report Wizard 200
  Creating a table
    Adding fields 42
    Choosing Data types for fields 42
    See also Databases, designing 42
  Creating relationships between tables
    70
  Creating Subform 238
  Creating Subforms
    With a wizard 238
  Creating two levels of subforms 245
  Creating unbound controls 209
  Creating boxes
    Check Box 127
  Creating forms
    Creating a forms using a wizard 90

Criteria
  Filter 147
  filter 147
  Query 147
Crosstab Query
  Creating Crosstab Query, see also
    queries 187
Current Date 224
Customising a query 163

D

Data
  Backup xiv, 155, 195, 320, 325, 329,
    345, 346, 347, 348, 350, 352, 359
  Changing 45, 46, 82, 84, 102, 103,
    107, 116, 119, 225, 340
  Checking xiii, xiv, 252, 253
  Copying data 264
  Deleting Data 275
  Encrypting 343, 376
  Entering, See Adding Data 3, 27, 30,
    38, 51, 70, 75, 89, 94, 104, 106,
    121, 126, 128, 151, 186, 226, 227,
    233, 269, 303, 378
  Exporting, See Exporting Data xv
  Finding Data 143
  Restoring data from backup 349
  Restricting access 104
Databases
  Compacting 5, 354
  Converting into MDE files 341
  Creating 4, 21, 25, 27, 30, 35, 40, 42,
    44, 58, 67, 70, 89, 93, 126, 131,
    155, 184, 188, 194, 200, 201, 238,
    240, 241, 245, 275, 281, 298, 300,
    305, 322, 326, 345
  Encrypting 376
  Encrypting/Decrypting 343, 376
  Repairing 5, 354
  Restoring 349
  Switchboard see switchboards 27,
    297, 298, 299, 300, 301, 302, 303,
    305, 306, 307, 308, 309, 311
Database Window 37, 72, 73, 94, 161,
    164, 200, 201, 262

Database Wizard 23
Datasheets
  Adding Records 74
Datasheet view 40, 54, 74, 85, 96,
    148, 152, 160, 376
  Field Properties Section 39
  Switching between views 41
Data Access pages
  Creating a Data Access Page with wiz-
    ard 277
  Creating with Autopage 276
Data Entry
  See also Adding records 288
Data Types
  Setting field data type 46
Dates
  Automatically entering date 39
Date functions
  Setting Default property to current
    date 105
Decrypting 344
Default Value Property 55
Default View property
  Continuous form 111
Delete
  Fields 31, 42, 46, 48, 71, 80, 91, 156,
    158, 166, 170, 238, 246, 254, 255,
    257, 291, 292, 295
  primary keys 3
  Relationships 3, 4, 7, 8, 9, 63, 64, 70,
    72, 202, 244
  Tables see also delete objects xv, 6,
    8, 31, 33, 37, 75, 156, 213, 249,
    262, 324, 366, 370, 372, 375
Delete button 307, 309
Delete Query 193, 195, 375
Deleting Controls 215
Designing
  databases xiii, 21, 23, 24, 297, 341,
    343, 345, 370, 377
  forms xiii, xiv, xv, xvi, 3, 4, 5, 9, 10,
    21, 22, 23, 27, 44, 46, 60, 63, 89,
    93, 96, 108, 116, 121, 132, 149,
    154, 249, 266, 274, 275, 283, 299,
    311, 317, 322, 327, 341

382

queries xiii, xv, 4, 10, 21, 23, 27, 57, 63, 70, 154, 155, 160, 165, 166, 183, 187, 193, 194, 197, 198, 248, 249, 274, 281, 291, 341, 375, 378

reports xiii, xiv, xv, 3, 4, 5, 10, 21, 27, 46, 60, 63, 93, 116, 154, 155, 200, 201, 248, 251, 266, 298, 317, 322, 327, 341, 376

subforms 111, 245, 247, 248

Design view
in forms 44
in tables 1
See also switching to datasheet view 40

Documentation 4, 356

E

Encrypting 343, 376
Entering Data 37
EXPORTING DATA 359
Expression
Entering an expression 375
Expression Builder 104, 169, 212, 214, 222, 224

F

Field
Renaming A Field 44
Fields
copying 4, 264
data types 7
Field List
Displaying field list 58
Field Names 364
Field Name column, 59
Filters
applying 61, 85
Removing 165, 321, 335
Find command 143, 147
Font
Changing font sizes 114
Footer 219, 220, 221, 222, 231, 232, 235, 236
Formatting
Controls xiv, xv, 45, 46, 60, 98, 100, 103, 107, 114, 116, 119, 120, 121, 136, 206, 208, 209, 215, 216, 217, 222, 226, 245, 282, 283, 379
Format property xiv, 35, 102, 103, 104
Forms
Adding page breaks 136
Creating a form with a wizard 90
Customising a Form 208
Subforms see subforms 237, 243, 250, 378
Form Wizard 91, 92, 238
Freezing 88
Functions 154, 212

G

GroupInterval property 232
GroupOn property 232

H

Help xv, 15, 16, 17, 18, 19
Hiding
Duplicate values 167
HTML files
Importing/Exporting 369

I

Importing
Databases xiii, 21, 23, 24, 297, 341, 343, 345, 370, 377
Tables xv, 6, 8, 31, 33, 37, 75, 156, 213, 249, 262, 324, 366, 370, 372, 375
Indexed 376
Indexed Property 376
Indexes
Creating 4, 21, 25, 27, 30, 35, 40, 42, 44, 58, 67, 70, 89, 93, 126, 131, 155, 184, 188, 194, 200, 201, 238, 240, 241, 245, 275, 281, 298, 300, 305, 322, 326, 345
Inserting
Page Numbers 222
Pictures 26, 40, 98, 138, 140, 200, 379

Internet 20, 270, 271, 272, 274, 275, 290, 376, 377

L

Layout
  Customising a Form 208
  Form layout 92
Linking 251, 359, 372, 377
List boxes
  Create a list box 122

M

Many-to-many relationships 64
Microsoft Access xiii, xiv, xv, 1, 3, 4, 5, 6, 13, 14, 15, 16, 18, 21, 27, 29, 30, 32, 33, 34, 36, 38, 39, 40, 43, 44, 46, 47, 50, 51, 52, 54, 56, 57, 58, 60, 61, 63, 68, 69, 70, 71, 75, 76, 77, 82, 83, 88, 89, 90, 92, 93, 94, 96, 98, 100, 101, 102, 103, 104, 107, 114, 124, 128, 131, 132, 134, 135, 138, 139, 140, 141, 143, 145, 146, 148, 151, 152, 154, 157, 159, 165, 169, 170, 172, 175, 177, 179, 180, 184, 186, 191, 192, 193, 194, 196, 197, 198, 200, 202, 203, 206, 207, 208, 210, 211, 212, 214, 215, 218, 220, 221, 228, 229, 230, 232, 234, 237, 238, 241, 248, 249, 250, 251, 252, 255, 258, 262, 266, 267, 270, 272, 273, 274, 275, 276, 277, 278, 279, 280, 281, 283, 285, 290, 297, 298, 303, 304, 310, 311, 312, 313, 317, 321, 323, 325, 326, 329, 330, 331, 334, 335, 346, 353, 354, 355, 356, 358, 359, 360, 361, 362, 363, 365, 366, 368, 369, 370, 371, 372, 375, 376, 377, 378, 379
Modules xv, xvii, 262, 375
Month 174, 188, 191, 193, 232
Moving
  Controls xiv, xv, 45, 46, 60, 98, 100, 103, 107, 114, 116, 119, 120, 121, 136, 206, 208, 209, 215, 216, 217, 222, 226, 245, 282, 283, 379

Moving Controls 114

N

Navigating between records 80
Navigational buttons 81

O

Opening
  a Database 256
  a Form 263
  a Query 291
  a Table 256
Operators 169

P

Paste button 169, 212, 213, 223
Permissions
  Modifying 192, 208, 281
Pivot Table xv, 90, 160, 290, 293, 378
Primary keys
  Creating a primary key 36
Printing
  Print Preview 201
  Print report 298
Print button 268, 305, 357

Q

QBE grid 158, 164, 166, 177
Query button 189
Query Design
  Adding Fields 42
  Adding records 112
Query types
  Action query 155
  Crosstab query 184
  Delete query 155
  Make-table query 155
  Parameter query 184
  Select Query 154
  Update query 155

R

Records
  Adding records 155

Current record symbol 317
Deleting records 70
Editing records 95
Filtering records 147
Selecting records 171
Referential Integrity 69, 70, 71
Relationships between tables
One-to-many relationship 195
Relationship button 72, 73
Renaming
Renaming a field 44
Reports
Customising a report 206
Setting report properties 226
Resizing
Controls 114
reports 200

S

Saving
Automatically 313
Manually 356
Sections
Sizing 115
Security
User level security 320
Setting
Field size 35
Passwords 320
Sizing
Controls 115
Smart Tags 60, 61
Sorting 146, 179, 228, 229, 230, 231,
233, 378
Starting
Microsoft Access 39
Startup 297, 309, 313
Subform/Subreport 243
Switchboard
Editing 297

T

Tables
Adding Fields 42
Deleting records 95

Importing 359
Primary key 362
Relationships 3
Tab Order 104, 107
Text
Sizing 108
Text boxes, see also controls
Creating bound text boxes 99
Creating unbound text boxes 101
Deleting 112
Moving 114
Text Files
Delimited 360
Text files
Exporting data 370
Importing data 370
Tools
Check box 19
Combo Box 121
Command button 133
Label 215
Line 69, 72, 73, 82, 90, 118, 136,
200, 210, 356
List box 332
Total button 175, 176, 178

U

Users
Adding Users 329
Assigning users to groups 329
User level security
Groups (see groups, security) 322
Permissions, modifying 322

V

Validation
Validating rules 56
ValidationRule Property 105
Validation Text Properties 105
Values
Default Value 124
Null value 175
Viewing
Data Access pages 275
Forms 266

Query Results 168
Reports 266
Tables 316
Views
  Datasheet 196
  Default 46
  Design 46
  Form View 93

W

WIFs 326, 330, 331, 379
Windows
  Database window 343
Wizards
  AutoForm 89, 90, 375
  AutoReport 200, 201, 375

Form Wizard 89
Query Wizard 155
Report Wizard 200
Table Wizard 263
Workgroup 320, 323, 325, 326, 327,
    329, 330, 331, 334, 379
Workgroups
  Commands 330
  Creating 322
  Default 323
  Ids, assigning 327, 338

Y

Yes/No data type 184

ABOUT THE AUTHOR

Sheila Ababio is a computer professional with a degree in Business Information Systems (MSc Business Information Systems). Sheila has been working with databases for more than 15 years. Currently specializing in training business users and building database applications.

www.ingramcontent.com/pod-product-compliance
Lightning Source LLC
Chambersburg PA
CBHW080146060326
40689CB00018B/3864